The God Of Many Things

The Life And Works Of Arundhati Roy

GEW Humanities Group

Global East-West

World Literature.
A Global East-West Series.

First printing, 2025.

Contents

Preface by Hichem Karoui

Arundhati Roy: Writing As A Combat Weapon

I. Introduction

Arundhati Roy's writing isn't just about spinning a yarn—it kinda turns into this gutsy tool that pushes back against a whole mess of social ills. In our world, where the prevailing stories often just keep that old oppression rolling, her words come in like an unexpected punch against a status quo that many of us take for granted. I mean, she shows off, in a raw and offhand way, how folks on the fringes suffer—a reminder that all these different power plays (including that messy talk on militarisation and, uh, twisted ideas of manhood) tend to mix together. It's been said (and, honestly, it sticks with you) that when you let militarised notions of masculinity drive how conflicts get seen and handled, you end up stuck in this never-ending loop of violence (Sharoni, S. 2008). And then, there's that whole bit where everyday fears get morphed into slick political moves—as if our anxieties are just another card being played in the system—which really drives home the point that Roy's insights break apart these tired old ideologies. So, in a way, her work lays down a kind of foundation for viewing literature as more than just art; it's a battle cry against a system that, well, seems determined to hold us back.

Overview of Arundhati Roy's literary contributions

Arundhati Roys literary contributions extend beyond the boundaries of conventional storytelling, merging narrative with a potent political critique that reflects the complexities of contemporary South Asia. Her debut novel, The God of Small Things, serves as a poignant exploration of personal and historical trauma, depicting the intersection of love and societal constraints within a patriarchal framework. Roys body of work also engages with pressing social issues, embodying the struggles of marginalised communities and advocating for justice. As observed, contemporary South Asian women writers have created a significant literary space in challenging both cultural values and the dynamics of linguistic representation (Lau et al., 2002). Roys essays further exemplify writing as a combat weapon, confronting authoritarianism and environmental degradation, while also engaging with global discourses on nuclear politics and identity as seen in its intersection with race and ethnicity (Williams, Paul, 2011). Through her multifaceted contributions, Roy continues to illuminate the resilience and voices of those often silenced.

The concept of writing as a form of resistance

Writing emerges as a vital form of resistance, particularly in the context of Arundhati Roy's work, where it serves not only as a medium of expression but also as a weapon against oppression. Roy's narratives challenge prevailing socio-political norms, illustrating how literature can confront and disrupt dominant ideologies. This concept of writing resonates with critical discussions around militarised masculinities, as the experiences of soldiers reveal the complex relationship between personal narratives and broader power structures (Sharoni, 2012). By documenting stories and experiences often silenced by hegemonic forces, writers like Roy contribute to a de-mystification of violence and oppression, allowing for a reconceptualisation of resistance. Furthermore, in an era increasingly dominated by technology, the act of writing asserts its revolutionary potential by transforming fear and complacency into a reclaimed space for community and dissent. Through this lens, Roy exemplifies how writing functions as both combat and liberation.

II. The Role of Fiction in Activism

Fiction plays a crucial role in activism by offering a compelling medium through which to critique systemic injustices and engage the public imagination. Arundhati Roy exemplifies this dynamic in her own works, which often provoke considerations of societal issues such as environmental degradation and human rights violations. By invoking narratives similar to those found in recent Caribbean science fiction, which question the implications of nuclear supremacy and its impact on marginalised communities, Roy highlights the transformative potential of storytelling. For instance, in works like Rey Emmanuel Andújars Gameon, the geopolitical ramifications of nuclear war are explored, emphasising the need for proper mourning and remembrance in the face of destruction and loss (Ginsburg, 2020). This aligns with broader discourse on racial and ethnic representations in nuclear narratives, as examined in Race, Ethnicity and Nuclear War, where diverse voices challenge the dominant violent rhetoric and envision alternative futures (Williams, 2020). Through such narratives, fiction serves not only to illuminate pressing real-world issues but also to inspire activism and resistance.

Exploration of themes in Roy's novels that challenge societal norms

Arundhati Roys novels intricately weave themes that confront and dissect societal norms, ultimately functioning as a potent form of resistance. Within her narrative landscapes, Roy exposes the deep-seated inequities embedded in traditional Indian society, challenging the structural status quo that has largely remained unaltered despite centuries of external influence (Muzaffer, A. 2011). Her work reflects on the complexities faced by South Asian women, navigating the intricacies of identity, agency, and cultural expectations in a rapidly changing context. These themes are particularly salient in contemporary South Asian literature, which has emerged in reaction to postcolonial legacies and current social upheavals (Lau, 2002). By artfully articulating the struggles of marginalised voices, Roy establishes a critical dialogue on patriarchy and oppression, asserting literatures role as a transformative tool for social change. Her narratives not only depict personal stories but also resonate with broader movements against entrenched societal norms.

The impact of storytelling on raising awareness about social issues

Storytelling emerges as a pivotal tool in raising awareness about social issues, revealing the deep interconnectedness between individual experiences and collective struggles. This form of narrative not only personalises abstract societal problems but also fosters empathy among audiences, enabling them to step into someone else's shoes and understand diverse perspectives. Arundhati Roy exemplifies this impact through her literary and activist endeavours, effectively utilising her narrative voice to illuminate the intricacies of social injustice and environmental degradation. By portraying the lived experiences of marginalised communities, she compels readers to confront uncomfortable truths and motivates them to engage in critical dialogue. Moreover, storytelling holds the potential to transcend geographical boundaries, reminding us of a shared responsibility towards our environment—an integral tenet in Indian traditions that regards the Earth as a nurturing mother (Nandhikkara, J. 2015). Thus, storytelling not only informs but also mobilises collective action towards significant social change.

III. Non-Fiction as a Tool for Advocacy

The role of non-fiction as a tool for advocacy is prominent in the works of Arundhati Roy, who masterfully intertwines personal narratives with broader socio-political critiques. Through her essays, Roy challenges dominant narratives, drawing attention to marginalised voices and local struggles that resonate on a global scale. This approach aligns with the concept of a small cosmopolitanism that reaches out to global audiences by highlighting local injustices, prompting readers to cultivate empathy for diverse experiences. She effectively uses non-fiction to illuminate the consequences of neoliberal globalisation, arguing for a re-evaluation of societal values in ways that resonate deeply with her audience. By positioning her advocacy within the framework of personal and collective narratives, Roy mirrors the work of other postcolonial authors who similarly encourage a nuanced understanding of interconnectedness. Such literary strategies reinforce the necessity of advocacy in the contemporary cultural landscape, as explored in (Macwan et al., 2018).

Analysis of Roy's essays and their influence on public discourse

Arundhati Roys essays serve as a formidable intervention in public discourse, illuminating critical social, political, and environmental issues that resonate profoundly within contemporary society. By employing a narrative style that merges personal anecdotes with rigorous analysis, she effectively engages with themes that challenge dominant paradigms, mirroring the dynamics of postcolonial gothic literature, as seen in the works of writers like Roy herself. Her essays reflect the nature of home and nation, prompting readers to confront the unsettling realities that lie beneath the facade of national identity (Azzam, 2007). Furthermore, as a South Asian woman writer, Roy navigates the complexities of language and cultural representation, positioning her work as part of a broader movement of contemporary South Asian womens writings that critique systemic oppression while forging new narratives (Lau, 2002). In doing so, she not only contributes to literary discourse but also fosters a more inclusive dialogue regarding social justice and activism.

The significance of her critiques on globalisation and imperialism

Arundhati Roys critiques on globalisation and imperialism serve as potent commentaries on the intricate intertwining of power, identity, and resistance within modern societies. By dissecting the hegemonic practices endorsed by global institutions, she uncovers the often-neglected consequences these practices have on marginalised communities, highlighting the socio-political ramifications that arise from unchecked imperialist agendas. Roy's arguments challenge Eurocentric narratives that perpetuate structural inequalities and advocate for a reevaluation of ethical and political subjectivities in the face of these dominant discourses. In this regard, her work echoes the sentiments of emerging theories that question deterministic identities while calling for a counter-hegemonic global community, suggesting that the path toward liberation must navigate the complexities of race and racialisation in a global context. Moreover, as we already hinted, her insights reflect the urgent necessity to demystify militarised masculinities that sustain imperial actions, reaffirming the critical role of writing as a tool of resistance (Sharoni, 2012).

IV. The Intersection of Personal and Political

The interplay between personal narratives and political discourse in Arundhati Roy's works underscores the profound complexity of contemporary Indian identity, particularly within the context of globalisation. Roy's writing transcends mere storytelling; it serves as a combat weapon against social injustices, as exemplified in her second novel, The Ministry of Utmost Happiness, where she intertwines fantasy and realism to critique pressing issues such as environmental degradation, anti-globalisation sentiments, and caste discrimination (Monaco, A. 2018). This hybrid narrative format not only conveys the struggles of marginalised individuals but also highlights the resilience inherent in their lived experiences, reinforcing the notion that personal stories are inherently political. Moreover, the current generation seeks to redefine its identity against the backdrop of rapid globalisation, recognising literature as a means to explore the intersection of individuality, culture, and society. Thus, Roys narratives become vital vessels for both personal expression and collective political consciousness.

How Roy's personal experiences shape her political views

Arundhati Roy's political views are profoundly influenced by her personal experiences, which serve as a critical lens for her literary and activist endeavours. Growing up in a diverse India, her exposure to its myriad cultures and disparities shaped her understanding of national identity and social justice. As mentioned in contemporary discussions regarding South Asian women's writings,

Roy's narrative traverses the complexities of a patriarchal society that often marginalises voices like hers. This background informs her staunch opposition to militarisation and systemic oppression, drawing parallels with the broader feminist critique of militarised masculinities, which underscores the interplay between identity and conflict (Sharoni, 2012). Moreover, her works resonate with the themes of negotiating cultural identity and resistance against colonial legacies, as explored in studies of postcolonial literature, reinforcing her commitment to reclaiming space for marginalised narratives (Lau, 2002). The synergy of these experiences fortifies her advocacy for social change and human rights.

The use of personal narrative to connect with broader social movements

Personal narratives are potent tools for weaving individual experiences into the broader tapestry of social movements, as illustrated in Arundhati Roy's compelling body of work. By sharing her intimate stories, Roy not only humanises complex socio-political issues but also creates a bridge for readers to connect with larger struggles, such as anti-globalisation and environmental activism. This narrative strategy not only engages the audience emotionally but also incites critical reflection on systemic inequalities. For instance, soldier narratives reveal how militarised masculinities are deeply rooted in the fabric of power and violence, highlighting the urgent need for de-militarisation that challenges oppressive systems (Sharoni et al., 2012). Roy's narratives similarly emphasise the metamorphosis of personal grief into a collective struggle against injustice, resonating with the themes of transformation within her work, where individual experiences are contextualised amid the chaotic interplay of societal pressures and technological advancements (Blake et al., 2018).

Conclusion

In conclusion, Arundhati Roy's body of work serves as a powerful testament to the role of writing as a transformative tool against oppression and injustice. By weaving narratives that expose the complexities of military conflicts and societal inequalities, she challenges the dominant paradigms that often perpetuate violence and marginalisation. As discussed in various academic critiques, such as the necessity of de-militarising masculinities in contemporary warfare, her narratives resonate with the urgent need to dismantle systems of power and oppression. Furthermore, the adaptability and resilience of Indian society, which has historically embraced change while resisting functional loss, underscores the potential impact of Roy's writing in shaping a more equitable discourse. Ultimately, her literary activism reflects a larger struggle for human rights, making her work an essential component in the arsenal against tyranny.

Summary of Roy's contributions to literature and activism

Arundhati Roy's contributions to literature and activism reflect a profound intertwining of narrative craft and socio-political engagement, positioning her as a formidable voice in contemporary discourse. Her debut novel, The God of Small Things, garnered international acclaim, while its intricate portrayal of deeply entrenched societal issues, such as caste and gender, showcases her keen insight into the complexities of Indian society. Beyond fiction, Roy's essays, particularly in works like Field Notes on Democracy, illuminate urgent political realities, critiquing neoliberalism and advocating for marginalised communities. Her commitment to activism extends into the realm of environmental and anti-globalisation movements, emphasising the intrinsic connection between human rights and ecological sustainability. In examining subjects like nuclear imperialism and post-colonial identity, Roy's literary and activist efforts resonate within broader frameworks of decolonisation and social justice, emphasising that literature can serve as a potent weapon against oppression, as articulated in Race, Ethnicity and Nuclear War: Representations of Nuclear Weapons and Post-Apocalyptic Worlds (Williams, 2020) and regarding feminist thought in the context of the pandemic.

The enduring power of writing as a weapon for change

In the landscape of contemporary literature, the role of writing as a potent weapon for social and political change is particularly exemplified in the works of Arundhati Roy. Her narratives not only depict the struggles of marginalised communities but also challenge the prevailing narratives constructed by those in power. By weaving local stories into global dialogues, Roy cultivates a unique form of literary cosmopolitanism that resonates with broader audiences. This approach echoes the assertion that post-colonial authors can create alternatives to neoliberal globalisation through their literary expressions, as illustrated in the exploration of Roy's works alongside those of her contemporaries like Salman Rushdie and Amitav Ghosh (Macwan, 2018). Roy's ability to evoke empathy and inspire activism demonstrates the enduring power of writing as a transformative force, capable of dismantling entrenched systems of oppression and fostering a sense of collective responsibility among readers.

In a nutshell

Arundhati Roy is a remarkable writer and outspoken activist who has made an imprint in contemporary literature. Roy was born in Shillong, Meghalaya, India on 24 November 1961. She spent her childhood in Kerala, a southern strip of land in India which is famous for its picturesque beauty and also for having rich socio-political undertones. She moulds fiction, essays and activism together, making her unique in political and literary fields worldwide.

Roy first emerged to world attention with her debut novel *The God of Small Things* (1997), which is a love story blended with the socio-political drama of casteism and family feuds in India, set in the post-colonial era. The novel won the prestigious Booker Prize, capturing Roy's literary acclaim. Critically acclaimed for its stunning prose, distinctive structure, and exploration of unconventional romance bound by societal constraints and rules, the novel cemented Roy's place as a modern literary icon. Despite the overwhelming success of her first novel, she made a conscious decision to step away from fiction, focusing instead on prose and political activism. Roy has published texts such as *The Cost of Living* (1999), *Power Politics* (2001) and *Capitalism: A Ghost Story* (2014), which portray her uncompromising passion for social justice. Roy has been known to speak publicly against globalisation, environmental issues, and the misuse of corporate power along with state power that emerges in Society.

In her essays and speeches, she goes against the norm when discussing the Narmada Dam project, India's nuclear policies, and the growth of Hindu nationalism. Her activism has drawn praise as well as controversy, though it is clear that there is no denying that she sees the power words have in bringing change.

The Ministry of Utmost Happiness, released in 2017, marked her return to fiction and was an ambitious attempt to showcase Indian life through the eyes of its marginalised citizens – transgender women, Kashmiri militants, among others. Like her first novel, the latter features equally poetic prose and brutal social introspection. It further cemented Roy's status as a writer who skillfully weaves beauty with cruelty in her narratives. She has faced legal disputes and scrutiny for her activism yet continues challenging authority without compromising her principles. Roy's unique blend of fiction and non-fiction, art and activism, position her as a distinct voice in modern literature. We view Arundhati Roy as a creative spirit in defiance of convention.

Her life serves as a testimony to the unyielding might of narrative while simultaneously describing her life's unparalleled adventure. She has, without a doubt, embraced evolution in all of her existence.

References

Azzam, Julie Hakim (2007). The Alien Within: Postcolonial

Gothic and the Politics of Home. https://core.ac.uk/download/12209344.pdf

Ginsburg, Samuel (2020). Bombs, Bodies, and Ghosts : Navigating Rhetorical Legacies of Nuclear Technology in Recent Caribbean Science Fiction. https://core.ac.uk/download/372703350.pdf

Lau, Lisa (2002). Women's voices: the presentation of women in the contemporary fiction of south Asian women. https://core.ac.uk/download/6115520.pdf

Macwan, Sunil Samuel (2018). Literary Cosmopolitanisms of Salman Rushdie, Amitav Ghosh, and Arundhati Roy. https://core.ac.uk/download/213074423.pdf

Monaco, Angelo, (2018). Fantasy and History in Postcolonial India: the Case of Arundhati Roy's Anti-Global Novel. https://core.ac.uk/download/541253605.pdf

Muzaffer, Aliya, (2011). Tradition Versus Modernity: A Study of Shobha De's Socialite Evenings, Starry Nights and Snapshots. https://core.ac.uk/download/159343894.pdf

Nandhikkara, Jose CMI (Editor: 2015), Environmental Interface: Literature, Law, Science, and Philosophy, Dharmaram Vidya Kshetram, Bengaluru, India.

Sharma, K. P. (2024). The Defiant Faces: Intersectionality in Arundhati Roy's Resistance Narratives. *Rupkatha Journal on Interdisciplinary Studies in Humanities, 16*(4). https://doi.org/10.21659/rupkatha.v16n4.14

Sharoni, Simona (2012). De-militarizing masculinities in the age of empire. https://www.ssoar.info/ssoar/bitstream/document/28159/1/ssoar-oezp-2008-2-sharoni-de-militarizing_masculinities_in_the_age.pdf

Shellstrom, Rachel (2022). Becoming a More Empathetic

Leader and Person. https://core.ac.uk/download/519865718.pdf

Williams, Paul (2011). Race, Ethnicity and Nuclear War. https://core.ac.uk/download/478135700.pdf

Chapter One

Introduction to Arundhati Roy

A Life of Courage and Conviction

Contextualising Roy's Impact: Literature and Activism

Arundhati Roy is a remarkable author, who boasts an equally influential career in activism and claims a reputation for being fearless. Her unmatched capacity to bridge the gap between fictional creativity and unyielding sociopolitical activism firmly places her as a boundary-defying figure. It is within this contrariety that Roy's impact rests – in the mastery of the fine line between the art of storytelling and the responsibility of enacting change. Roy is a celebrated author best known for winning the Booker Prize – which is considered one of the world's most prestigious awards

– and who shot to prominence in the literary world after publishing 'The God of Small Things,' which became a worldwide success. Undoubtedly, Roy is one of the authors that reshaped the post-colonial literature regard as having a signature style and unprecedented thematic concerns. While defying the post-colonial literature categorisation, Roy's unswerving commitment to tackle social and environmental injustice is a blatant manifestation of her desire to make a difference. As a strong combination of creative art and activism, she has become the foremost storyteller who calls for deep self-assessment and challenges the existing order.

With both her speech and actions, Roy conveys an appreciation of the impact that both storytelling and public sociopolitical engagement can have. Her defying of conventional boundaries of a public intellectual showcases the strength of her understanding about the role of a public intellectual.

Encouraging Engagement: Initial Inspirations

Arundhati Roy remembers her life as a writer and activist as being shaped by her childhood and youthful experiences. She was born in 1959 in Shillong, India, and later moved to Kerala. With her early years surrounded by so much cultural diversity, she was educated in the rich traditions and social dynamics that would further influence her creative aspects. The natural beauty of Kerala and its multicultural society offered an outstanding opportunity to foster empathy and understanding that would surface with her activism and literary works. It was within this vibrant environment that Roy developed a deep appreciation for the complexities of human relationships, social justice and environmental sustainability. As she sharpened her observation skills and cultivated a deep sense of wonder, the need for storytelling and literature grew stronger for her, becoming a weapon against injustice and a medium for change. In Roy's life, this period of time can be marked as the time in her life which made her become one of the most influential writers and activists.

Also, her relatives and family friends, teachers, and even some local leaders contributed towards kindling a sense of responsibility or a more active positive transformation within society, which equipped her with the necessary will power to tackle injustices which were broad-based. These influences greatly impacted the emotional and intellectual development of Roy and her life was a mosaic of her encounters that brought forth the myriad ways in which she chose to interact with her environment, making an imprint on her activism and artistry. Roy's early life blended in motifs of cultural sophistication, social relations and social ignorance which had already begun to sculpt her strong resolve towards tackling major issues at a global scale through literature, activism and sheer determination.

Emergence on the Global Scene: The God of Small Things

In 1997 Arundhati Roy published her first novel 'The God of Small Things,' and as soon as it launched it won the hearts of people and critics from around the world. The story takes place in Kerala, India where, like all of Roy's other works, this novel captures her amazing storytelling ability focusing on complex emotions such as love, loss, and the oppressive nature of society's expectations. Along with vivid portrayal of nature, the author goes deep into the world of human relations and attempts to open one of many social issues.

Roy's writing, filled with vivid images and lyricism, presented her as a literary talent to watch out for. After winning the revered Man Booker Prize in 1997, The God of Small Things earned Roy international recognition. The triumph of the novel established the author's reputation as a great literary figure and drew immediate attention to problems of social stratification such as caste, gender, and other social inequalities. By masterfully weaving stories and displaying her understanding of societal structures, Roy became a forceful advocate for structural violence, revealing her as a brave woman who didn't shy away from addressing challenging realities. The impact of the novel extended beyond countries that were former colonies to include the identity of a postcolonial citizen and the aftereffects of colonialism. It prompted further debate on the boundary space for individualism and control by society. Arundhati Roy became a household name following the release of The God of Small Things. This was just the first step of what promised to be an incredible rise to fame not only as a bestselling author, educator and social activist but also as an environmentalist.

A Defining Moment: The Convergence of a New Form of Art and the Societal Needs

With The God of Small Things, Roy takes a remarkable leap in her career as a writer and activist. This marks the culmination of Arundhati Roy's intense work leading towards her first bestseller and also the first time she used her newly found global platform to speak up for issues of social justice and human rights.

The novel's depiction of caste, class, and gender relations in Kerala was matched by the real-life inequalities and injustices which antagonised and solidified Roy's commitment to initiating positive change. The attention The God of Small Things received for its discussion on identity and oppression demonstrated how art and politics are intricately linked and how storytelling bridged the two. Roy's storytelling expertly brought together the personal and political worlds, exposing the social wounds that required urgent attention. Roy's fame earned her acclaim as a writer, which shifted the focus of discussions surrounding power, resistance, and democracy towards her. She leveraged her fame to draw attention to systemic inequalities and injustices afflicting societies, giving her the novelistic power to change the world. It remains a mystery why she suddenly decided to abandon the role of a "storyteller" and transform into a voice for the unheard. In doing so, she defied the expected use of citizenship: shedding the rights of the dominated to reclaim the freedom of expression. In these acts of defiance, she confronted and recoiled against the power of oppressive rulers in the friction between free will, creativity, and political activism.

These shifts had a profound impact owing to defining moments in Roy's life circumstances, fully embracing her identity as a writer-activist who sought to combat inequality through literature and frontline social activism. The intertwining of art and activism placed Roy on a challenging but extraordinarily impactful legacy that transcends literature to bring about change in society.

Navigating the Dual Realms: Fiction and Reality

Arundhati Roy's life as a writer has been notable for striking a balance between fiction and reality. In her works, storytelling goes hand in hand with social activism, and the art of narration is very useful in highlighting real issues of social and political concern. In her novel, The God of Small Things, Roy narrates the story of a family, love, and loss within the volatile social structures of Kerala. Her characters are not merely fictional but endure real-life battles with rigid societal values and injustices. The audience and readers of the book are taken deep into a world of emotions and experiences and shown the bitter truths that are often ignored.

Roy's activism goes far beyond fiction as she works to address social and political issues. She tackles controversial topics, which transforms her from a simple storyteller to an active change agent. From her non-fiction accounts, it's evident that she deeply cares for marginalised communities, and she approaches their suffering through her non-fiction analysis of socio-political relationships with ease and confidence. Roy's ability to shift between the two spheres of storyteller and activist demonstrates her mastery of the relationship between fiction and non-fiction. Roy, as well, has never shied away from claiming the bilateral link of literature and activism. Through her candid, yet emotional narratives, she extracts the intertwined concepts from the two domains and merges them into a single cohesive unit. Her work is more than creative writing; it is also a tool for consciousness raising and social reflection. The fusion of reality and fiction in Roy's work is designed to provoke readers to come to terms with their reality while changing their perception of the world. As suggested, Roy's engagement in those two aspects has greatly contributed to contemporary literature. This has motivated emerging writers to tackle social and political issues of today.

Her method demonstrates how literature can change society, confirming the belief that storytelling is indeed strategic. While the distinction between fiction and reality becomes increasingly ambiguous, Arundhati Roy remains a central figure who demonstrates the importance of well-crafted narratives in the context of overwhelming social problems.

Unwavering Commitment: Advocacy and Public Life

Involved in an array of environmental and social injustices, Arundhati Roy has proven her credibility during her career by constantly advocating for social justice and global change. These stark issues and the manner in which she deals with them have made her a public figure. Outside of literature, Roy's concerns for the world and its inhabitants are critically deep; as such, she has employed the power of her voice to address matters of social injustice, the violation of aboriginal rights, environmental destruction, and many other forms of discrimination. As a result, Roy has become one of the predominant figures in public life, where she engages in discussions in the public sphere about contemporary issues and challenges society to act. Because of this, it is her advocacy and public life that serve her profound and empathetic understanding towards the vastness of human suffering because people take action only when they are set in crisis. To millions around the world, the compassion, justice, and equality embodied through Roy's fierce voice for the voiceless is deeply inspiring.

Addressing Controversies: Legal and Social Battles

Legal and social controversies have been a familiar sight for Arundhati Roy, her fiery persona often landing her in the middle of various disputes on a national and global scale. As is expected of a person willing to exercise dissent freely, Roy has found herself face to face with the more powerful and traditional interests. As is the case with powerful people, interests were injured, legal steps were taken, and societal discord ensued. For many, Roy's arguments against government policies and corporate power brought a paradigm shift in politics, society and culture that made her a paragon of virtue as well as a critic. One such episode that is of note is her extreme opposition to the Narmada Dam, which resulted in her taking up the cause of displaced people and indigenous folk. This brought her a host of legal troubles and public controversies. As a result, these conflicts showcase the difficulty in voicing support for marginalised communities in a society filled with social injustice and disparity. Moreover, Roy has found herself in the eye of the storm on account of her support for many social movements that have garnered sharp criticism from nationalists, leading to a marked change in public attitudes and extensive media coverage.

Even while personally attacked and legally harassed, Roy has been committed to equity and justice. The tenacity of her spirit and the depth of her convictions do not fail to astonish when she takes advantage of adversities as opportunities for multiplicative change. The social and legal struggles alongside her career have worked copiously as testimonials to her fierce spirit of activism guided by truth and relentless consistency. The steps she undertook served the suppressed, and now there is no getting out for the poor to escape poverty. These obstructions have not only crafted her self but also provided her indelible literary works with a powerful sense of action. If Roy continues to summon fearless strength while battling controversies, then she will be more than an author;

she will touch the heart of everyone wishing for a world where equity matters.

Philosophical Foundations: Influences and Beliefs

Roy's work is built upon different influences and convictions because philosophy is the basis of her activism. The first and most important component of her philosophy is empathy and deep commitment to social justice.

Roy recalls that during her childhood years in Kerala, India, she developed an appreciation for the interconnectedness of living beings and their ecosystems. This awareness greatly impacted the Roy family's environmental consciousness and continues to be visible throughout her advocacy and writing by highlighting the importance of ecological sustainability and respect for indigenous knowledge. The influence of Eastern philosophies, especially regarding non-violence and compassion, can be seen in how Roy harnesses her rage towards systemic oppression by calling upon peaceful resistance and solidarity.

Roy's immersion in postcolonialism and literary theory has given her a more sophisticated understanding of the relations of power and the covert operations of hegemonic forces. Following Edward Said and Gayatri Spivak, Roy uses the notion of subalternity and its necessary decolonisation in her advocacy work to give voice to oppressed and marginalised communities that have been silenced. Feminism through an intersectional lens is also part of her philosophy, which means and relates to feminism through the empowerment of women and cross-cutting struggles of different communities. Embracing diversity and inclusivity illustrates Roy's commitment towards confronting multiple hierarchies and promoting equity.

Roy critiques capitalism, particularly its neoliberalism, from a societal perspective, which she derives from her ties with movements on socio-economic equity and equity-based resource allocation. The particular aspects of her anti-imperialist and her community development approach give credence to her development philosophy. With these strands of deep and broad anti-imperial sentiment submitted to her multilayered, multi-philosophical perception of reality, Arundhati Roy's works are thoroughly infused with her ethical and social commitment to act for the political and social empowerment of the disenfranchised and vulnerable.

Critical Acclaim and Criticism: A Balanced View

Through the integration of Roy's literary and activist pursuits, one can easily identify the reception of her work in criticism and praise: a blend of a single criticism and praise of her work clearly indicates a complexity surrounding it. As a core element of literary criticism, Roy is remembered for her first novel, 'The God of Small Things,' which won the Booker Prize and remains a point of reference for many readers around the world, thereby making her a landmark figure in contemporary literature. The complexity of the novel's narration, the characters, and the social and political issues discussed comprehensively portray Roy as a dedicated fiction writer.

Regardless of praiseworthy feedback, Roy's environmental, anti-capitalist, and human rights positions evoke rather extreme responses. Many applaud her gall in confronting systemic injustices, whilst some condemn her as a dangerous radical whose beliefs and her heretical views challenge established norms and ideologies. Such variance in viewpoints stems from the deeply polarised nature of her public utterances and writings. Critics usually focus on Roy's blend of activism and art, and pose the big question: does her passionate advocacy drown her literary talent? Some suggest that her provocative non-fictions, written with heated passions and sharp criticism, eclipse her fictions. On the other hand, defenders argue that Roy combines art and activism and uses her pen to give voice to the voiceless and effect social change. This duality keeps the conversations alive on the expectations of writers in society. Also, the fury in Roy's criticism of globalism and neoliberalism has received its fair share of controversy as her opponents claim that her arguments are simplistic and her wording incendiary. Critics warn against idealising her opposing voice and rather ask for objective criticism of her insights.

Alternatively, supporters argue that her self-indulgent critique is vital in confronting systems and power structures as she advocates for challenging conversations in the contemporary world. In other words, the analysis of Arundhati Roy's reception is rather a fusion of praise and criticism reflecting the impact of arts, activism, and policies. It illustrates how urgently diverse views should be sought and how a society should consider the responsibilities of creation and intellectualism in the present day.

Paving the Way Forward: Legacy and Future Directions

While Arundhati Roy's legacy still unfolds, her contribution to literature, activism, as well as social awareness, remains highly felt. It is not hard to see the many ways this seemingly resistant spirit will further mark her territory, and that may very well serve as an indicator of the importance of her works. Roy's contribution is exemplified with one main feature of her legacy, which is the further encouragement of upcoming writers, activists, and intellectuals. With her activism and relentless fight for the less privileged, Roy has set the stage for emerging voices to take up and advance the social justice agenda.

Whatever impact Roy had on the literature and activism plots will forever elicit discourse and reflection on current issues of concern such as climate change and social injustices. There is no doubt that the issues she fought for historically will continue to dominate important conversations globally, ensuring her influence reverberates in the centuries to come. Observing Roy's storytelling skills and her ability to fight for a cause, it is intriguing to think about the new dimensions that advocacy will develop from storytelling. As humanity contemplates multidimensional issues, the demand for strong narratives that address deep-rooted forms of oppression and discrimination is becoming increasingly urgent. There is no doubt that Roy's works will illuminate the path to be taken by artists wishing to merge activism with artistry to propagate sustainable change. Besides, the digital era offers new avenues for audience engagement that could open up her works for discussions on various channels. Leveraging new technology can help replenish the activism spirit that Roy represents, and build a community that advances positive change across the world. The commitment Roy has shown in respecting humanity and championing the marginalised is illustrative of what individuals and groups can do to promote social change.

This lasting bequest marks the literary realm forever and stands as a memorial of benevolence, strength, and an unswerving sense of belief when one is confronted with misfortunes.

Chapter Two

The Early Years

Growing Up in Kerala

Cultural Heritage and Family Background

Roy enjoyed her formative years in the beautiful state of Kerala, India. Due to being born into a family that practiced art and intellectualism, she was accustomed to reading literature, art, and social philosophy. This dimension of her family heritage had a strong impact on creativity and expression in the form of various art in her family life. Roy was fortunate to grow up in a region rich in oral storytelling, providing her childhood with vivid stories and lessons that enabled her to pursue a career as a storyteller and social justice advocate.

This family background encouraged dissent and critical thinking, enabling Roy to appreciate sociopolitical discourse. Roy's family was also able to encourage her curiosity and awareness of social inequities, providing her with the necessary environment to shape her understanding from a young age. It is evident that, in addition to Rajiv's strong passion for literature and advocacy, he received ample support from his family background to build a strong base of support to challenge the status quo and give a voice to the oppressed.

Additionally, the blending of her family with the culture of Kerala allowed Roy to be taught different forms of art such as dance, music, and visual art. These experiences gave Roy a keen appreciation for the capabilities of different forms of art. Furthermore, the focus on family within her family greatly helped Roy develop a strong sense of community which later influenced her writing and activism work.

In summary, the mix of Roy's family history and Kerala's cultural history explains why she approaches life and art in a multifaceted way. These influences not only adjusted her artistic perspectives but also developed her compassionate understanding and critical analysis of society, which defines her work. From these experiences, we can see that Roy, as an activist and a writer, grew within the richness of her cultural background and the caring embrace of her family.

Formative Influences: Early Exposure to Literature and Art

During Arundhati Roy's childhood, her early affection for literature and art influenced the great works she constantly aspired to in the future. While residing in Kerala, she was surrounded by a culture that appreciated art and narrative in storytelling. The community folklore and traditions aided in building her love for words and images, as stories would always be a big part of her life and heritage.

As much as Roy enjoyed reading the popular classics, she was also drawn towards more modern and contemporary works that were somewhat controversial and had much to say about society and the oppressed. These greatly diverse literary backgrounds unequivocally shaped her writing into what is now considered melodious and brutally honest poetry.

Alongside literary works, the cultural atmosphere of Kerala helped to form Roy's sensibilities. The rich visual traditions such as mural paintings, temple art, and traditional crafts provided her with a vocabulary, which would later find expression in her evocative prose. The way she deeply assessed the relationship between culture, history, and visual arts helped her develop a holistic approach to storytelling, making it rich in images and symbols.

Moreover, the incorporation of literature with arts in the culture of Kerala fostered in Roy a comprehensive view of creativity as a means for social change. The visually artistic expressions, with the ability to defy prevailing norms and create new worlds to live in, are integral to her worldview. Such early exposure helped form a lifelong dedication to utilizing literature and art as advocacy tools to amplify marginalised voices and focus attention on critical social issues.

Through Roy's integration of literature and arts during her adolescence, she learned to craft and elaborate compelling stories that transcended emotional boundaries. The integration of aesthetics with social issues would later emerge in her writing, captivating the audience to confront the harsh realities of society.

Education in Kerala: Academic Pursuits and Inspirations

As a state blessed with natural beauty and a progressive framework, Kerala stands out for its unique relationship between education and culture. Arundhati Roy's upbringing was diverse and multi-faceted, providing her with countless sources of inspiration. Kerala's educational environment served as a constructive influence in the development of the author – from its vibrant intellectual energy to its lush green surroundings. The inclusiveness of the educational system of Kerala that integrates traditional modern and contemporary disciplines greatly encouraged critical as well as interdisciplinary thinking. As a local school and university student, Roy experienced first-hand the rich blend of culture and intellectual activity that the educational institutions in Kerala offered. She met numerous inspiring teachers and students who motivated her to write, advocate for social justice, and tell stories, which eventually gave birth to her artistic and activist self. While moving through the learning spaces in Kerala, Roy at the same time started questioning issues of identity and societal structures, which set the groundwork for her later portrayals of those aspects in her literary endeavours.

The combination of her classroom education and the world outside her class helped her to appreciate the complex social structure created by tradition, modernity, and dissent. Roy's Kerala education provided the first phase of her interaction with the profound discrimination and rebellious attitude that exists in society. To sum up, the primary education she had in Kerala not only gave her an academic structure, but also an inspiring reservoir which shaped her writing and activism for people beyond the state.

The Social Landscape of Kerala: A Tapestry of

Traditions and Change

Kerala is known for 'God's Own Country' because of its vigorous Kuṭiyattam's rich cultural pipe. With modern Kerala society being actively developed around the concept of cultural uniformity alongside the diversity which is prevalent, the state is capturing the world's attention through the interface of religion, traditions, modernisation, and innovations. Kerala society's phenomenal transformation throughout the years is also due to great focus on education, urbanisation, and mass media. Moreover, modern literacy and educational art are exploited with multi-disciplinary approaches that serve sociological and anthropological ramifications. Special attention progresses in the form of social work, areas of underprivileged sections of the society such as women and oppressed religious communities assist to make the norms in civil laws on women in non-governmental organisations. The essences arising from Polycomplexity blend the paradigms of social inclusion create unique dialects.

The fusion of change with the preservation of heritage has helped to create a society that balances the challenges of modernity while celebrating diversity. Furthermore, the social reform and social welfare commitments of Kerala have greatly assisted in cultivating a socially conscious citizenry that is ready to grapple with issues of social justice, human growth, and holistic development. Examining the details of the social fabric of Kerala, it is clear that the complexity of its patterns of tradition and change has fundamentally transformed people and their perspectives, beliefs, and hopes.

Impact of Family Dynamics on Personal Development

No single person has a perfect character, but the family they come from dictates a great deal of it. In regard to Arundhati Roy's childhood in Kerala, the family structure was quite complex and it had a lasting impact on her worldview as well as ambitions. In this regard, her life is emblematic of the intertwining family systems present in the Roy family, for each module had its own cherished values, practices, and norms. The intricate clash of heritage and modernity affected the understanding of the society deeply for the younger Arundhati. The balance of these relationships provided her with a strong sense of belonging and identity filled with expectations and traditions. Among complex family dynamics, the young Arundhati began to learn social organisation, sexual division of labour, and sociology that formed the basis of her active and literary life. Along with identity, she was also exposed to the socio-political environment of the country including caste, class, community, and religion at such a tender age which helped eliminate confusion about these issues later. The Roy family was complex, with multifaceted structures and relations which contributed significantly towards familial beliefs, meanings, and identity.

Additionally, the assistance and obstacles provided by family members shaped her support, resilience, and intellectual curiosity, all of which influenced her future endeavours. It was within these family dynamics that Arundhati Roy's primitive notions of justice, equity, and selfhood were refined, and prepared her for what she would later achieve both in literature and social activism. The effects of those family relationships on her evolution demonstrate the significant role that such experiences have on a person's life.

Early Encounters with Gender and Identity

The processes concerning gender and identity developed gradually in comprehension in Arundhati Roy's life. She attended primary school in Kerala, one of the southern states famous for its multicultural and sociologically rich cultures. In Roy's family, like in many others, there was a clear division of gender roles and expectations that was accompanied by traditional cultural norms. Her family helped shape her first ideas about gender and identity, teaching her about the social realities that she would later seek to reject in her literature and activism. Roy keenly analysed the struggles for power that her family members went through and learned early on how, in everyday life, women often had less access to opportunities than men. As such, she began to think of issues of gender identity and how such identities affect one's freedom to act.

Roy's self-examination of her role in these structures prepared her to critique societal norms in the future. Furthermore, the vast range of people living in Kerala offered a different perspective on gender and identity. Different aspects of culture such as tradition, art, and literature made Roy conscious from a very young age of the existence of different gender representations and the notion of multiple identities.

This openness towards different views helped her to have an all-embracing worldview and added depth to the description of roles for the people in her novels. At the same time, the unique social structure of Kerala provided subtle illustrations of the relations of class, caste, and religion to gender, which helped shape Roy's approach towards dismantling systemic biases as an intersectional feminist. To sum up, the interplay of family relations, social norms, and the complex culture of Kerala deeply influenced Roy's thoughts about gender and identity from a very young age and prepared her for her later critical engagement with these issues.

The Role of Nature and Environment in Shaping Imagination

During her childhood, Arundhati Roy's imaginative skill was deeply influenced by the picturesque green backwaters, tropical forests, and flora and fauna of Kerala. The coconut palms swaying in the wind, along with the monsoon rains, served as a backdrop to her creativity. These experiences fostered a deep respect towards nature and came with an understanding of the ecological balance in the area. Roy's keen observation of life and the different ecosystems formed by the Arabian Sea and the Western Ghats awoke her to a variety of emotions. She was able to draw inspiration from nature around her, which became a motivation to write stories reflecting the world as it is. Nature provided her with stories to tell, genuinely transforming the world into one echoing with vivid descriptions of nature intertwined with the culture of Kerala.

The cultural ethos of Kerala, which is greatly attached to nature, nourished Roy's understanding with a variety of customs, highlighting how the people's perception of the nature around them nurtured it. Roy's literary sense was also cultivated by the rich soil of Kerala, which grew various crops and plants, and provided an inspiring setting for the clash of human beings and nature. The visual appeal of the riverbanks, lush green paddy fields, and coconut tree groves were greatly enticing and served as an inspiration for Roy to examine human beings' experiences in relation to nature. Roy's deep encounters with the wilderness of Kerala and its astonishingly rich biodiversity created within her a great eco-consciousness to advocate for environmental causes in the future. Therefore, the unmatched beauty and diversity of Kerala helped shape Roy's empathetic depiction of characters and their relationship with nature, leading her on a path to becoming a distinguished author.

Broadening Horizons: Experiences Beyond the Village

During the formative years Arundhati Roy spent in the village of Kerala, the world beyond the borders of the village began opening up for her. It was not merely geography that was changing, but a whole world of institutions and cultures that was waiting to be explored. During this time, the new writer in Roy was beginning to awaken, and the world beyond her childhood home started to pull her towards it.

As a child, Roy was interested in reading and storytelling which proved to be her greatest teachers. The literature written by authors from different regions and cultures opened up her perception and understanding of the world. In addition to new cultures and traditions, this literary exposure provided different perspectives. Such experiences stimulated a yearning to explore new vistas, far beyond the boundaries of the familiar village.

All this helped her gain the confidence to explore new towns and cities that had previously been off limits. Roy nurtured this newfound confidence by exploring the more modern and urban parts of the countryside. Along with the beauty of these regions came new reasons to challenge the still rustic way of living which added to the thrill of urban life. Together, this made it possible for her to move beyond the simple life as a villager which matured her sense regarding life and its complex nature.

Her physical interactions, or engagements with people from various backgrounds, were a level deeper than self-exploration. These interactions fostered the gentle wings of compassion and a welcome desire to understand what it means to be human, enabling her to engage with the complexities of life through literature in her later years.

Roy's imagination was also influenced by changes in society and new global phenomena. With the world becoming more integrated and changes happening on a bigger scale, she began to appreciate the concept of different stories being tied together, and was motivated to peel apart the layers that join people from different societies.

Every new encounter added a new layer to her worldview, filling her imagination with tales and feelings alongside sharp perspectives. These emotionally rich and politically pointed events are what gave rise to a new type of writer whose stories evoke emotion and compassion towards the people around the world. Therefore, with Roy, we reach an end where the events of her life give sense to everything coming before, for her life epitomises the sum of all international relations and deeply combines the entire human race.

Early Signs of Rebellion and Non-conformity

During her youthful years, Arundhati Roy was characterised by a deep nature of rebellion and non-conformity. This segment will analyse how Roy, even in her adolescent years, would actively display acts of disobedience toward basic societal standards and expectations. In the context of family, friends, and the larger community, Roy made great attempts aimed at defining public attitudes and profoundly resisting them. This stubbornness was usually rooted deeply in a sense of justice and systemic discrimination. These experiences shaped her later identity as an activist and a passionate defender of the silenced groups of people. It was through challenging social constructs of gender, social order, and hierarchy that Roy's journey in fighting for social justice began. Roy's desire to seek the truth and achieve social justice constantly placed her in conflict with existing beliefs, and she ended up playing the role of an outspoken activist for social change.

While travelling through the beautiful scenery of Kerala, it became evident that Roy was already drawn towards ideas that were different from the popular ones, which indicated that she would later prefer to travel on unconventional roads in her life both professionally and personally. This chapter presents in detail the changes and events that developed the defiant attitude of Roy, focusing on the deep impact of her early experiences with child injustice and inequality. With such context, one is able to appreciate the distinct impact that Roy has had over literature and activism in her life as she is known as an icon of social and literary oratory in the world.

From Kerala to the World: The Seeds of a Global Perspective

Arundhati Roy's initial years in Kerala helped shape her worldview and her writing perceptions. While growing up with the vibrant culture of Kerala, Roy appreciated the value of diversity and interdependence from an early age. The exposure she received from the multitude of customs, languages, and religions practised in her area reaped a global awareness that nurtured deep empathy and understanding towards the plights of people around the world. Her initial involvement with pluralistic culture fuelled her interest in the common human life that was limitless by geography.

Roy's passions in literature and her insatiable desire for knowledge opened her eyes to literature outside of her environment and region. She practised literature as a tool for travel, with every new work bringing her closer to the differences and commonalities that unite humanity and society's struggles. She learned to appreciate the idea of all people being deeply connected, preparing her to advocate for social justice and marginalised communities on a global level.

Now, because of her engagement outside her state, Roy's experiences have provided her with an understanding of a larger world, and along with it her travels and interactions with different people brought various ideas that strengthened the fabric of humanity. Roy captures the motives and expectations of international politics and social relations which influence her desire to fight for change and empower the unheard revolution.

Having a strong sense of belonging to Kerala's specific culture, now juxtaposed with the rest of the world, allowed Roy to obtain a perspective from which she could later write her cross-border narratives. From a unique perspective, Roy crafted compelling stories with unparalleled accuracy, cultivating the understanding of local and international forces. From the calm sceneries of Kerala to the chaotic cities in distant continents, these places Roy travelled to provided her with a great sense of how deeply connected human beings are to each other, shaping her literature and philanthropy across the world.

Chapter Three

The God of Small Things

Literary Triumph and Global Acclaim

Introduction to 'The God of Small Things'

The author Arundhati Roy, 'The God of Small Things' is a novel that not only made her a household name, but captured many readers with its beautifully crafted story that appeals to one's deepest emotions. The first idea that Roy had for the novel was a way to make space in the literary world by trying to defy the norms India has to offer. With her eyes set on India's state of Kerala, Roy embarked on a writing journey that would go on to change Contemporary Literature for years to come. 'The God of Small Things' is of extreme importance and gives Roy's career the height of achievement that she has earned due to the book, but also shows the ability and depth with which she is able to comprehend and express the human condition. It proves beyond doubt Roy's ability to blend deeply personal stories with social and political issues, which she later boldly advocated for.

Throughout the coming sections where we analyse the inception and writing process of 'The God of Small Things', we are going to witness the very beginning of a masterpiece that still touches the lives of readers around the world.

Inception and Writing Process

The God of Small Things is a turning point in Arundhati Roy's life marked by skilled literature and intense creativity. Forming this novel was not an intellectual affair, but rather a deeply personal and emotional journey drawn from Roy's ability to appreciate human behaviours and social norms.

Roy's writing style and methods are not typical as she bases them on her recollection of the world. The novel has a complex narrative structure with a non-chronological order which indicates great care and attention during its crafting. The multi-dimensional characters in the novel were all elegantly designed to blend in the predominant issues of love, caste, and societal norms.

The specific environment where writing takes place profoundly affected the construction of the novel itself. The bond Roy shares with her native land of Kerala is present in the novel and affectionately reflects the place and history of the region. A place of great imagination and a canvas for her literary journey, the author's very strong imagery and descriptions throughout the book illustrate, to great effect, her fondness towards the setting.

Moreover, the thematic underpinnings of the novel emerged

from a confluence of diverse influences, ranging from familial dynamics to socio-political upheavals.

Exploration of Themes and Motifs

Analysing themes and motifs in 'The God of Small Things' reveals a complex structure of literary attributes that aid in understanding the novel's timeless relevance. Arundhati Roy's multi-faceted storytelling uncovers different thematic layers such as social, family, relational, romantic, and tragic themes. The motif of forbidden love set against the backdrop of a steeply stratified society easily becomes the focus of attention and highlights the sharp consequences of breaking societal rules. Roy intricately portrays the complexities of forbidden love alongside the harsh truths of traditions and the overpowering societal expectations.

The motif of social innocence within the sphere of social discrimination and power relations enhances the narrative perspective. Roy vividly captures the imagination of readers through her tender depiction of the twins' life, Estha and Rahel, and their naïve interactions with a world full of bigotry and anger. Their experiences reflect the larger injustices that exist within Ayemenem.

Centrally, the still recognisable theme of identity and cultural alienation is present in the novel, providing a valuable consideration in relation to personal conflict and self-objectives vis-à-vis societal expectations. This understanding of identity is anchored on the characters' development, which illustrates the reality of cultural normativity vis-à-vis the need for self-freedom.

Roy intersperses the themes and motifs into the storyline and feels the reader drowning in the complex emotions and social problems of the society. She understands people and social systems so well, she is able to create an inviting space for the readers to grapple with issues as grave as love, freedom, listlessness, and social norms. All these themes and motifs play a significant part in the appeal of the novel and make it possible for a wide range of people around the world to understand its message, making 'The God of Small Things' one of the most important books in modern literature.

Characterisation and Narrative Structure

The important features of Arundhati Roy's 'The God of Small Things' are its character development and its highly literary techniques of narration, which give the novel its profundity, as well as its breadth. In this novel, the different characters are crafted in such profound detail that the readers sympathise with the characters' journeys, conflicts, and emotions. Every character is portrayed with particular motives and contradictory multi-faceted features that are a reflection of the reality of life. In character portrayal, Roy captures the individuality and interdependence of her characters, Rahel, Estha, Ammu, Velutha, and the rest who, with or against the forces of social life, are controlled by the interplay of the societal social structures and relationships.

Roy's narrative structure is just as striking, as she incorporates a multitude of timelines and vantage points into the same story. This form of storytelling weaves events and feelings together as one whole set. This method of storytelling is also more complex since the reader has to piece together information that is given out of order with respect to chronology to understand the characters' past and present states. Roy's manipulation of time and perspective works to engage the reader's discernment and appreciation of the internal struggles and external conflicts the characters undergo.

Additionally, the themes that recur throughout the novel are aided by symbolism and metaphorical elements within character development and the plot of the story. Roy constructs complex imagery and allegorical representations of her characters and their experiences and the socio-political context in which those experiences embrace them. This multi-faceted method of character portrayal and arrangement of the story provides fresh understanding of the novel and challenges readers to think of the deeper meaning that is coded in the story.

Moreover, the relationships that the characters have with one another within the plot serve as another way to grapple with themes of identity, social class, and familial or cultural obligations and their effects. Through these skillfully devised relations between the characters, Roy asks why people connect, why they betray each other, or stand strongly resilient which evokes deep thoughts about humanity's multifarious condition.

To sum up, the delicate care for the characters together with the advanced plot structure used in "The God of Small Things" portray the essentials that the novel possesses which makes it uniquely fascinating in literature. Through the created characters and the other constructions of the plot, Arundhati Roy presents a story that enchants its readers and speaks to many cultures which results in its prominence till today.

Cultural and Historical Contexts

In analysing the cultural and historical contexts that envelop "The God of Small Things," it is important to examine the multi-layered socio-political backdrop against which the story is set. The novel is set in Kerala, India, during a period of turbulence and change. It intricately captures the interplay of caste relations, social stratification, and the political turmoil characteristic of post-colonial India. This rich context is beautifully portrayed through the Syrian Christian community, who stand at the crossroads of modernity and tradition. The novel's examination of the caste system reveals the impact of systemic historical injustices and offers striking commentaries on the societal conditions that shape individual existence.

Moreover, deeper meanings of the narrative are clearer when placed alongside events such as the rise of communism in Kerala or the impact of colonialism. These are illustrative of the historical context. Roy captures the spirit of the times, describing the palpable sense of conflict between rebellion and obedience, freedom and control. The novel does not limit itself to the issues of its immediate context. It provokes thoughts on the issues of domination, discrimination, and defiance that are global in nature.

Incorporating cultural and political features, 'The God of Small Things' proficiently covers the features and characteristics of Kerala. It describes the Kerala landscape in rich detail and captures its customs and traditions in such a manner that the readers feel them deeply, which makes the words 'come alive'. This masterly mixture of cultural aspects not only grounds the story within India but accentuates the reality of human life that creates empathy and understanding across various countries.

Due to the complex combination of cultural and historical elements, the story becomes more interesting; 'The God of Small Things' becomes a true snapshot of the reality of the existence of individuals and societies in the modern world. Through the commingling of the intensely personal and the dramatic social context, Roy tells a stunning story, deeply anchored in the particular history and culture of its environment, to which it is always alive and valid.

Reception and Critical Acclaim

It is safe to say that the novel received rave reviews from the global audience. With such intricate details and intertwining stories, the prose is bound to receive critical acclaim. As for the motives, the novel deliberately highlights the infamous Indian caste system within the dual socialistic policies of Britain and India, which have their roots buried deep in Communism. Not only did it triumph in the depth and breadth of social issues, but also the symbolism of 'small things' is a perfect articulation of the relationship between childhood and innocence. It captures micro events which have macro consequences. Even within the cloak of 'magic', real life complexity of relationships along with societal norms adds to the wonders of a tale.

Roy received international exposure and fame after winning the prestigious Man Booker Prize 1997 along with diverse accolades and literary honours making the novel even more visible with queuing readers. It is a gem of contemporary fiction and as such is swathed in a variety of accolades. With such recognition from both institutions and global literary circles, Roy has truly cemented her status as one of the greatest literary forces of modern times.

Critics lauded 'The God of Small Things' for dealing with forbidden romance, caste system intricacies, and the effects of colonialism on Indian culture. Roy's finesse in analysing power politics and emotions was appreciated by readers and thinkers alike. The novel's prose, which included social critique, crafted the way for identity, oppression, and traditions to be discussed and debated in a sophisticated manner.

Despite the critical appreciation, 'The God of Small Things' generated views and self-contemplation in literary and scholarly forums. Different scholars presented their views on the novel's topics, symbols, and themes, which contributed to the discussion on post-colonial literature and feminist literature. Roy's novel suppressed the literary canon and the stereotypical view of western literature and representation.

The novel is an enduring one, as seen from the book's frequent mention in literary and educational circles all over the world. 'The God of Small Things' acts as a foundation for new writers and thinkers and helps in providing insight towards cultural power domination, intersectionality, and the use of literature as an advocacy tool for social reformation. The book's relevance in today's time proves the literary excellence of Roy, who crafted her words in ways that crossed borders and resonated with people universally.

Awards and Recognitions

Roy's The God of Small Things, the author's first novel, received tremendous reception from the literary world and it gained remarkable critical reviews across the globe. The extensive marketing success the book achieved was further supported with the vast list of eminent awards and commendations which Roy received, marking her as an important author. All these achievements were, without a doubt, remarkable, but her most notable one was received in the year of 1997 – the Man Booker Prize. With this award in hand, Roy's name reached every corner of the world while also painting her as an author that is both insightful and adept. One of the objectives of the prize, that is to publicise 'The God of Small Things' - which, by the way, is of immense note, was successfully achieved, thereby ensuring an everlasting hallmark of the book. Besides those, it received the Giller Prize in Canada in 1996, which goes on to prove the 'transnational' character and gripping storytelling of the book. Its fame was not limited to Canada, but transformed it into a triumph that went, with a level of importance, international. Also, the book was extremely popular, and as a result, in 1997 it was awarded the National Book Critics Circle Award for Fiction and the Irish Times International Fiction Prize in 1998.

These accolades illustrate Roy's profound storytelling abilities, including her heart-wrenching examination of family relationships as well as love and societal expectations. Noted equally is the universal relevance of the novel as 'The God of Small Things' also won the Eurasian Commonwealth Writers' Prize for Best First Book. Such awards affirm the novel's claim as an important work of literature that covers wide-ranging borders and cultures, speaking to a myriad of people. Further, this masterpiece of Roy's was adopted by many literary bodies and institutions which is why it won the Crossword Book Award and Rajagiri International Award for Literature, amplifying her and his name in global literature. These awards simultaneously recognise her important contribution to literature as well as the importance of 'The God of Small Things' in world literature. With these awards, Roy's captivating storytelling, sharp distribution of satire, and her unique prose are appreciated internationally, earning the status of a classic novel. The testimonial evidence by the various awards and commendations given to 'The God of Small Things' speaks to its greatness and influence on modern literature, and proves that the novel is a work that will inspire people for ages to come.

Impact on Indian Literature

Arundhati Roy's first work of fiction, 'The God of Small Things', profoundly impacted Indian literature. The book's multi-faceted prose, unorthodox narrative structure, and prosaic social critique rewrote the storytelling paradigms in India. Roy's unique ability to blend the deeply intimate with the politics surrounding her characters' lives was a radical development in contemporary Indian fiction. As the book climbed the popularity charts, it did not only cast Roy in the limelight as an author, but Indian literature as something that could hold value abroad.

'The God of Small Things' set a precedent for any Indian literary work in the telling of Indian experiences, wringing out stories which previously seemed implausible and seeing the world with Indian eyes. Her willingness to discuss subjects which are considered forbidden as well as her willful disregard of the existing literary traditions gave birth to a new Indian writer who does not shy away from orthodox modern complexities of his culture.

In a similar fashion, the widespread popularity received by The God of Small Things brought attention to Indian literature which was not the case before. It redefined what Indian writing is and can be, resulting in a change that encouraged more diversity and inclusion in the world of literature. This change also allowed many other Indian writers to tell their stories to the world, giving way to a deeper understanding of India's complex culture.

The novel also contributed to conversations about caste, gender, and social class in India, making it possible for self-reflection and discussions to take place in the Indian literature circle. It urged writers and academics to address the uncomfortable realities and start engaging in discussions that were previously regarded as unspeakable or marginalised. It is from this perspective 'The God of Small Things' is revered and scrutinised as the most effective piece of literature that led to the change that is necessary for Indian literature to be more widely understood and appreciated.

In conclusion, the consequences of the God of Small Things in the arena of Indian literature are profound. The focus on innovation within the narrative structure of the story, the underlying themes, and the international reception of the novel have put it on the pedestal where it can single-handedly shape the future of Indian storytelling and proclaim the importance of Indian literature to the rest of the world.

Global Influence and Translations

Roy's book 'The God of Small Things' is an acclaimed piece of literature in India but also on the world stage. The themes of the book and the manner of storytelling are so gripping that it has been translated into many languages and is read throughout the world. The book's treatment of emotions alongside the fabric of society enables an audience to connect on a deeper level. Furthermore, the incorporation of traditional Kerala culture seamlessly blended into the story enables readers abroad to gain insight into a unique heritage.

The book delves into the stirring aspects of love, loss, and the societal norms that bind people, striking an empathetic chord with individuals from different cultures. This analysis also explains why 'The God of Small Things' is so popular. Everyone can empathise with the situations portrayed in the book. The examination of complex relationships of power, dominance, and social order produces debates about justice and equity across the world, making the book a point of discussion on many international platforms, and who would not want to engage in thought-provoking discussions.

Adapting the novel to different languages has had its benefits and drawbacks. A translation project hopes to convey the basic message of the original text in a way that takes into consideration the culture and region's peculiarities. Furthermore, translation enables the dissemination of Roy's narrative to people who do not have access to the English version, increasing the readership and impact of the novel.

Moreover, 'The God of Small Things' has been an important tool in promoting cultural communication and cross-border interactions. Because of its translations, this novel becomes an instrument through which various cultures can view and appreciate the intricacies of another society and thus enhance mutual understanding and cultural dialogue. Its translation into other languages has surely established it as one of the world's greatest literary works, which is now believed to have the power to conquer the world's geographical, cultural, and linguistic boundaries.

To summarise, the reach and translations of 'The God of Small Things' demonstrate the deep impact that Arundhati Roy's story has on a global scale. The novel's ability to resonate within the heart of readers past language barriers speaks to the significance and influence of the novel, assuring its place as one of the most important works of literature in the world.

Reflective Conclusion: Legacy of the Novel

The legacy of "The God of Small Things" is much richer than the book's primary literary success and its international popularity.

Arundhati Roy's first novel has tremendously shaped the evolution of modern literature and continues to impact thousands of readers, writers, and scholars across the world. The ability of the novel to poignantly reflect and critique societal norms has made it one of the most central pieces of literature that describe the human condition across cultures and times. Its characters and relationships themselves, coupled with the unique structure of the novel, inspire debates on socio-relational complexities and personal liberties.

Arundhati Roy's contemporary style of engaging with issues of love and loss, caste and politics, sets a new benchmark for other writers to take on contemporary social issues boldly. In more than 40 languages, and done so in a way that attracts an audience from all over the world, the novel has kept its central theme intact, which explains the enduring impact of "The God of Small Things." This novel remains crucial for academic institutions across the globe, signifying the continuing importance of the book in contemporary literature, postcolonial feminist, and experimental narrative studies.

Moreover, the legacy of the novel can be captured from the impact it has had on later literary movements and emerging writers. The innovative style Roy employs in 'The God of Small Things' that fuses prose with poetry together with sharp observation has redefined 'story' and inspired writers to write with an intent to provoke. Therefore, as with many new emerging writers wanting to experiment with styles, so with the case of 'The God of Small Things' it remains influential.

In social discourse, just like in literary criticism, the novel's legacy or impact theory can be observed. The novel's ability to demonstrate the intricate blends of tradition, the modern, and globalisation leaves the reader questioning the changing nature of a society and what it means to undergo cultural integration. The gaps within the social and political fabric is what the novel focuses on – having deeper implications towards the understanding of 'The God of Small Things Anantagiri' and the world today.

In summary, The God of Small Things is an example of how literature can change people's thoughts and perspectives. Its legacy serves as proof of the fact that storytelling is not only beautiful but also crucial in facilitating meaningful conversations. While the novel promises to provide intrigue and difficulty to readers at the same time, one thing is for certain; its legacy is lasting, having inspired countless people.

Chapter Four

A Voice for Change

Transition into Activism and Non-fiction

Introduction to Activism: Catalysts and Motivations

To a greater extent than most people, Arundhati Roy's entry into activism stemmed from powerful motivations and was propelled into action by a variety of compelling catalysts. With rich details of her life experiences and her observations of societal injustices, one could easily trace the origin of Roy's passion for activism. Over the years Roy spent in Kerala, India, she encountered privilege and deprivation, giving her a first-hand understanding of the surplus inequalities embedded within society. These vivid memories, blended with her understanding of empathy, drove her innate desire to challenge systemic inequities. For Roy, social justice and the fight for marginalised communities was like a spark that set her on a journey to bring meaningful change to the world. Roy, as a literary figure and an academic, had to come to terms with the power dynamics and the nature of oppression, all of which Roy was acutely aware of, and all of which drove her activism. The different kinds of social injustices she stood for and the failure to speak for the silenced and forgotten, and the determined pursuit of truth and justice became the reasons and the means for Roy to propel into advocacy.

This is where Roy's nuanced understanding of the Indian sociopolitical space, particularly concerning environmental issues, indigenous affairs, and social class conflict, did capture her attention and basically provided sparks that set her in motion. These influences combined created for Roy a resolve that seemed to be petrified, which motivated her to use her power and influence towards real change in society. In this chapter, we analyse the complex patterns of Roy's activism to demonstrate how the antagonistic forces and motivations of her life irreversibly changed the course of her activism.

Initial Forays into Advocacy: Early Campaigns and Initiatives

The shift of Arundhati Roy from an exceptional fiction author to an activist was accompanied by some defined campaigns and actions that took her to the high pedestal of social and political activism. After the unprecedented success of her novel, The God of Small Things, Roy started grappling with concepts that pertained to social justice and human rights, which gave birth to the desire in her to bring about positive change to the world. While she started her initial activities in advocacy, Roy tried to advocate for the silenced poor people, seeking to raise their voices against oppression.

One of Roy's earliest campaigns sought to bring attention to the suffering of marginalised populations in the context of large development projects like the controversial Narmada Dam construction. In attempting to understand the intricacies of displacement and destruction of nature, she spoke with passion that captivated the public and brought her cause unparalleled attention. Her efforts on behalf of the marginalised people, along with her articulate communication skills, made her one of the leading voices against unjust state and corporate neo-colonial oppression.

Roy's participation in a myriad of grassroots efforts and civil society actions deepened her commitment to the socio-political inequities of her context. She single-handedly attracted the world's attention to local issues while building coalitions with other activists and organisations through her participation in public debates, marches, and rallies. This approach was key to Roy's vision and showed others that change is possible when people unite, thus building a strong base for her anti-establishment literature and activism.

As Roy's authority was expanding, so was her involvement with a wide range of issues, be it indigenous advocacy, gender bias, discrimination, or even freedom of speech. With such wide-ranging engagements, she began to establish a presence at the intersection of literature and activism, championing an idealistic social order that seemed almost utopian. This phase in Roy's life was the starting point of her determined activism, which later morphed out of the traditional confines of activism into fierce non-fictional prose.

Charting New Territories: Shift from Fiction to Non-fiction

Roy's move from fiction to non-fiction was another defining moment in her life because it made her step away from the world of fiction towards one that is more rooted in reality. With this change came a new set of responsibilities that stemmed from a genuine need to address the reality of the present, paired with a potent capability to inspire change and initiate critical discussions.

With Roy's step into the non-fiction realm, it was evident that she was ready to face harsh truths and use her pen as a weapon. She wasn't just an observer; writing for her became an act of rebellion. As a self-defined public intellectual, she set out to do the unthinkable: break the established order and the narratives surrounding it, while also inviting the audience to think critically about the order and norms set by society and the government.

Switching from fiction to non-fiction gave Roy the chance to tackle complex issues in great depth with a focus on sidelined and marginalised issues and topics. From corporate environmental destruction to human rights abuses and state violence, she brought attention to these issues and many more through critical and profoundly deep research. This metamorphosis showcased her relentless search for justice and equality, which deeply affected people both nationally and internationally.

Using her experience and first-hand encounters with people suffering due to social injustice, Roy visited new places with compassion and claimed authority where it was warranted. With her literary skills, she backed these arguments with stories that were moving and greatly appealing as they went beyond intellect, delving into the workings of the systems of power and oppression.

Moreover, the shift into non-fiction enabled Roy to participate in a discussion that went beyond the boundaries of her fictional works. Her works sparked debates, shaped policies, and triggered activism, underlining the critical function literature serves in social transformation. Using the pen as a sword of defiance, she took on the powerful with unmatched vigour, evoking the internationalism of the oppressed and those seeking a just society who had long been dormant.

In summary, the shift of Arundhati Roy from fiction to non-fiction represents a decisive stage in her life, one that is imbued with a strong sense of urgency and didacticism. Needless to say, her storytelling mastery in fiction is profound, but her non-fiction pieces showcase her unwavering intention to challenge the status quo and champion the oppressed. This change was not only a fresh contribution to literature, but also set a fresh and strong reminder of the relationship between art and activism which still fuels the endeavour towards a more inclusive and humane society.

Influential Essays: Articulating Vision and Dissent

Arundhati Roy's entry into the realm of non-fiction writing enabled her to engage with various socio-political issues and, as controversial as it may sound, express her vision and dissent with an unmatched sophistication. Her Independent essays are a few of the most remarkable expressions of critical thinking on contemporary global issues. Through these writings, Roy takes the liberty to subvert and redefine the contours of dominant discourse and power. We cannot ignore the underlying strength of her essays that are carefully crafted to draw attention, discussion, and encourage action.

In Roy's case, it is her remarkably keen observational skill and ability to reflect on current events that make her stand out among seasoned writers. The essays she tackles on the topics of climate change, violations of humanitarian rights, wealth disparity, and the socially dangerous phenomena of capitalism speak on their harshest points. She generously lays out her grand ideas, which, when put together, form a whole that is bigger than the sum of its parts and serve as an invitation to the readers to think and act towards the world we live in. With every word carefully chosen and arranged, Roy exposes her bedrock beliefs about the pursuit of truth and justice, revealing how profoundly the public discourse is shaped by such brilliant minds.

And of course, these essays provide a window into Roy's powerful convictions about these communities who have been silenced by the very systems designed to protect their fundamental human rights.

With relentless determination, she reveals the injustices caused by dominant power structures and calls on the readers to make an effort towards achieving a more balanced and fair society. Through her nuanced storytelling and sharp analyses, Roy's essays come alive beyond the borders of traditional debate, asking the audience to work alongside her to craft a kinder and more inclusive global community.

In a nutshell, Roy's powerful essays possess the remarkable ability to galvanise people, evoking motivation to transform, and encouraging them to take centre stage and lead societal change. As she tackles difficult subjects and presents bold viewpoints, she dares the reader to reconsider the familiar sphere of social contract and move beyond the narrow value of reality. Thus, she takes the baptism of public debates and ensures that there is no vacuum or neglect of emerging discussions that matter. Roy uses written language to call readers to action to create a world imbued with justice, compassion, and unwavering unity.

The Role of Public Intellectual: Engaging Wider Audiences

Beyond her work in literature and activism, Arundhati Roy is a public intellectual whose voice has a profound impact on society. While engaging with wide audiences, she drives the efforts to discuss essential socio and political issues that are available. In her critique and passionate advocacy, Roy goes beyond the traditional parameters of discussion and uses her social platform to talk about issues that matter. It is this multidimensional approach that not only engages but also mobilises existing supporters as well as reaches out to audiences with opposing views.

Roy is able to tap into audiences from different walks of life due to her relaxed manner combined with an unwavering dedication to social justice on her part. Through lectures, public interviews, and even rhetoric in public forums, she manages to break the barrier of complex themes and presents them in a way that everybody can relate to. Her skillful articulation of intricate concepts makes her a sought-after figure for discussions on topics ranging from environmental conservation to economic inequality and human rights.

Moreover, Roy uses her power to raise the voices of the oppressed in both national and international fora. She understands the significance of narratives and uses them to explain the stories of the less heard. With her profound literary skills, she constructs heart-touching stories with a view to nurturing compassion towards the people and cultures, in epic proportions.

Roy comes to the fore in this era of technology through different media and communication channels. From social networking sites to writings and visual recordings, she makes use of almost all modern technology to communicate her ideas. By using such platforms, she can personally connect to an audience irrespective of their location or culture.

Additionally, Roy is not limited to traditional audiences and makes the best of them. She participates with other artists, filmmakers and musicians in search of new ways of advocating and creating. Her participation within other disciplines transforms how she deals with activism and rational discourse, bringing new excitement to the everyday.

In short, as a public intellectual, Arundhati Roy is crucial in mobilising larger audiences, cultivating debate, and advocating for social change. Her tireless efforts in voicing the voiceless, coupled with her ability to communicate sophisticated ideas, make her one of the foremost modern-day writers and activists in the world today.

Controversies and Challenges: Navigating Opposition

Contesting dominant norms and structures is often considered a scope for opposition. For a celebrated novelist turned activist, Arundhati Roy, opposition in the form of critique has always resonated along the lines of her life and career. During her involvement with social and political controversies, she aggressively and single-handedly opposed multifarious challenges on a local and international scale.

Roy is known to have taken an actively unapologetic 'in your face' stance against certain phenomena like environmental and human abuse as well as gross socio-economic disparity. Along with other controversies, this led to the emergence of hundreds of issues such as public character defamation, legal controversies, and a variety of public backlash. Her unilateral scrutinisation of governmental policies, extreme corporate influences, and the glorification of nationalist sentiments were, in turn, used against her to try and silence or eliminate her.

Some ferocious frictions did not arise only from outside sources but also from various sections within society that were adverse to change or perceived her views as being too radical. Managing and manoeuvring through these exploding dynamics became very challenging. On top of that, as is common with most divided and polemic issues, these topics strongly offended defenders of the status quo which amplified the need for silencing these voices even more.

The intricacies of competing with one's juxtaposed identities and beliefs remain just as challenging as competing with opposition. Roy was criticised for provocation and outspoken advocacy for CLR, as well as for her opposition towards systems of power that undermine others. This resulted in critics pushing back against her initiating opposition because it undermined the traditional narrative of power structures being incorporated within them.

Beside this, Roy also challenged hegemony's stereotypes, telling them that there is no such thing as absolute control to counter. These counterarguments seem simple but are exceedingly complex within overbearing narratives socially accepted. Encompassed within them are preposterous justifications of American democracy and civilisation, which one can only fathom. Roy's antagonists sought a resolution through glaring failure, redirection to reverse prey-and-predator structures fully ignored. Leverage in such circumstances is typically unforgivingly abused. Encountering such horrendous assertions causes silence to seize for most; however, the opportunity was seized instead of sanctioned.

Roy's active and idle life has decisively fostered her change, and these contradictions uncovered extremes of horrendous cruelty she was compelled to face as an outworking of bounding.

Collaborative Efforts: Alliances with Social Movements

The shift into activism and non-fiction writing for Arundhati Roy began with her participation in collaborative social movements. Understanding the need for social movements, Roy sought the cooperation of grassroots and advocacy organisations, as well as oppressed groups, in order to multiply the benefits of her advocacy efforts. She realised that to bring about meaningful change, there was a need for people's solidarity and diverse experiences to unite towards a common goal.

Roy's social movement alliances included a myriad of issues such as anti-globalisation, environmental and indigenous peoples' rights, and even wars. Associating herself with movements like these, she aimed towards achieving the social struggles which called for multiple issues to be addressed in an inclusive way. She did not just passively support these causes but actively aided them by using her social power and knowledge, which, in turn, helped garner attention to these critical issues regarding social justice.

Furthermore, Roy was directly involved in advocacy work, including participation in mobilisations and demonstrations. Such actions earned her a spot in the media and at the same time made the causes she supported more visible thanks to the media coverage she received. Her activism aided in building real relationships with people suffering from systemic injustice and deepened her understanding of their lived realities.

Beyond the activism, Roy's literature helped bring attention to the activists and leaders of the social movements. She not only wrote, but made public appearances to give a voice to people who were often sidelined. This writing approach gave power to the powerless and helped broaden the discussion on social justice and change.

The impacts of Roy's work with different groups gained attention for more than just the awareness created. These movements integrated into powerful campaigns for change that progressively shifted public policy, public sentiment, introduced legal reforms, and changed people's attitudes towards social movements. Additionally, Roy's collaboration with a wide range of movements helped build greater unity among various causes and enhanced the overall progressive movements for social change.

In the end, Roy's coalitions with social movements showcased her personal investment in a better world constructed with the collective efforts of citizens. By appreciating the role and skills of grassroots organisers and broader society's unsung heroes, she showcased how solidarity can tackle societal problems and work for positive social change.

Impact Analysis: Measuring Success and Influence

The consequences that stem from Arundhati Roy switching her focus to activism, and non-fiction writing, are hugely noteworthy, which is why they need to be analysed thoroughly. In this setting, success and influence are not only defined with traditional literary trophies, but also with societal transformation, political conversations, and the visibility given to the oppressed. By analysing the intangible changes alongside the tangible results, we can understand what impact Roy's advocacy has had.

While analysing the impact of Roy, one critical aspect to keep in mind is the real changes that followed her participation in social movements and causes. This includes changes in laws, changes in policies, and changes at the organisational base which stem from her activism work. All of these structural changes are measurable and can be evaluated in terms of their enduring effects on the various communities, so they provide a straightforward means of measuring success.

Moreover, the impression that Roy's non-fiction and public activities have created is equally important. A single speech can galvanise public sentiment and instigate active debate on critical socio-political matters and she has done exactly that through eloquent essays and speeches. Here, the dissemination of ideas and amplification of the submerged voices are equally and significantly impactful within the scope of her activism.

Beyond the tangible changes, social justice education, human rights infringement, and environmental concern deserve special attention because of actively engaging the public through these issues. Additionally, Roy's ability to mobilise a wide range of people and groups for action indicates that she wields great power over a multitude of audience which is, indeed, her enduring influence.

An interdisciplinary approach to impact analysis assumes Roy's work has had an impact on academic circles, and it is her contributions that have evoked fresh debates and responses from different disciplines. Such activity is certainly beyond immediate practical outcomes, but it gives rise to enrich the discourse and perform deeper examination of the intersection of literature, politics, and human rights.

In the end, the nuanced consequences of Roy's activism and non-fiction writing need to be assessed in a comprehensive manner that both measures and considers the more complex changes in attitudes, policies, and storytelling. Understanding the intricacies of her influence and assessing its implications over time helps us understand the advocacy's impact on the world while fundamentally grasping the extent of her life's work.

Reflections on Activism: Personal Narratives and Insights

In a strange twist of paradox, the stories that accompany Arundhati Roy's activism are possibly the most mundane, yet contain the deeply personal insights that shaped her journey through life and continue to do so for many others globally. In these reflective narratives, Roy provides a glimpse of the psychological and emotional aspects of activism and recounts in her own way, the fight, motivation, and tenacity behind her holistic commitment to social justice. She recounts the intimate episodes that have ignited her zeal for change and describes her deep emotional connection with marginalised communities and individuals whose stories have shaped her worldview. By bringing these personal stories to the forefront, Roy humanises her advocacy work in a way that is incredibly powerful and empathetic, moving her activism beyond words into action. These stories harbour some degree of paradox too, as in equal measure of compassion, empathy, and hope, there exists the deep lament of the toll that the deep structures of power take on those who navigate the tumultuous waters of dissent.

Her thoughtful activism provides invaluable perspective into the ethical concerns and moral struggles accompanying efforts towards any meaningful transformative change. Additionally, Roy offers remarkable criticism on activism and the construction and deconstruction of social movements within the context of global issues and the new globalised world. She stresses the importance of mobilization and unified grassroots movements with strong intersectional coalitions on sociopolitical transformation based on her vast experience. With these remarks, Roy contributes to the discussion on activism and prepares future social change advocates by explaining the multifarious facets of social change phenomena. Roy's insights on activism reflect far beyond her personal life and narrative in essence and serve as a rich depository of wisdom, courage, and compassion, while offering constant encouragement to those who tend to dismiss the avenues through which humanity needs empowerment and help. Such insights will never age, evidencing the need for an individual's will to act and the community working together to redesign and reshape the world we all live in.

Transitioning Forward: Future Paths and Aspirations

Arundhati Roy's life as an activist and a writer has been dedicated to working on social justice, environmental issues, and human rights. As she looks forward, she aspires to continue performing work that sheds light on and elevates marginalised communities as well as systematically oppressed people. She aims for diverse communities to engage with one another in a manner that allows for empathy to be cultivated in a world full of conflict and division. Roy remains resolute in addressing land rights, indigenous issues, anti-globalisation, and other movements which are powerful and require constant attention. She is eager to promote younger writers and activists in the hope of fostering a critical and empowering legacy. With the intention of using educational and mentoring projects, she anticipates encouraging and inviting younger generations to be a part of societal change. Roy imagines continuing to blend fiction and non-fiction writing, using narrative storytelling as an agent for social change as she moves forward.

What Roy is aiming for rather is a focus on fostering transnational solidarity through art in order to address both global cooperation and the Indian challenges such as economic inequality, climate change, and geopolitical conflicts. She pushes further by envisioning the use of digital technology to reach wider audiences because virtual spaces have the capacity to mobilise people for action and build awareness. In conceiving her intended path, Roy has reflected on the complexities of the pursuit of justice and equality. She notes the need for an approach that outlines the reality of discrimination and oppression and recognises that these encircle whole communities. Most importantly, she intends to participate in conversations and projects that transcend geographical boundaries and are meant to empower people from all parts of the world. The advancement of Roy's mastery in the literary world continues to guarantee her commitment as a writer and animator of socio-cultural life whose agenda captures the attention of the contemporary world for change.

Chapter Five

Exploring the Richness of Narrative

Thematic Elements in Roy's Fiction

Thematic Exploration

Thematic exploration in Arundhati Roy's works reveals a myriad of ideas, feelings, and social problems. Her stories encompass complex human relationships and family dynamics, which form an underlying current of her plot development. Roy masterfully describes the relationships and the interplay of individuals and families with their roles and families. The exploration of social relationships and family is a recurrent theme and provides insight into the human experience and the impact relations have on structures of society. To analyse her narratives, Roy poses the questions to be answered through the text: what role does family play in one's self-identification? How does one's past family history shape their present? What can love and loss do to a person within a family context? This part prepares the ground for analysing the various aspects that characterise Roy's literature and examines the emotions and societal critique present in her stories.

Human Relationships and Familial Ties

Arundhati Roy's fiction reveals family relationships as the emotional anchor of the story while integrating them into the plot. She intricately navigates through family systems, exploring the diverse relationships, clashes, and attachments that define the life of her characters. Familial bonds are regarded with concern as they exemplify both the beauty of love and the intricacies of its intimate circles. Roy encapsulates the essence of love, loss, betrayal, and redemption amidst familial relations and mirrors humanity through them. Through robust characterization and gripping narratives, she depicts the immense joys, persistent battles, and unrelenting tensions within families and makes readers walk through the characters' emotional experiences.

Additionally, Roy's examination of family relationships also has a social and cultural scope. She shows how people's relationships are shaped by traditions, social norms, and the passage of time by intertwining personal stories with societal structures. Roy masterfully tells the tale of how individual and collective histories are woven together simultaneously, focusing on the socio-cultural dimensions of family relationships. Her stories unravel the myriad ways families are structured, revealing the underlying current of historical, cultural, and power relations that shape her narratives. Thus, Roy thematically deepens the understanding of her works' fundamental issue.

Also, Roy's understanding of human relations goes beyond biological and legal dimensions of family to include chosen and found families and unconventional relationships. She richly develops the idea of human relations by showing her readers characters who receive support, comfort, and companionship outside the traditional definition of family. In these other relationships, Roy captures the tenacity of the human spirit and the ability to love and nurture in unexpected ways. Such an approach enriches the thematic scope of her fiction while providing insight into the importance of family, compassion, and relationships in a changing world.

Ultimately, Roy's fiction demonstrates how relationships, connections, and social interactions have bearing on one's identity, impact a sense of community, and even society as a whole. Through compelling narration, she brings readers deep into the exploration of emotions—how people and cultures intermingle, fundamentally transforming them and showing them the true meaning of human connection.

Post-Colonial Contexts and Cultural Identity

It is crucial to analyse post-colonial contexts along with cultural identity as these are the essences underlying Arundhati Roy's remarkable literary work. Roy masterfully balances the impact of colonial rule and cultural identity that is uniquely woven in India's fabric. Roy also talks about the aftermath of colonialism—the struggle to find cultural identity through modernity's lens—and the oscillation between native culture and foreign culture heavily affects civilisation. Through her diverse narratives and rich settings, Roy also poses questions regarding the impacts of embracing modernity on traditions and belief systems.

Roy's work is remarkable in its portrayal of the intricate aspects of cultural identity in post-colonial societies. She fuses history with contemporary life so vividly that readers are offered an incisive glimpse into the processes of individual and communal struggle and triumph. Her narratives also illustrate the latent complexities of cultural amalgamation and the unique ways in which people grapple with their cultural legacy in the wake of globalisation.

In Roy's work, the exploration of post-colonial contexts is not limited to India. She deals with more complex themes of imperialism, nationalism, and resistance. Roy's subversive stories profoundly challenge the prevailing hegemonic powers as they wrestle with the complex intertwining of oppression and subjugation. Through layered cultural memory and collective trauma, Roy captures the enduring impacts of colonial legacies, allowing readers to consider why contemporary societies function the way they do.

Additionally, in Roy's depiction, cultural identity is not only about representation, but also a representation that calls for self-reflection and conversation. By weaving together personal stories and societal conflicts, she compels readers to confront the burdens of colonial legacies and invites them to partake in the difficult conversations that foster unity. Through powerful prose, she dismantles stereotypes and incites empathy, building a society that is more caring and accepting.

To summarise, Roy's analysis of post-colonial contexts and cultural identity is a remarkable demonstration of the tenacity and vibrancy of peoples and cultures as they navigate a multifaceted world. It goes without saying that this evolving aspect of her narratives deepens them and simultaneously encourages contemplation at such great lengths that one goes through an enriching process of self-exploration and reflection on society.

Social Injustice and Caste Dynamics

Social injustice and the caste system has been one of the key aspects of concern in the works of Arundhati Roy. Through her writing, Roy examines the intricate nature of Indian social systems, revealing the persistent brutalisation of people of the lower castes and their relentless impact on families and societies. Her stories vividly portray the plight of subordinate groups and systematically unfold the discrimination and violence done against them in different spheres of life.

Roy has made it clear that social injustice and the caste system is entrenched in every aspect of social life and exposes the deep-rooted inequality system. It demonstrates how the processes of social stratification are interlaced with other forms of discrimination like racism, sexism, and classism, and more where such issues define the existence of her people. Roy brings these problems to the forefront to make her audience uncomfortable, making them make way to the resolution to deep-seated biases of society.

Also, Roy's approach to social injustice is not only one of concern, as she weaves it into captivating stories that force readers to confront the struggles of people at the nadir of the caste system. Her dramatised depiction of the plight and the hope of the oppressed increases the need to tackle caste discrimination and inequities in modern-day India and beyond.

Roy's novels demand societal and collective responsibility while arguing for action to eradicate socially unjust discriminative frameworks and divides rooted within the caste system. With the power of her narratives, she pleads for compassion, acceptance, and togetherness, so that the oppression is realised and active steps towards creating a just society can be taken by everyone.

This way, Roy's criticism of the social injustices women face through the lens of the caste system deepens the conversation around inequity while forcing action towards it. This dimension of her writing does not only add value to her works but also offers considerable insight and shifts the focus of debate toward equity and justice through literature voiced by many around the world as they confront caste marginalisation and social change.

Memory and Time: A Non-linear Approach

It is evident from Arundhati Roy's fiction that her non-linear approach to time forces the reader to engage with it and memory in an unorthodox manner. Roy artfully arranges the order of her narratives in such a way that they seem to interrupt linear narratives while presenting emotions and events through a shattered prism that resembles how humans remember things. This is how Roy examines the nature of time, memory and the non-linearity of the human experience.

In Roy's works, time is not merely a chronological sequence of events easy to track, but rather, is an elastic concept that stretches and snaps to the will of memory and perception. These concepts are interlaced components that weave together, flow together and merge with each other in an orderly but still disorienting manner that begs one to ponder the intricacies of human recollection. The essence of non-linear human memory that Roy strives to convey takes the form of emotions capable of transcending boundaries of meaning and the constraining elements embedded in time and time itself.

Moreover, the non-linear method used by Roy enables the examination of trauma, resilience, and collective memories on a micro and macro level. Memories come and go while blending with the present to give shape to a deeply woven narrative that represents both personal and societal trauma. Roy's deft handling of temporal layers allows for the infusion of urgency and emotional weight into her stories, all while conveying a deep understanding of the consequences of historical discrimination.

Invoking non-linearity permits Roy to bypass conventions of narrative structure, drawing attention to the interwoven tapestry of personal and communal histories. Non-linearity empowers readers to remember the past alongside the character and engage in constructing the fractured puzzle that demands empathy towards the complex inner world of the characters. Thus, Roy's unconventional grasp of memory and time moves her works past the limitations of literature, offering her audience an alluring realm where time flows naturally, memories are palpable, and life defiantly prevails.

Gender Roles and Feminism

In Arundhati Roy's literary works, gender roles and feminism are some of her most profound topics because of her attempts to include marginalized voices and the societal frameworks that are at play. Roy goes beyond traditional frameworks, exploring power structures like identity and gender, as well as the ways through which patriarchal order is inverted. In her fiction, she portrays the Indian woman's plight and struggle, her resilience, and her agency working within oppressive systems. Roy navigates gender alongside other social identities like caste, class, and religion, enriching her take on intersectional feminism. Her stories offer nuanced representations while at the same time dismantling stereotypes that travel across the globe, making people critically examine the systemic oppression and deep-rooted impacts of gender discrimination. Roy ardently advocates for women's rights, which, alongside gender equality, becomes the focal point of her narratives. She tells the stories of those who have been neglected or marginalized. Her characters are not passive; they break free from the socially constructed restraints, capturing the spirit of feminist defiance and strength.

Not through Dabri Roy's feminism literary critique, Roy exposes the capitalism underlying the patriarchal oppression of women, defining new boundaries of misogyny and offering possibilities of alternative futures. Roy deepens the image of sympathy of her readers by inseparably weaving together gender, power, and freedom relations through striking language and vivid imagination. Arundhati Roy advances the discussion with her feminism literature remarking Indian and women's position within social structures and deeply impacts literature alongside social justice activities.

Environment and Place as Characters

In Roy's novels, we see that the environment and place do not function as a mere background to the action; they serve as integral characters in their own right. The intricate details of nature and geography serve westernization not only as the scenery of action, but also as the driving force of the tale. In 'The God of Small Things', Kerala is described in the most beautiful and spellbinding manner, and it's not just the description, but part of the invaluable embrace shaping the story's curve. The dialectics of beauty and fury are captured indelibly into the very walls of the Kerala backwaters, and so the domineering waters and hot-tempered beauty capture the spirit of the characters' emotions throughout the events.

Roy's treatment of the environment incorporates a wider scope including ecological devastation, the socio-economic and political displacement caused by development projects, and the overarching impact of political hyphenated logics. Her stories deal with the aftermath of human impacts on nature, focusing on the disruption of life due to violence as a consequence of nature's counteraction. Through masterful narration, she illustrates the bond that exists between the environment and the people within it, showing how shifting weather patterns or biology can be seen as answers or responses to social changes and vice versa. This multifaceted reality is what enriches her stories beyond imagination, where nature plays an active role in the conflict.

In Roy's works, the notion of place serving as a character device is strikingly prominent. The rough and dreary landscape of war-torn Kashmir serves as setting and for characterization, as well as the fiery protests against land acquisition depicted in 'The Ministry of Utmost Happiness,' where the landscapes become a representation of the socio-political reality of the people inhabiting them. By attributing agency to these places, Roy changes the narrative, converting them from mere backdrops to active forces that significantly affect the lives of the characters.

Roy's evocative blending of the environment and space with human life enhances the emotional scope and relatability of her stories. She depicts the environment and place as social actors who shape the fates of the characters, making the readers interrogate their connection with the world and the consequences of people's actions on the places we live. In doing so, she breaks the conventional limits of storytelling and creates a rich narrative landscape where the environment and place are prominent protagonists.

Silence and Voice: Power of the Marginalised

Roy masterfully captures society's marginalised in her works using the dual silence and voice. The hybrid silence is often a product of social subjugation, political dominance or discrimination. This agency brings the voices of the marginalised to the fore. Roy intricately interlaced narratives to showcase the struggle of discrimination within dominance. Closing one's mouth, for one reason or another, has a purpose and is blanketing one's identity or life experience. The absence of a voice is a powerful weapon that continues the subjugation and disempowerment of a particular target group. Roy's protagonists struggle with a phenomenon called silence. They traverse a disempowering society that is self-perpetuating and seeks to erase their social agency. On the other hand... amplifying voice serves the potent act of reclamation. Without a doubt, silencing individuals leads to the erasure of identities. Roy showcases the preservation of power that lies in storytelling, claiming the tagline – available for all. Storytelling indeed prevents the cancellation of narratives and offers the oppressed and invisible the chance to claim their identity. "That is effectively coming out of narratives and declaring their existence along with the forming rigid oppressive systems." Roy's nuanced representation of this dialectic captures the importance of constructive narratives for achieving fairness and balance within societies. By revealing the complexities of silence and voice, Roy urges readers to confront the privileges that come with speaking, listening, and witnessing. This exploration of themes resonates acutely in contemporary socio-political landscapes, prompting consideration of the ways in which silencing practices continue to reinforce marginalisation and inequity. Roy's poetic prose answers the call to action by showing us how we need to shift the focus to those whose voices have been silenced, dismantling the mechanisms that perpetuate these narratives, and challenging the narratives themselves. In this way, discussions about silence and voice in Roy's fiction showcase the power of storytelling while calling on people to take up the responsibility of amplifying marginalised voices, building empathy, and nurturing active solidarity.

Interweaving Personal and Political Narratives

Roy's literary creativity can be best understood through the integration of personal experiences within a political context. In each of her novels and essays, she unites the unique phenomena of individual life with socio-political realities. This union is emblematic of the struggle for human existence and society's system of dominance and control that one tries to break through.

Roy's personal motive is fixed in the complex fabric of life, and that which is personal is political. She depicts how different characters are able to exercise their agency in the context of their relationships, the choices that they are presented with, and the struggles that form the other side of the coin around them. This intersection profoundly affects and is affected by the complex array of national and international reality, the intersection of the individual and the collective.

Roy does more than depict ideas; she gives voice to real people by interweaving personal narratives that challenge the existing dominant beliefs. Readers come to empathise with fictional characters while at the same time realising their anger due to the lies hidden behind the façade of politics, revealing how the lives of ordinary people are shaped by the decisions made by those in power.

The combination of the personal and political dimensions of her story enhances its appeal and relevance, provoking consideration of and dialogue about important social concerns.

Roy's blending of personal and political stories is valuable in resisting hegemonic narratives and highlighting neglected narratives. By focusing on personal matters within a broader socio-political context, she constructs counter-narratives that challenge the dominant discourse and depict neglect. This blending removes the distinction between the personal and political and compels readers to acknowledge the impact of unacknowledged power dynamics.

To sum up, Arundhati Roy's literature is encased in deep intimacy, emotion, and relevance due to the aplomb she uses to combine personal and political narratives. With her profound storytelling, she argues about the fate of lives suspended in the torrent of history and speaks about the need for their lives to be transformed by literature and discourse about justice, equity, and societal changes.

Conclusion: Synthesis of Themes in Roy's Literary Canon

In the post-reading of Arundhati Roy, it is clear that the depth of her stories is beyond mere storytelling. It is a striking feature of her work where themes of human connections, memory, gender, post-colonialism, social injustice, and the environment are interconnected; personal history and political events are deeply interwoven, revealing an intricately woven tapestry of multidimensional literature. This cross blend is a reflection of the complexity of society, human experience, and social interactions that Roy captures with unparalleled insight.

Chapter Six

Political Engagements

Narmada Dam and State Critiques

Historical Context: The Narmada Valley Development Project

The Indian government initiated the Narmada Valley Development Project as one of the largest river development projects in India. It intended to develop irrigation facilities and hydroelectric power stations on the Narmada River in order to harness its water resources. It was supposed to provide water and electricity to millions of people living in poverty-stricken areas of Gujarat, Madhya Pradesh, and Maharashtra, stimulating socio-economic development in those areas.

Still, the goals of the project were too ambitious, especially in regards to land acquisition and relocation costs for displacing indigenous populations, which led to further complications. The construction of dams and reservoirs resulted in flooding vast areas that required the relocation of thousands of families, submerging promising farmlands, thriving forests, culturally significant places, and historical treasures. These repercussions led to immense unrest and opposition from the communities that were affected and resulted in protests and advocacy movements on both national and international levels.

Apart from that, the Narmada Valley Development project cut across major issues of more social concern including sustainable development, social justice, and indigenous people's rights. Detractors noted the adverse impacts on the environment due to dam construction, while also considering the mitigation of imbalance in resource levelling which ignored indigenous and marginalised people alongside the vulnerable groups.

The undertaking also mandated a review of government policy and decisions concerning the level of consultation and participation of the communities in the project's planning, implementation, and execution. The conflict of interest between the vision of the stakeholders for the Narmada region led to the realisation of the need to balance development with environmental and social justice, making the development project heavily oversocialised in nature.

All in all, the Narmada Valley Development Project served as the profound subject of dispute concerning the issue of the interrelationship between development, equality, human rights, and environmental concern giving room to incredibly long debates and movements throughout the Indian community and beyond.

Roy's Introduction to Activism: Early Involvements and Influences

Her sympathy towards the underrepresented, royalty neglected people and deeply oppressed became visible during Roy's early life in her home state of Kerala. As part of a progressive family, she still continues to remember the very first discussions she had regarding social inequality and political fights. With education from the National Institute of Design in Ahmedabad, she got greater focus as well as understanding of various issues related to socio-politics. This was able to put her in touch with movements that campaigned for the environment, social issues, as well as basic human rights and the impact was overwhelming. The turning point for her was the Narmada Bachao Andolan (NBA) as well as the struggle against the Sardar Sarovar Dam. Roy's perspective was changed completely as she came face to face with development-induced dislocation and devastation. The aftermath of these activities and the preceding environmental degradation forced her to realise the extent of damage that the people of the country are having to suffer due to disgusting development policies. The circumstances made use of the works of leaders like Gandhi and Ambedkar and pro-activists to formulate ideas that helped express her disagreement both at the societal and political level and do politics.

Through her first novel, 'The God of Small Things,' Roy captured the landscape of India, both sociologically and politically, shaping her image as an author and as an activist. Along with Roy's emergent literary recognition came an ever-growing engagement with social activism, as she began to use her platforms to address the deep-rooted inequities faced by marginalised people. These experiences of engagement and the influences around her not only set out the path for her as an activist, but also made her recognise the need for action and responsibility that comes with power.

The Real Cost: Understanding Displacement and Human Impact

Displacement resulting from large scale development initiatives like the Narmada Valley Development Project is a complex issue that affects an entire region and a vast number of people and communities. It is equally important to look beyond the salient statistics and appreciate the intricacies and humanity that comprise the story of displacement. The cost of displacement is not simply the loss of homes or employment. It represents, perhaps more acutely, the erosion of cultural and social set identities.

At the core of this conversation is the intense disruption faced by people who were forcibly removed from their lands. The mental impact of displacement is something that is extremely difficult to quantify as people try to cope with the feeling of being severed from connections to the landscapes that formed the basis of their identity. The displacement caused by relocation creates fractures within a community which undermines enduring social relationships and support mechanisms.

It is important, however, to note the other consequences of such large scale infrastructure projects, namely the personal consequences as well as the environmental costs. These changes in ecosystems and natural settings result in a form of displacement, not just limited to human beings but also extending to displaced wildlife. Environmental devastation increases the degree of hardship faced by already vulnerable communities placed on marginal land, worsening their suffering.

Exploring the real consequences of displacement requires looking into the power relations and interests which are responsible for such calls for development. The fusion of policies from the state and companies along with corporate interests subsidies raises important questions about the social inequities masked by these projects which require deep scrutiny. Through the analysis of power, Roy makes it clear that sociopolitical discourse and activism is needed to mitigate the concerns of powerless people affected by such policies.

Recognising the true expense of displacement is to consider it a humanitarian violation on a very fundamental level. It needs immediate action from decision makers, social groups, and the entire world. To foster constructive discourse without being defined by figures enables us to feel the real impact of human suffering that comes through displacement and makes it relatable.

Sustained Campaigns: Mobilisation and Advocacy Strategies

The problem of the Narmada Valley Development Project posed a multitude of issues, and Roy Arundhati dealt with them with utmost care. Her perseverance with campaigning through unique methods alongside understanding the deeper context framed her multi-tiered advocacy approaches, which made all the difference. The campaign would not have been as effective without the right context and narrative.

Over writers marketed the project and made testimonials from people who previously worked with micros placed templates in-line. Combined with Tavakoli's work supplementary guides, these testimonials painted a broad outline that was further fortified by detailed scaffolding constructs. At the heart of her campaigns, Roy manufactured materials that catered to secondary school kids, which made high school seniors excited to drive those outcomes through. Alongside town hall meetings and community outreach programmes, this set the stage for positive shifts stemming from overwhelming public paradoxes.

Roy formulated powerful advocacy plans to make sure that the complaints of the displaced people were heard by important decision makers. Through petitions, marches, and other public events, she tried to highlight the very human aspects behind the numbers in the project's figures. In doing so, not only did she underscore the suffering of the people most affected, but also the most serious ecological and humanitarian impacts the dam's construction would have.

Besides direct contacts with affected communities and other stakeholders, media advocacy was an important component in Roy's campaigns. Through the use of press, television, radio, and the internet, she told the stories of the marginalised, creating compassion and support from audiences of different social and economic classes.

Also, Roy effectively used some international collaborations and partnerships to promote the Narmada Dam issue more globally. She worked with well-known local and foreign environmentalists and human rights defenders and specially drew their attention to the need to deal with the issues of forced displacement and environmental destruction. This approach not only expanded the campaign outreach, but also created partnerships that supported the credibility and effectiveness of the movement.

These long-lasting campaigns marked by systematic advocacy

showed how Arundhati Roy has fought for the elevating of silenced people as well as for sociopolitical injustices. Roy's impassioned yet strategic approach sparked movement both domestically and internationally, profoundly impacting India's environmental and social activism landscape.

Engaging with Policy Makers: Dialogues and Debates

Social justice and environmental conservation advocacy for which Arundhati Roy is known have been formed from policy engagements that contended for social change through meaningful debates. Dialogue as a method of negotiation, Roy has sought policy makers at the global, continental, national and local level to hear her arguments suggesting changes through her critique reasoning and argue concerning policy considerations. Here we attempt to explain the various aspects of Roy's engagement with policy makers noting some of the approaches Roy brought forth concerning the methods policy makers and even the general public arguing to make policy and societal change. Constructive engagement with policy makers, as Roy exemplifies, 'demands' deep-seated commitment to achieve outcomes that blend vivid confidence with tactic strategy. Shifts in policy often only take place when officials, lawmakers and the policy influencers are reached; this is often referred to top-bottom advocacy from community grassroots. In these efforts, Roy has come to engage for those suffering through policies that strive to raise ill-informed policies. Roy proposes that settlements aimed at bringing empathy and understanding to policy makers usually tend to fail. Those who do not care to cede some ground and are ready to grapple with difficult arguments across worlds of existing orthodoxy garner support from change advocates seeking systemic transformation.

Roy's dialogues have served not only as forums for expressing disagreement but have also triggered deep rethink among policy makers, challenging them to grapple with the harsh realities of vulnerable groups. Roy has dismantled deep-seated biases and misconceptions through compelling debates, providing challenging alternatives rooted in kindness and understanding. Recognising dialogue as a catalyst for change, Roy has utilised her pen to champion the causes of the powerless and expose the humanitarian crises neglected by bureaucratic systems. Her passionately crafted speeches and penetrating analyses have sparked debates that propelled policy makers to acknowledge the need for reforms. This interplay between Roy and the policy makers highlights the power and magic of engaging in meaningful discourse while demonstrating the transforming potential of civilised dialogue and thoughtful discussion for the advancement of social good. This emphasises both positive change and development.

Media Engagement: Amplifying Voices Through Literature and Interviews

As a prominent writer and activist, Arundhati Roy has mastered media advocacy as a campaigning technique to voice the plight of the underprivileged and marginalised communities in society. She has powerful literature that portrays the plight of people who have suffered because of state policies and environmental concerns. Furthermore, through her interviews and public engagements,

Roy has been able to advocate for the marginalised people, question the status quo, and engage the public on critical issues that need urgency from society.

Roy is aware of the power that literature has when it comes to awakening people towards social movements and revolutions. One of her most distinguished novels, 'The God of Small Things,' earned praise from many quarters including literary experts and audiences. It also shed light on the socio-political issues in Kerala while discussing themes such as caste, class, and gender in Indian society. Additionally, her essays and non-fiction works have provided sharp insight and commentary towards the socio-economic and political dynamics of today serving as great motivation to citizens and activists who care about the issues around them.

Apart from her literary works, Roy's insights and analysis have reached a wider audience through her interviews, public talks, and panel discussions. Roy's interactions with journalists and other media personalities enabled her to focus international attention on the struggles of marginalised peoples, where their voices are often ignored. These issues became public through Roy's articulate expression, with the impact of people starting to challenge the existing power structures and fostering empathy and solidarity.

Through the media, Roy has focused the audience's eyes on the understated human narratives behind political decisions and their resultant policies. Such active engagement showcases Roy's belief that every story, in every form of media, is a chance to make advocacy for social change. These comments amplify those who are silenced all too frequently, redefining the role of literature and journalism through her writing.

To sum up, it can be argued that the social media actions of Arundhati Roy show her strident commitment to social justice and advocacy. The intersection of literature, media, and activism has broadened the scope and impact of her message. In Roy's work, there is a sense of urgency and relevance that our world desperately needs today. The ongoing struggle of Roy to highlight the muted and challenge dominant discourse motivates emerging writers, activists, and every individual working towards a just and humane society.

Critiques of State Policies: Challenging the Consensus

Critiques of state policies form a crucial component of Arundhati Roy's engagement with socio-political issues, particularly her vocal stance against the controversial Narmada Valley Development Project. Roy's critique transcends mere opposition; she meticulously deconstructs and challenges the consensus surrounding government policies that perpetuate injustice and exploitation. By scrutinizing the impact of state decisions on marginalized communities, Roy exposes the inherent power imbalances and the detrimental consequences inflicted upon vulnerable populations. Through her literary prowess and incisive analysis, she illustrates how state policies often serve to consolidate the privilege of the powerful at the expense of disenfranchised groups. In meticulously confronting the prevailing narrative propagated by state authorities, Roy raises profound questions about accountability, ethics, and governance. She scrutinizes the underlying motives driving state policies and unmasks hidden agendas often obscured by officialese and propaganda. Roy's relentless interrogation of state policies forces a reappraisal of entrenched beliefs and challenges the unquestioned authority of governmental institutions, offering an alternative perspective that amplifies the voices of those who are silenced or ignored. Furthermore, by shedding light on the intricate web of interests that underpin governance decisions, Roy empowers readers to critically evaluate the ethical ramifications of bureaucratic actions and hold leaders accountable for their choices. Her articulate and compelling rhetoric effectively articulates the perspectives of marginalized communities, positioning their narratives at the forefront of discussions surrounding state policies. Ultimately, through her sustained and eloquent critiques, Roy advocates for a more equitable and just societal framework, thereby reshaping the discourse on governance, democracy, and societal responsibility.

International Perspectives: Aligning with Global Environmental Movements

Arundhati Roy's advocacy work goes beyond national boundaries as she participates in and supports the global environmental movement. By working at the intersection of political, social and environmental justice, she has established herself as a significant voice in global conversations around ecological conservation and sustainable development. Understanding the interconnectedness of environmental problems and the need for a collective response, Roy recognised the global... authored powerful writings and speeches for public audiences that underline the need for urgent climate action to conserve biodiversity. Aligning with global environmental movements, Roy has actively participated in diverse forums, workshops and collaborative efforts simultaneously aimed at solving critical environmental problems not only at her home but across the world. Beyond participation, her work has raised awareness as well as policy discourse and actionable steps on the environment around the world. Roy's work across different environmental organisations and platforms have enabled the exchange of perspectives, approaches and best practices towards collectively working to reverse environmental damage and enhance sustainability. Her explanation of the consequences of corporate and infrastructural development on ecosystems and marginalised peoples is compelling to many environmental advocates around the globe.

Roy seeks attention to vulnerable populations suffering due to environmental crises by actively joining global movements. Her international activism underscores the need to go beyond nation-specific conflicts and borders when dealing with common crises. Thus, Roy helps in developing the awareness needed to appreciate the relationship between all forms of life and the natural world. It demonstrates her willingness to participate in global environmental movements which helps to build international cohesiveness and action for unity towards improved wellbeing of people and nature.

Resistance and Repression: Navigating Adversity

Roy's journey toward social and environmental justice activism has not come without challenges. The chapter focuses on the unyielding attempts from state authorities and powerful stakeholders to silence her dissenting voice, and the equally remarkable resolve Roy showed in refusing to yield to repression. With her advancing activism, there was a clear multi-pronged strategy aimed at demonising her and attempting to curtail her influence. This chapter explains the legal and extralegal strategies to silence her activism, looking at how those in power worked to suppress her voice. It summarises the complex aspects of resistance while providing an enabling description of the stark inequalities in resources and access that existed as Roy sought justice. It also reveals, amidst struggle, the deep emotional and psychological scars that were imprinted due to constant confrontation, illustrating the reality of unrelenting pressure. While Roy fiercely countered attempts to limit her influence, a broad range of aligned forces came together in deeply damaged solidarity which she reached out toward. The chapter explores the variety of repression such as character assassination or legal limitations, revealing the reality of power control in civil society.

It also provides a deeper evaluation of the effects and impacts of these oppressive strategies on broader struggles for change. With powerful stories and chronicles, it explains the indomitable nature behind Roy's resistance and how that shaped contemporary activism. In essence, this part captures the essence of the struggle against hardship through transformative advocacy, showing the importance of courage and strength against organised oppression.

Long-term Impacts: Reflections on Activism and Outcomes

It is important for us to remember Arundhati Roy's work and its aftermath; her sociopolitical activism left a lasting imprint on society and the world as a whole. With her works and exertions, the way people think now and the conversations they have are largely different than before. One of the main achievements of

Roy's work is the emphasised attention on critical human social concerns focusing on social justice, environmental protection, as well as human rights. Because of her ardent support and disapproval of government, Roy brought a lot of change to society and public perception, which has inspired societal advancement on multiple fronts. Her influence is testimony to the power of her earlier activism far beyond the narrow context of agitation, which remains significant even today. Furthermore, the causes she championed have repeatedly outstripped confining specific clashes or campaigns, while providing enduring ecosystem shifts and improvement in policies. Not only did the Narmada Bachao Andolan movement try curbing dam construction, it also broadened the development discourse towards providing resources to people living in poverty or those who can't afford an ease of life, disenfranchised communities and prospective development. Roy turned the art of activism for social causes into literature by using her social endeavours to radically change the way people perceive art and literature.

Her various works have deeply shaped the understanding of multifaceted social problems and further prompted more extensive reflections around sociopolitical themes. Moreover, through her international work, she has built a global network of activists and thinkers that has furthered the scope of her work beyond national boundaries. As a result of her relentless efforts to achieve justice, there is, for example, considerable activism's impact in the legal sphere where case law, judicial activism, and other trailblazing legal constructs emerge from her activism. Finally, the results of Roy's activism are found in the sustainability of her messages and stories that critically challenge the relations of power along with the social order. In reflecting on the long-term outcomes of her activism, one appreciates fully the accounts of Roy's literature, activism and social change.

Chapter Seven

Navigating Controversy

Legal Challenges and Public Perception

Controversies: A Contextual Overview

The activism and writing of Arundhati Roy have demonstrated the damage of unapologetic nonconformity and defiance, often resulting in conflicts of a legal nature and public outrage. Controversies are an unescapable part of Roy's life as a vivid author and outspoken advocate for social and environmental justice, and this stems from her uncompromising boldness. Roy has faced legal issues from mocking government policy to fighting corporate theft, demonstrating her unyielding energy. Roy has sustained legal battles during her lifetime due to her fearless approach, showcasing the power of modern contrarianism. Furthermore, her involvement has cemented her reputation as a fighter for justice, but also symbolises the unwavering strength of literature juxtaposed with activism. Analyzing Roy's life through the lens of these controversies reveals the complexities and impactful force of dissent that shapes the narrative of society. Most importantly, however, it fosters an understanding of how such misrepresented dissent and conflict reconfigures the notions of artistic expression and activism.

Legal Entanglements: Analysing Key Court Cases

In Arundhati Roy's controversial life, we see that she has faced multiple legal battles due to her fierce activism and a mouth that does not mince words concerning issues that put her at odds with powerful systems. This part of the book focuses on some of the most important legal battles in Roy's life. One such battle is as recent as 2002 when she was charged with contempt of court for openly criticising the judiciary's treatment of a divisive dam project. This case thrust Roy into a legal storm, but it also became a focal point for debates around the world regarding the right to express dissenting opinions and free speech. Her participation in numerous human rights and environmental movements conflicts with the overreaching power of the state, marking the personal conflicts with the legal regime as battles capturing the distressing clash between individual advocacy actions that prompt state responses. These clashes in the courtroom were crucial for Roy's personal story: they fuelled her image – already radicalised from earlier writings – as a fervent champion of justice and human rights. Moreover, the way her battles in the courtroom were portrayed highlighted the struggles in India's socio-political situation, systemic problems people have to deal with, and the scope of civil liberties that exist in the country.

We reveal the intricacies of balancing activism through the law's lens—and the impacts of those who defy powerful order—after reviewing these court cases.

Public Perception: Media Representation and Impact

We cannot dismiss how Arundhati Roy has been put in the spotlight because of how the media has manipulated and had an effect on her work. The depiction of Roy in newspapers, television, and other media platforms greatly influences the way she is perceived and how she is embraced as a social and political advocate. The media representation and public perception work hand in hand and are multifaceted.

There are several debates on the accuracy of her messages and views as they are presented to the public through the media. Despite the advancement of communication technologies, traditional media remains dominant. Time and again, controlling public perception has given the media the chance to either defend or destroy people's reputation. Both graciously and harshly, this has presented itself to Roy, punishing and praising her for her bold takes on issues that greatly divide public opinion.

Also, the effect of media representation on Roy goes further to include her identity as a writer and an activist. Reviews, interviews, and feature stories consolidate her public image which affects how she advocates and how her writing is perceived. Furthermore, how her work is dealt with in the public domain has the potential to influence their expectations of her and interpretation of her work, adding to the importance of media representation in analysing the reception of her literary and activism efforts.

Moreover, how media representation interacts with public perception impacts the socio-political context in which Roy operates. The representation of her actions and ideas has the capacity to shape public perception and influence discourse on meaningful issues she addresses such as environmental justice, human rights, and economic disparity. Hence, media representation not only shapes perceptions of Roy as an individual but also transforms perceptions at the media level and shapes the level of engagement with the causes she promotes.

Considering these various angles, analysing media representation in light of public perception is crucial in understanding the dynamics around Arundhati Roy's public image and the attention given to her creative and activist undertakings.

The Role of Censorship: Challenging India's Legal Frameworks

Censorship, either by the government or society at large, has profoundly affected the creative scope in India. In this regard, issues surrounding Arundhati Roy have attracted severe controversies regarding the globalisation of culture and law. Roy's works in particular have sparked critical debates on the Indian and international legal systems which are in place to protect creative expression as well as the author's rights. Censorship, as defined legally or culturally, does pose an issue to the modern-day legal system of India and its freedom of expression.

Roy critically discusses that the legal infrastructure of India is fundamental for censorship because it derives from law which gives the government overreaching power to control if the entertainment industry undertakes despotic actions or is even incendiary in nature. This always leaves conflict with the legal prerogatives given in the constitution and provides a never-ending dilemma for societies. Having been the subject of many creative containment mechanisms, Roy appreciates her acceptance that the government has the right to mandate policies that control expression and societal portrayal.

India faces community censorship in addition to state-sponsored censorship. This can come in forms such as violence, economic sanctions, and even mere social avoidance. Such forces restrict freedom of expression. Roy's experiences exemplify navigation through the multifaceted barriers in the face of censorship beyond laws.

Roy, alongside her allies, has initiated movements to defy and eradicate the oppressive censorship practices. Whether it is through legal action, advocacy campaigns, or movements from international allies, they have worked towards greater freedom of expression and creative thought. Their efforts have safeguarded open debate in scholarly discourse and creative activities. Roy's national endeavours towards truth and social change have sparked discussions on the need for one of the country's legal structures, while weakening its control over the domain of protected creative work.

The persistent struggle with censorship highlights the critical contributions of artists, scholars, and public figures in the maintenance of democracy and the practice of constructive conflict. It calls for a review not only of the legal boundaries but also public opinion concerning artistic creation, emphasising the importance of collective and active defence of freedom of expression. While the conversation develops further, Roy's activism for uncensored expression showcases the willpower of many who defend creative expression and freedom of thought while facing attempts at silencing.

Support Networks: Allies and Advocates in Times of Crisis

Arundhati Roy has been fortunate during times of crisis. She has always had a support system of friends and allies ready to come to her aid in times of need. Roy considers herself lucky as many individuals came to her assistance providing help in various forms, emotionally as well as practically. She had to face legal battles and scrutiny from the public which was made easier due to the assistance she was receiving. Numerous writers and activists were ready to support her, along with legal experts and relevant NGOs which made her support system very multi-dimensional. One important factor of these support systems is that people help Roy with utmost faith that she will use her voice in the right way and will advocate for social justice. This aids in developing new ways of collaboration and support. Moreover, the support provided for Roy also brings focus and attention to other concerns like freedom of expression and even human rights, thus initiating the much needed debates and communal movements. Alongside moral support, she received help and guidance from advocates willing to strengthen her legal defence and further her message.

Whether it is through pro bono legal representation, fundraising, or providing strategic communication services, these allies have been crucial in protecting Roy's ability to continue working under strain. Their support has also helped moderate the impact of efforts to marginalise or discredit Roy's reputation, bolstering her within the literary and activist communities. This chapter will analyse the collective support networks during a crisis and reveal the relationship of an individual figure to the people who support him or her. By examining particular examples of support and advocacy, we are able to understand the complex network of relationships that defend and empower those who oppose power structures. These relationships create strong support networks to ensure that collaboration within the network is successful in resisting and standing resilient against adversities.

Critics and Detractors: Voices of Opposition

Arundhati Roy's powerful literary works alongside her political activism have stirred controversy and sparked debates that capture the attention of many. Critics and detractors of Roy, which include political rivals as well as cultural critics, have expressed counter opinions on her work and stance. Some of these critics have taken issue with her literary fiction blending too seamlessly with advocacy arguing that it erodes the aesthetic value of her prose. Other observers, scholars and commentators alike, noted that the blend of social issues and politics along with the overemphasis on the message of the work losing its substance marked a marked decline in literary quality.

Authors and groups holding other perspectives have provided responses to her coping advocacy, bold attitudes, fierce posited socio-political contrasts and the agenda informing their reasoning. In this case relevant to critiques, she has been accused of depicting more complicated issues in overly simple terms and framed as being divisive rather than fostering productive dialogue. The scrutiny surrounding her advocacy, however, has been multifocal; some critics of her advocacy wonder how accurate her interpretations are and claim her advocacy is riddled with discrepancies barring her from the required supporting context. Moreover, claims have been made regarding excessive dramatization of events alongside selective retelling of facts, which those countering her claims dislike becoming increasingly angry and dividing opposing groups.

In the public eye, media critics alongside opinion leaders have analysed and debated Roy's views for better or worse contributing to the polarized discussions. She has, in the eyes of some, been lionised, claiming the mantle of a courageous dissenting voice for speaking truth to power. Others, however, have condemned her as someone who seems more inclined to creating turmoil than productive arguments. There is considerable conflict over the discourse regarding her activism and its reception in public debate which showcases the varying divides within society.

Furthermore, in the academic world, the combination of art and activism in the work of Roy has been deemed pejoratively as literature by some scholars who, citing the lack of evidence, express concern as to the bias she applies in her work. Heated debates persist on the matter of social responsibility of writers, with some advocating that a clean boundary between the two spheres should exist, while others support a more blurred distinction, claiming there is a necessity to merge art and activism.

Arundhati Roy has defended herself and her work fiercely, even when faced with the most intense criticism. She also paid heed to criticism while emphasising the importance of actively tackling uncomfortable truths. Particularly unconventional truths and consequences associated with them that dissenting perspectives harbour. Roy motivates the world to confront difficult realities while brazenly claiming space for marginalised voices who are silenced. All in all, the harsh scrutiny Arundhati Roy received for her multifaceted works demonstrates the lively debates of contemporary society and blended topics of literature, politics, culture, activism, and public image.

Standing Firm: Roy's Responses and Repercussions

By drawing those multifaceted bitter realities, Roy gets to define her confronting literature in a sharp-edged manner. Facing the fury of competing voices, Roy strategically takes a critical approach with words balanced to suit both the surface and rooted meaning. Even when receiving intense criticism, like Roy, all push back using a composed structure, astoundingly clear communication, and refined decision-making blended with profound energy in every stance she encounters. Roy chooses to respond with intellectual bearing through critique that tactically advocates the change of action while protecting the identity of her work and activism.

Roy's responses tend to reflect a profound sense of responsibility towards the issues she supports, further highlighting her efforts in social justice and human rights advocacy. She has demonstrated perseverance in the defence of marginalised people and in the confrontation of power structures, which many admire but some oppose. She has profoundly impacted the public dialogue concerning divisive issues by articulating them with compassion and understanding, which positioned her as a powerful contemporary voice in literature and activism.

The consequences of Roy's adherence to these positions have

extended well beyond public perception. She has faced legal and institutional backlash, with her work often provoking fierce public debate and legal scrutiny. Regardless of these obstacles, Roy has remained steadfast, guarding her artistic expression and criticism of society's structures. While such resolve has incurred struggles and personal costs, it has fortified her reputation as someone who unapologetically takes on social justice inequities, ready to face significant challenges along the way.

Roy's controversies have had an impact on literature and activism as a whole. It has sparked discussions on how constructively intellects and artists have to intervene in social problems and what ethics, if any, they think are appropriate in exercising their voices. Her actions have exemplified the idea that the real art is not just creating, but rather marking different in the norm.

While exercising the dual role of an activist and a renowned writer, Arundhati Roy has been shown as the outcome of the sheer will of the authoritative consequences aimed towards courageous advocacy. Her rigidity encourages contemplating the boundaries where creativity meets action and reminds us of the responsibilities and difficulties that come from using one's skills to change society.

Intellectual Freedom: Balancing Artistry and Activism

For the longest time Roy has been known as an activist and a writer, employing Roy's intellectual freedom to navigate the worlds of artistry and activism cuts deep into Arundhati Roy's public persona. Striking this balance has not only elevated her as a creative figure but also as a social change advocate. The two shed empirically diametrically opposed views that have drawn sharp inspiring support and equally strong condemnation, demonstrating the struggle to balance harmony between the two spheres.

Roy's works avoid the crux of reflecting if artists have an obligation to use their skills to create art that comments on socio-political happenings. She leads through literature championing the voiceless through her works which is fundamental towards her strife towards change. By claiming and maximizing the scope of intellectual freedom, Roy's literary skills seek out systemic injustices and the challenges besetting the powerless, challenging traditional societal introspection in regions where it is restricted.

At the same time, Roy's alignment with controversial matters and her public criticism of the state's actions have sparked discussions regarding the limits of artistic freedom. Critics argue that there is too much in politics and that literature, as an art form, suffers because it is overly concerned with themes and subjects that interfere with its absolute beauty. On the other hand, Roy's staunch defence highlights her belief that it is impossible to ignore the fact that writers have responsibilities that require them to go beyond the written word.

Creativity intertwined with social and artistic forms of expression requires carefully calibrated strategies for the exercise of intellectual freedom. It is asking to be subjected to deep critical examination of the moral obligations that rest on the shoulders of the artist and force them to consider whether it is necessary to do something about the unjust suffering people, and in doing so, limits freedom of creativity. This puzzle is best solved through Roy's remarkable blend of narrative and sociological imagination that demonstrates her great command over the balance between the demands of creative discourse and politics.

Through the bi-focal lens of intellectual liberty, Roy integrates art and activism as she forges a body of work that goes beyond literature—transforming it into a means of genuine impact. As her powerful writing captures the essence of social issues, it demonstrates both strength and compassion, reflecting the profound essence of intellectual freedom wielded for the improvement of society.

Crisis Communication: Managing Public Relations Strategically

The term 'crisis communication' relates to the management of controversies regarding public figures and, in some cases, the work of intellectuals such as Arundhati Roy. Every so often, a public figure will face legal repercussions along with a fair share of public debate, and the management of public relations becomes central to the protection of reputational concerns and professional relationships.

Conciliatory communication is heavily integrated and embedded in the policy, structure and qualities of the organisation or person. In this context, preemptive means are deployed to solve problems and calm various stakeholders. In Roy's case, these approaches involve operating on the assumptions that critics are working with facts and that they must be provided with coherent narratives sympathetic to her principles and convictions. In Roy's particular situation, the use of press releases, interviews, and social media provides opportunities to communicate with and positively interact with the wider society.

Crisis communication entails restricting the flow of contacts to supporters and allies but opening the flow of information to the wider community to facilitate communal support and mitigate any fears.

Justifiably, Roy was insightful in reaching out to her audience, fellow activists, and civil society organisations to sincerely acknowledge their commendable efforts during challenging times. These efforts bring people together and help consolidate her reputation as a figure who resolutely fights for social justice.

It is also equally important to discuss the role the media plays in influencing public opinion and offering information during a crisis. In these periods of public attention, controversies need to be framed to provide as much drama as possible. Roy's understanding of this realm has enabled her to work with journalists and media personnel whom she knows will do justice to her perceptions. By engaging in selective conversations that include her in actively constructed nuances of debates, she has used her platform to highlight the controversies surrounding her while also challenging viewers to reflect.

Moreover, integrating negative perception management with sustained evaluation for detailed public scrutiny and profiling results from both ends can be considered effective crisis communication. Roy has exercised control over the perception of her legacy amid controversy while acknowledging that there is a purposeful focus on her work and ideas.

Her advocacy work and creative writing have allowed her to maintain her relevance and reaffirm her resilience. This, in turn, helps create a legacy that transcends her hardships and advances her cherished causes.

Long-term Ramifications: Shaping a Legacy Amid

Controversy

Controversies, along with many legal battles, can tremendously alter a person's legacy. This is particularly true when discussing literature and activism. Each of Roy's controversies, whether legal or public, has significantly impacted the legacy she leaves behind. How these challenges are dealt with tends to determine the public's perception of the individual, as well as the figure's impact on society. In this case study, I focus on the seldom-discussed power dynamics of controversies, how they shape public memory, and their indelible impact on Roy's legacy. Each of Roy's controversies has deeply influenced the legal arena as well as the court of public opinion. Fixating too much on potential outcomes and a single global image has the potential to entirely shift public narrative. Controversies surrounding a public figure's name, identity, and career almost always yield the same consequences. Positionality continually alters public perception, and avoiding it is nearly impossible. Such decisions determine how history, gentle or unyielding, remembers you long after you are gone. In Roy's case, his presentation and intense support of Indian nationalism framed his rise to fame, but his relentless iconoclastic critique of modern geopolitics made him equally detested. Overstated consequences tend to lead to conflict rife with public scrutiny and legal entanglements.

They obscure the anticipated reception of an individual's work, ideology and impact on social discourse. It is within this framework that we delve into the various angles of constructing a legacy amidst controversy. Thus, Arundhati Roy's legacy becomes critically intertwined with the controversies she has survived and the legal battles she has waged. However, it is not only the controversies, but her determination, deeply held principles, and fierce advocacy that ensures her legacy will endure. As bold debates regarding the boundaries of intellectual and artistic expression versus social duty continue to unfold, Roy's legacy stands strong as a powerful reminder of the impact that art and activism can have. The impact of her response to the controversies and legal hurdles she faced is her enduring mark on literature, activism, and the public psyche. Roy masterfully navigates crises while remaining resolutely true to her beliefs, ensuring that she is remembered as a character of courage, integrity, and resolve devoted to real change.

Chapter Eight

The Resurgence in Fiction

The Ministry of Utmost Happiness

Introduction to 'The Ministry of Utmost Happiness'

Arundhati Roy's novel, 'The Ministry of Utmost Happiness', attempts to sketch the multifaceted portrait of India as it intricately sets its main geography in Delhi. The novel brings forth the vivid representation of a maze-like India where different people from different parts come together in a single ecosystem. The narrative opens with a beautifully crafted scene that evokes tenderness and heartbreak at the same cadence, something which resonates strongly in Roy's books. It's quite clear that the intent Roy had was to shed light on the often neglected multiple struggles of people, which in a society is often termed a mosaic. The substratum that the novel revolves around serves as a city microcosm representing the entire modern day Indian society and serves as a rich setting where deeply woven destinies are still untold in times of unnatural chaos.

Contextual Re-entry into Fiction: The Timing and Motivation

Literature enthusiastically welcomed Roy back into prose after years of absence with 'The Ministry of Utmost Happiness' in 2017, which she had written alongside her activism. The novelist's 'The God of Small Things' was already globally popular. She undertook fiction much later, mixing a broad range of social issues, including economic meltdowns and political destabilisation that seemed to fuel Roy's life decisions around mid-2017.

It appears Roy had retained a plethora of unsaid words in her head that were screaming to be penned down in a form of prose. Her main aim was to colour the reality that lay before her and give life to the unheard branches of families and individuals in the subcontinent. The writer put all her thoughts into the masterpiece 'The Ministry of Utmost Happiness,' aiming to immerse her readership into contemplation while instigating sensitivity towards complex social issues.

Roy's engagement with pressing socio-political matters such as the rights of indigenous peoples and environmental justice, along with state violence, further influenced her decision to switch to fiction at this point. The combination of her writing and steadfast advocacy demonstrates her assumption that fiction, like every other form of art, can be a powerful tool and a change agent in society.

Roy's departure from non-fiction highlighted her belief that there is a deep necessity for a shift in society and that art is a powerful tool for facilitating dialogue and understanding.

The specific context of 'The Ministry of Utmost Happiness' explains both the timing and passion of Roy's return to fiction. This renewed focus, selective and partial, is an invitation for readers to go beyond understanding literature as mere entertainment and to appreciate a nation undergoing profound internal shifts.

Character Development: Portraits of a Diverse India

In 'The Ministry of Utmost Happiness', Arundhati Roy furthers her literary mastery with the rich character development of India's multifarious people. Each character in the book is unique, and meticulously crafted to bring out different aspects of the Indian space and its dynamics. Roy's vivid portrayals serve to explore the deep-rooted aspects of social stratification, communal violence, and politics in India. Every character, either protagonist or supporting, is instrumental in shedding light on the philosophical conflicts, mental crises, and the indomitable will of humanity during difficult times. These characters capture the multifariousness of India in all of its identities, beliefs, and violence through a single narrative. Ranging from the oppressed to the elite, Roy creates a compelling ensemble of people whose lives merge and separate at different points in time, portraying the striking depth of Indian society. She captures these people with incredible astuteness and empathy, revealing the conflicts, hopes, and contradictions of their lives. Also, the relations within the set of characters emphasise the idea of humanity above class, nationality, culture, and race. In creating such a compelling Indian ensemble, Roy carves identity for the pluralistic India by reframing from single representations.

Her psychological comprehension is as profound as her particulars, and both bring life to each character, making them deeply authentic and relatable. The characters' struggles reflect the modern India's blend of issues concerning gender, sexuality, tradition, and modernity. Roy intricately intertwines the threads of familial and romantic relationships with the socio-political fabric of India's constantly changing landscape and depicts the country's perilous beauty. Placing themselves in the characters' shoes allows readers to experience a multitude of contrasting emotions, perspectives, and narratives, each revealing new layers to the ever-complicated reality of India. In essence, 'The Ministry of Utmost Happiness' proves that Roy surpasses everyone in her capacity to create such refreshing and deeply authentic characters that define the social, cultural, and political history of India woven together.

Narrative Structure: Interwoven Lives and Destinies

The wonderful complexity of Arundhati Roy's characters, each with their own story to tell, adds to 'The Ministry of Utmost Happiness's intriguing narrative structure, where the diverse characters possess their interwoven lives and destinies. The novel shifts smoothly from one tale to another, enabling readers to experience different areas, classes, and even layers of the history of India.

Roy's ability to integrate the stories of her characters is remarkable as she manages to blend different lives into one single narrative, showcasing how the human experience is intertwined. She masterfully narrates the tales in such a way that reveals the multitude of relationships irrespective of civilisations or borders, illustrating how one person's life can alter so many others.

Roy's non-linear approach adds a different dimension to the story, as the events chronologically relate to one another in a seemingly chaotic fashion, just as life does. Readers are offered the perspective of piecing together the lives of the characters as they are presented through multiple frameworks. Roy fluidly moves between the past, present, and future, and captures the essence of time's nature along with its impact on human beings, resulting in a timeless tale.

Moreover, the specific way the novel is written helps reveal key aspects such as determination, self-efficacy, and the lasting ties of companionship and affection. By interweaving different stories, Roy highlights the depth and complexity of emotions and struggles, reinforcing the humanity present beyond cultural, societal, or geographical divisions. This synthesis of destinies explores the complexity of interpersonal relationships alongside the broader socio-political reality in which these lives are situated.

By analysing the converging lives and destinies of her characters, Roy skillfully navigates around the understanding of identity in a multi-ethnic and multi-national society. Through the lens of varying experiences, she addresses the issues of exclusion, forced relocation, and belonging and, in the process, attempts to show how some people define and adapt to the social reality that exists in modern India.

In this sense, the arrangement of events in 'The Ministry of Utmost Happiness' reflects Roy's talent in narrating a story, where readers are welcomed into a domain where the intricacies of the loom of fate have woven tender explorations of the human experience.

Themes of Displacement and Identity

Arundhati Roy addresses the particular notions of displacement and identity in 'The Ministry of Utmost Happiness' with incredible care and insight. The plot develops in the setting of India which is very colourful and diverse, at the same time being inhabited by people from marginalised communities who come to terms with the reality of their displacement and the search for belonging. Roy artfully captures the realities of both sociological concepts of displacement alongside the psychological and emotional chaos wrought upon a person by being forced to leave a place that one is accustomed to. As portrayed in the narrative by Roy, the rough voyage of people who are displaced because of evolving concepts and socio-political changes in the world puts them in a situation where they have to indelibly change their sense of self. Roy highlights how identity is constructed by looking through the kaleidoscope of identity through numerous characters which socio-political events have overshadowed. She highlights the plight, discrimination and struggle for recognition of transgender people, hijras and numerous others who live on the margins, and in doing so tells the story of their fight for self-acceptance. By narrating the lives of different people such as these with prominent socio-political changes, Roy explains the complex nature of identity.

Additionally, she interrogates the fixed paradigms of identity and constructs encouraging readers to embrace boundaries in human experiences. Through her vibrant and powerful prose, Roy enables the readers to encounter the harsh and sobering realities of people struggling with displacement and marginalisation, which evokes profound understanding and empathy towards their situation. Exploration of these issues resonates universally reminding us of the shared experiences of humanity's desire for home, grappling with the world's fragmented identities, while searching for belonging in a world filled with chaos, inequality, and violence. In this way, 'The Ministry of Utmost Happiness' is a vivid depiction of the indomitable quest for dignity, affirmation, and the enduring grace of humanity amid the stormy seas of life.

Symbolism and Allegory: Unpacking Roy's Metaphors

Arundhati Roy is praised for the sophisticated use of symbols and allegory in 'The Ministry of Utmost Happiness'. Throughout the text, Roy skillfully constructs metaphors that prompt readers to explore the meaning hidden beneath the surface. Social justice, identity, and the resilience of the human spirit are some of the most important themes in the book. One of the most striking symbols in the novel is the graveyard, representing both death and the possibility of resurrection. Roy gets to ponder over the themes of death, memory, and mortality by using the graveyard as a focal point.

Graveyards serve as symbols for contemporary India; the socio-political condition of the country is such that their history is concealed, but never truly erased. Moreover, Anjum's transformation from male to female identity also has a wide scope of symbolism in regard to accepting a fluid identity and challenging the mainstream expectation of a rigid identity. This adds complexity to the discourse on class, gender, and religion.

Additionally, the whole of the novel encompasses Delhi, a living city that captures the hopes and struggles of its people. Roy gives the city life and spiritual meaning asserting heavy influence on its environment to reflect its people. Delhi is more than a geographically defined place in this novel. Through various metaphors, 'The Ministry of Utmost Happiness' is transformed from a passive vessel of narrative into a living text that demands deep reflection and captures symbolic meaning. These metaphors do not derive like magic but stem from diverse symbols Roy constructs as strategic tools to unravel societal complexities, proving her elegance as a writer. This part encourages the reader to explore the allegorical and metaphorical world that maps the contours of her literary prowess.

Critiques and Reviews: Reception in Literary Circles

Reception of 'The Ministry of Utmost Happiness' in literary circles has led to a great deal of discussion and critique. With respect to Arundhati Roy's second novel, scholars and critics have placed significant focus on undertaking multiple interpretations of its overarching themes, narrative style, and socio-political context. The depth and multifaceted structure of the story has required numerous interpretations, which adds to the rich discussion bubbling around the book. One of the many points of critique has been Roy's use of allegory and symbolism because, while some critics support the notion of multi-layered meanings, others argue that her intricacy leads to obfuscation. Moreover, the portrayal of the politically oppressed communities in storytelling and the contemporary Indian state politics has been subjected to the parameters of authenticity and ethical representation. Many notable authors have expressed their opinions regarding the work's broad ambition and the problems of dealing with such heavy topics. The most notable discussions have arisen from the novel being stylistically and thematically different from 'The God of Small Things,' which made people talk about the direction of Roy's artistry and how it affects her body of work.

Some critics have attempted to position 'The Ministry of Utmost Happiness' within the wider context of post-colonial literature focusing on how the novel participates in the discourse of identity, power relations, and colonial scars. Some of these critics have marked its lack of traditional storytelling techniques, while some others have commended its willingness to step beyond norms as a bold reflection of contemporary society. Roy's distinctive voice and relentless critique of societal constructs have also been the focus of some reviews, leading to debates on her role as a public intellectual and literary intellectual activist. In one way or another, all literary debates about 'The Ministry of Utmost Happiness' tell the story of how Roy's work rides criticism which travels beyond classical literary scrutiny.

Comparative Analysis: Contrasts with 'The God of Small Things'

In her new novel, 'The Ministry of Utmost Happiness', Arundhati Roy drastically shifts her focus when compared to her former work, 'The God of Small Things'. The latter captures the family melodrama set against the socio-political milieu of Kerala, while the former ventures into the territory of postcolonial India. The two novels are fundamentally different in how they explore and approach a narrative. 'The God of Small Things' is centred on the small worlds of its characters and the emotional conflicts they are engulfed in, while 'The Ministry of Utmost Happiness' encompasses its protagonists within wider societies estranged in turmoil. It is clear how much Roy has grown as a writer when contrasting the intimate familial perspective of her debut with the sprawling politically-influenced setting of her second novel. One more notable difference is how the narrative is structured. While 'The God of Small Things' uses a straightforward chronological approach, 'The Ministry of Utmost Happiness' employs a multilayered and nonlinear approach to the lives of the characters throughout time and space. This approach highlights Roy's development as a novelist willing to venture into new realms of narrative style and structure.

The depiction of gender and identity evolves from one novel to the other. In 'The God of Small Things', gender is explored more narrowly through the prism of a particular family, while in 'The Ministry of Utmost Happiness' there is fuller treatment of gender that includes people from many different backgrounds and experiences. This change shows Roy's increasing concern for the marginalisation of people in her stories, as well as their oppression and resilience on a wider scale. The juxtaposition of both 'The Ministry of Utmost Happiness' and 'The God of Small Things' reveals Roy's artistic evolution and underscores how she moves beyond the parameters of her initial triumph to grapple with sophisticated and urgent global concerns.

Public Engagement: Author Readings and Discussions

Arundhati Roy's engagements in the form of author discussions and readings have been essential for understanding her creativity, motivations, influences, and deep-seated sociopolitical views. She does not shy away from engaging with her readers as these events offer an opportunity for Roy to explain her works at a deeper level than mere literary appreciation. Given her long literary career and the lasting relevance of her stories, these sessions are crucial to understanding her literature. Her eloquence and intellectual vigour are on full display in these interactions, enriching the encounter for everyone present. In her vigorous discussions and enlightening readings, she takes the listeners into the sophisticated worlds of her novels. In these discussions, gentle but powerful insights concerning the characters, places, and themes of her novels help strengthen the readers' appreciation for her artistry while deepening the relationship between the author and the audience. Additionally, these interactions provide one with a different approach to the broad sociocultural issues that are extremely relevant to the understanding of the narratives. Discussing the story in detail, she provides a deeper understanding of the subtle intersection of the experiences of voiceless people, power, and contemporary India.

The unique structures of society along with individual agency allow for introspection that stirs discussions far deeper than the event itself. The dialogue interacts meaningfully with the audience, allowing learning to happen on different levels that mimic her ideas. Her controversies showcase her concerns for the social literary world which she uses to raise pertinent issues for public consideration. These gatherings serve to celebrate her artistry which enables the analysis of the impact of her words in juxtaposition to global issues. In describing the content of her prose, she creates space for questions that can be relayed towards the complex sides of the stories encompassed in her prose. There is no doubt that the audience communities profit immensely from these interactions and, together with other scholars, seek to problematise the narratives she weaves. These sessions expose Roy to deeper sociopolitical issues in her literature unlike anything that came out previously. Roy captures all these paradoxical shifts with ease; her strife is to bridge compassion, critical thought, and active contact with worlds beyond text.

Implications for Future Works

The output of 'The Ministry of Utmost Happiness' signals a defining moment in Arundhati Roy's career and considers her prospective literary undertakings. The matrix of characters, themes, and geopolitical aspects in the novel gives enough scope for Roy's prospective writings. As readers and critics grapple with the nuances of her narrative and the sharp criticism contained in her lines, it is clear that consequences for her future works are profound and many-sided.

To commence with, the depth and clarity of the themes in 'The Ministry of Utmost Happiness' indicates how much of India Roy is still eager to explore. The socio-political injustices intertwined with personal stories of indomitable spirit show the author's longing for capturing the diverse contemporary India, as well as the outside world. This multidimensionality sends a message about the need to deepen research in many areas and thus enriching her contacts in future literary works.

The impact of 'The Ministry of Utmost Happiness' is not limited to the customary boundaries of fiction, but rather illustrates a whole new scope of commitment and social responsibility.

As a result, the impact of future works suggests an increased focus on change through fiction. This is evident in Roy's mastery of intertwining both activism and artistry. Roy shifts focus to fiction that not only entertains the audience but also compels them to think and act upon important societal issues. This possible combination of her literary skill and social activism ensures that her work, which is expected to be harshly critical, blunt and beyond the dimensions of conventional fiction, will be profoundly powerful.

Additionally, the reactions to 'The Ministry of Utmost Happiness' offer Roy developmental insights. With all the criticism, scholarly critiques, and community conversations generated by the book, the author observes the multiple ways she uses the voices she wrote into her characters. This perception with her new words increases her grasp on how her text ranges fuels responsibility; one direction puts significant pressure on the creativity in her next works to make sure they deliver increased impact. While honing her skills along the changing processes of culture, politics, and literature, Roy is ready to tackle the issue of producing texts that will stand the test of time and also resonate with the present mood.

To conclude, the outcomes of Arundhati Roy's new book, 'The Ministry of Utmost Happiness', inspire potential future works filled with seemingly limitless thematic depth, creativity, boundary-fuelled art, and advocacy blended together erasing the distinction of Roy being just a writer but an authorial figure leading an emerging metanarrative.

While Roy commences her new projects, these implications stand as warnings towards the change in narrative structure, the shift which could dramatically change the reception of contemporary fiction and her future works unlike any other.

Chapter Nine

Literary Duality

Blending Fiction with Advocacy

Introduction to Literary Duality

The aspect of literary duality is important for a holistic understanding and depth in narrative works, especially with authors who seek to combine fiction with advocacy. Through understanding literary duality, writers are able to create cohesive themes and concepts that merge with the human experience and societies to form multidimensional perspectives. This allows writers to blend different elements such as personal stories and socio-political commentary, capturing the entire essence of storytelling. Because of the blending of opposing forces and ideologies, the story becomes more complex and detailed, inviting readers to understand real-world problems and moral dilemmas. Using this duality gives writers the flexibility to build two parallel narratives that serve as artistic expression and advocates for social change at the same time.

This blend of writing and advocacy enables readers to understand, not merely appreciate, the creative side of fiction but also to critically engage with the socio-cultural issues that are essential to the world.

Moreover, literary duality allows writers to blend emotion-filled stories driven by socio-political critique, catalysing readers to face the disconnect between life and fiction. Through the integration of various perspectives, literary duality also provides a seamless construction of intricate interconnecting plotlines and character arcs that contribute to a unified representation of human experience within the context of societal change. On the other hand, the intertwining of socio-political critique and emotionally driven stories encourages readers to confront the disconnect between life and fiction. The melding of socio-political criticism with character-driven narratives evokes profound introspection, compelling readers to face societal issues alongside their transformed perceptions spurred by the narratives. Ultimately, the concept of literary duality signals to authors eager to address themes such as advocacy, social controversy, or injustice while still pursuing artistic sophistication, assuring that the unification of fiction and reality adds artistic depth and moral clarity.

The Intersection of Fiction and Advocacy

Social change fiction has long instigated advocates and continues to encourage self-reflection and societal change. Arundhati Roy's works have profoundly impacted society's introspection. Fiction evokes character to construct realities that help readers engage deeply with critical issues such as social justice and equality. This intersection is a harmonious blend rather than a juxtaposition of genres, amplifying the impact of fiction on the active world. Empathy can be fostered towards different cultures and communities through marginalised voices. Roy has initiated conversations through her books about human rights, political equity, environmental sustainability, and more. People no longer see her writings as mere entertainment; instead, her books truly transform aspects of life beyond fiction. These narratives encourage activism and policymaking beyond the pages of the books. The blend of advocacy and fiction sheds light on various social issues in a framing that encourages readers to understand the dynamics of our society.

The ability to reflect and take action is brought forth through storytelling, and when used for advocacy, fiction acts as a beacon of hope, guiding society towards positive change. Readers who engage deeply in literary works encompassing the themes of fighting for justice and equality become part of the journey towards improving society. The timelessness of literature that drives genuine change is captured in the intersection of fiction and advocacy, which, through Roy's masterful works, showcases powerful literature.

Themes of Social Justice and Equality

The life of Arundhati Roy demonstrates a relentless commitment to achieving social justice and equality in society. Her powerful narratives in the form of stories shed light on the complexities of human life and explore the unheard voices that are not considered part of the popular. Within her work, the overriding focus is to redress the realities of injustice, abuse, or bias. Roy tells stories in a manner that helps readers to contemplate the uncomfortable, harsh, but real situations of people whose lives have been pushed to the margins. Her social justice work is not bound by culture and community; it extends beyond physical boundaries to elicit a response from people. In Roy's books, one sees the struggles and triumphs of people's day-to-day lives as they strive to survive the brutal reality of systemic injustices around them. This reality is also a responsibility, as it pushes the readers to reflect on what they do to create a better world. Through her characters, she tells stories about how people navigate a complex world filled with power and privilege, where some enjoy being on top while others are forced to remain in the dark.

Additionally, Roy masterfully incorporates strands of intersectionality into her stories, noting the complexity of the forms of violence, discrimination, and oppression an individual can face simultaneously. Her nuanced representations capture the struggles of people living at the intersections of race, gender, caste, and class, promoting a more holistic understanding of injustice. Furthermore, Roy's depiction of societal structures such as political, economic, and cultural ones reveals the embedded discrimination that nurtures systemic inequalities. She sparks important debates on how to transform entrenched relationships of dominance and systems of oppression. By doing this, Roy does not only lament the systems in place but explains how those systems could potentially be redesigned into one of equality and justice. Undoubtedly, Roy's stories are shaped by her unyielding stance on social equality and justice, influencing the perceptions of her audience and motivating them to become advocates for a just world.

Character Development as Societal Reflection

In advocacy literature, character development is employed to encapsulate societal reflections within a narrative. Developing or arcing fictional constructs as representations of real-world individuals' struggles and complexities enables authors like Roy to portray authentic character journeys that resonate with readers. These characters are not mere constructs of an author's imagination; they encapsulate real-world experiences and, more disturbingly, the societal injustice, inequality, and adversity that exists in the world.

Roy employs character development techniques to showcase the varying scopes of social structures and their subsequent impacts on individual lives. From the sharp caste and class divides to gender and power balances, she paints a complex picture of reality through fictional characters. Such a granular focus on characters' life histories allows the audience to sympathise with them and understand their complex realities.

Moreover, character development as social critique aims to confront deeply embedded societal constructs and viewpoints. Through the depiction of complex characters, either from underrepresented groups or from the outskirts of society, authors reveal the societal discrimination, neglect, and social injustice thriving in the world. Throughout their developmental journeys, readers observe, and alternatively, resist these dominating narratives that attempt to confine them within social hierarchies, oppression, and subjugation, actively exercising their self-determination, agency, transformation, and resilience.

Exemplarily, character development becomes a powerful tool for addressing the undocumented experiences and impacts of the historically voiceless and, therefore, hidden. The characters who undertake these journeys tend to struggle with personal and societal boundaries. The mainstream provides some of the social discourses for individuals who escape the peripheries. The characters do not passively accept reality; they confront the reader with hard truths and compel them to unravel the social biases that exist. In this way, they disrupt the silence, challenging readers to acknowledge these realities.

Additionally, character development as a sociocultural phenomenon opens up more complex discussions around the need for systemic change and the selfless agency needed to enact it. This focus on injustice results in characters being actively engaged with the reality where they exist. As readers, we are expected to grapple with the existing realities and think beyond the unjust oppression systems to a world that is equitable and fair. When readers witness the radical change these characters go through, they also question their own actions towards societal issues and imagine a world that is kinder and more inclusive.

In advocacy literature, character development goes beyond the scope of fiction, reminding us of the different aspects of human life and of human beings and invoking strong emotions, creativity, and reaction out of the readers. Through the blend of artistic storytelling and advocacy literature, writers like Arundhati Roy offer readers the chance to shift from passive consumption to becoming active participants in working towards a just and peaceful society.

Narrative Techniques in Advocacy Literature

Advocacy literature uses a broad range of diverse techniques in both written and oral form to engage readers and select audiences for social and political change. The use of character voices and first-person narratives, where characters recount and interpret their experiences, emotions, and viewpoints, is a particular skill which works greatly to evoke empathy by humanising the author's issues. Understanding isn't limited to intellectual comprehension; advocacy literature attempts to immerse the reader into the lives of neglected people or communities whose realities are very different to their own. A clear example is Arundhati Roy's work, where she masterfully weaves personal narratives into larger sociopolitical commentary. Advocacy literature makes the statistical portrayal of characters' lives relatable and urgent through breathtaking and truthful narration because without data we cannot understand complex issues.

Employing multi-perspective narratives allows advocacy literature to encompass every angle of an issue, broadening the understanding of a singular problem, thus encouraging the development of maturity and a sense of difference in understanding. Using various perspectives gives different authors the chance to address the societal problems that challenge assumptions and are addressed in imaginative ways. Other than that, imagining advocacy literature allows deeper profound thoughts with the use of symbolism and allegory. The use of metaphors, motifs, and allegorical features in the portrayal is vividly done so that there is not a shallow meaning the reader can interpret. Roy does a stunning job of depicting images symbolically and this reinforces the idea of "the figure of speech". Apart from these literary devices, blending history into the story also serves as an anchor for any piece of advocacy literature, allowing readers to understand the motives of history's turning points. Abiding by factual history enables the readers to contextualise the injustice and need for change. Employing non-linear writing approaches or unique narrative structures can grab the focus of the readers, breaking traditional literary frameworks. These techniques make the work more dynamic and change the lens through which issues are perceived. That is made possible through Ms. Roy's writing in "The God of Small Things", which binds the past and present and reveals societal constraints and individual acts of defiance. What makes advocacy literature stand out is not only the evocative imagery that they paint in the reader's mind, but also the action entailed in their words, depicting shifts toward a reasonable society.

The Role of Setting in Political Narratives

Within the politics of a narrative, the setting as a constituent chapter is fundamental when it comes to plot and meaning. The setting of a narrative integrates the location where it takes place, the timeframe, social setting, and even the culture within which the narrative is placed. For writers like Arundhati Roy, the setting is important in framing the intricacies of any political situation as well as social concerns.

In description, Roy's work illustrates setting as political theatre used for framing, context, and constraining possibilities. Moreover, it is herself shaping an era. It also is a vital function of chronicle. All of these devices serve a function in political narratives. As Roy depicts in "the God of Small Things", a constant device is the mundane or familiar. Mundane tedious things set social relations so the narrative action can begin. It is through social relations that the setting reveals itself.

The setting is dully functional, mundane, but it serves a deep purpose. With such detailed descriptions of the places, whether they are rural, urban, or territorial, authors are able to highlight the socio-economic conditions that exist for power relations and inequality in a society. That way the readers are provided with foundational insight on the underlying problems that exist and are far deeper than what is presented on the surface. Such clear descriptions enable readers to understand more than what is literally presented.

The movement of a setting captures the attention of the audience, as it also acts as a character that adapts along with the shifts in the belief systems and the goals of the protagonists and supporting characters. Known for her deep understanding of India's political drama, Roy uses settings with skill to demonstrate the discrimination, cultural complexity, and the chronicles that mould the characters and their choices. For example, the contrast between the rural and urban settings comes to epitomise the class structures and the socio-economic inequalities highlighting the correlation between space and power structures.

Furthermore, the setting functions as an outline for a work of art, wherein the combination of ideological politics, revolutions, and reformations are vividly showcased, demonstrating their impact on schemes and people. Placing the characters in certain historical contexts or into modern-day socio-political movements allows for the depiction of the different aspects of the society that shape, control, govern, and dissent that intertwine within reality and makes people ponder about the reality and how they relate to it deeply concerning structure and people, "contending that we're dealing with the system of politics that these people exist in."

In the realm of political stories, the use of a setting is capable of bringing about emotional changes, sympathy, and deeper insight into existing issues if such settings are subject to skillful crafting. In portraying settings convincingly and in a vivid manner, authors can with the clarity of political suffering not only grapple with but also compel readers to ponder the far-reaching consequences of policies, conflicts of ideas, and campaigns.

To sum up, the place of setting in political narratives is that of a multifaceted device imbued with much more than contextualising the sociopolitical reality of the character's actions and constructs, rather nudging the audience towards the complex associations between power and existence. Moving forward into Roy's works, it becomes startlingly striking that setting is not only essential to the chronotope but is also integral to the narrative's structural components and the thematic core.

Symbols and Metaphors: Unpacking Deeper Meanings

It is clear that symbols and metaphors are important devices in literature that help express deeper meanings and interpretations. Within advocacy literature, the employment of symbols and metaphors is particularly important because it enables writers to convey intricate social, political, and economic realities within a story framework. Drawing from her rich symbols and imagery, Arundhati Roy has utilised a great deal of symbols and metaphors that have both enhanced her storytelling and engaged critical thinking on real issues. This can be exemplified in her notable text, 'The God of Small Things', where the pickle factory attracted attention in the family of Kochamma. The factory's emblematic significance represents stagnation and decay of tradition as opportunistic modernity advances. It is also suggestive of post-colonial India's contradiction of growth. On the other hand, the other part uses metaphors in Roy's writing to explain the human condition and society, which tends to call on the exploration of her themes such as power, oppression, or resistance. Roy's creativity through word and image enables readers to consider the underlying message of the symbolism crafted for them.

In doing so, she addresses disturbing norms of society and considers other possibilities, shaping her audience's empathy and critical awareness for the deep-seated issues existing within society. Roy goes beyond basic literature through the storytelling and the Mehta allegories that infuse her work with deeper meaning and insight beyond her pages. Readers are invited to interpret these symbols and metaphors as they add layers of meaning, including cultural and historical context that deepens understanding of the people whose lives Roy's literature explores. In other words, Roy's advocacy literature is enabled through deep metaphors and symbols, enhancing the quality of storytelling while creating a lasting impression and meaning in the complexity of life.

Balancing Artistic Expression and Activist Intentions

Perhaps the most intricate part of creating fiction for advocacy is incorporating self-expression within artistic activism. It is no secret that social justice narratives shackle authors like Arundhati Roy under the multiple layers of literary creativity and demands of changing rhetoric. It involves making compromises to reality; fiction tends to force storytellers to act and incite reflection, and at the same time leverage the power of fiction. Integrating artistic expression with activist intentions requires striking the appropriate ethical balance as a critique of society. The ethics of authorship space, where characters and stories must be representative of real-life experiences, emerges. There are harmful representation tropes that can exploit people, which is not what this attempt seeks. From the opposite view, the infusion of intent embraces discomforting truths; those who should have the chance to speak often do not. Suppressing them usually means ignoring the inequities that are rampant in society, even the ones that dominate this narrative prose.

Nevertheless, there exists an unsteady balance between artistry and advocacy that requires a skillful approach and commitment to crafting narratives that inspire reflection, understanding, and challenge development instead of purely entertaining. This marks the approach of writers like Arundhati Roy who use different literary devices and narrative techniques to invite readers' participation beyond the story, the characters, and the plot to the socio-political commentaries within. They unlock the door to social engagement through the deliberate employment of figurative expressions known as symbolism, allegory, and metaphor. Social issues face penetrating scrutiny, standing boldly beneath these instruments designed to elevate discourse. The combination of art and activism requires a keen awareness of the repercussions that words can inspire and how narrative strategies can be aligned to fight for just change. Ultimately, this argues that there's always a 'sacrifice' that encountering creativity requires - the 'sacrifice' in question comes with solving to resolve issues emerging from conflicts intentionally crafted to represent social issues through artistic and activist endeavours.

Critiques and Applause: Audience Reception

Audience reception is one of the most integral facets of determining the impact and success of fiction that seeks to combine art with advocacy. Each work of fiction that employs the art of addressing societal issues wants to be heard and has the potential to receive both positive and negative criticism. In analysing the audience reception of such works, it becomes equally important to study the criticism and the greater scope of positive responses to it. From analysing audience reception, one is able to tell whether an author was successful in attempting to incorporate advocacy in fiction.

Criticism stemming from works integrating fiction advocacy often criticises the advocacy as being too overt, lacking nuance, or compromising artistic merit for propaganda. Critics often pose questions on the balance between storytelling and the advocacy agenda. Moreover, some audience members may feel uncomfortable grappling with difficult social and political issues portrayed through fiction, whereas some audience members argue that dealing with such issues enhances their experience of the text.

In contrast, appreciation for that type of literature arises from the intended ethical reasons explained without losing the narrative proficiency of the fiction. Supporters of these works highlight the authors' attempts to confront societal challenges with creative storytelling and celebrate the reality-denying impact such stories can have on society. Moreover, supporters argue that these works not only entertain but also shape critical empathy and discourse.

These all facilitate effortless focused attention to empathy and ethical reflection. Unlike the prior points, it is important to note that the audience reception aspect is homogeneous for all, even when noting there is versatility in understanding due to experiences, cultural identity, and beliefs. Some diehard readers consider the fusion of politics to be an eyesore exaggerated, while many appreciate the blend as a sound political address for relevant sociological discussions. Including people who criticise literature alongside those who admire it, striving for a mix of attributed fiction and creative advocacy fiction shows how intricate the goal of conscious literary readers is.

An assessment of audience reception highlights the importance of these constructions as well as the conversations that such works initiate. Through studying the diverse reflections brought about by these stories, authors are able to achieve specific intent that aids in societal change and advocacy.

Conclusion: The Power of Storytelling in Advocacy

Stated in the simplest way, storytelling is one of the most powerful forms of communication and has been in use for centuries to impart messages, emotion, and inspiration for change. The book highlights the remarkable reality of Arundhati Roy, where fiction collides with activism, and her ability to reach out to people from across the world. Ending this discussion makes one thing apparent—the power of storytelling in advocacy is immeasurable. There is no doubt the ability of a story to portray social issues, give voice to the voiceless, and help dismantle systems of power is unmatched. Roy's works showcase the perfect marriage of artistry and activism, reminding us of the enduring power of storytelling in advocating for social justice.

Remarkably, Roy seamlessly intertwines captivating storytelling with critical social and political issues that warrant extensive human attention. It is evident that through her fiction, Roy attempts to advance deeper than just expressing art and telling vivid stories as she seeks to build empathy and provoke important conversations. In so doing, Roy's multifaceted and multi-dimensional characters, along with elaborate storylines, are compelling enough to draw readers in. Moreover, through fiction, Roy's evocative storytelling addresses and attempts to resolve readers' engagement with real-world struggles along with the complex and often ignored socio-political dilemmas hidden within them.

Additionally, Roy motivates her readers to ponder their lives and take action due to the deep-seated connection because of the power of storytelling, describing vivid spaces bereft of empathy devoid of hope. Empathy and understanding become possible factors that reach out to various people. Faced with oppression, Roy vividly constructs immersive fictional worlds that mirror the challenges and triumphs people encounter in real life. By bridging the gap through fostering empathy, the readers of her characters gain profound insight, transcending the boundaries of distant realities with a profound connection that helps effect positive change.

Furthermore, the persistent importance of storytelling in advocacy has its origins in the ability of narratives to spark action and fuel social change. Roy's stories work as vivid examples that call for action, asking audiences to face the deeply rooted inequalities that are present and work towards resolving them. She literally compels audiences to change their stubborn minds and take action towards attaining justice and equality by telling them emotionally powerful stories. Roy's literature portrays her assertion that people are morally obliged to help in creating a just, benevolent society, and she empowers them to do so.

Roy's works showcase storytelling's power in advocacy. This goes to show how literature can be a catalyst for change and construction in society. Fiction blended with real life advocacy is a unique form of art that serves numerous purposes: protecting empathy, merging a sense of oneness, alongside dealing with imbalances of society while still enduring for a long time. Each of her stories contains great examples where people work together for the greater good, showing humanity in its most raw and beautiful form. This highlights the power and impact of collective action. Through Roy's work, it is clear that both sides of her stories bring attention to how we need to employ storytelling as a method of advocacy and inspire the world to see stories differently: as reliable options for meaningful change.

Chapter Ten

Global Conversations

Influence Beyond Borders

A Review of the Global Effects Relating to Roy's Works

As of now, Roy's literary work and corresponding activist work have had enormous effects globally, with her being regarded as a central figure in contemporary studies. The way Roy seeks universal relevance through social justice, environmental protection, and humanitarianism showcases how her work is treated all across the world. The literary world and political world coming together has always been a topic of conversation. These conversations later go on to advance the understanding among the different cultures and people across the world. Roy, being one of the major voices in postcolonial world literature, appeals to and works on the discourse coming from the marginalised voices. Such reactions can be seen from all the continents. On the other hand, her portrayal of India, with all its socio-political considerations, captivates readers globally. This draws them to the realities that exist in India. Talking about Roy, she has indeed become a symbol of interactions across various cultures because of her powerful statements on critical issues. Readers and even people who actively follow geographical boundaries tend to be invited by Roy's writings because she talks about the limitations placed on us. Because of this, we see Roy being considered a global scholar who brings forth the issues of disparate academic disciplines. With the purpose of studying Arundhati Roy on a global level, this chapter is looking to aid understanding of the scope of her contributions and movements.

Cross-Cultural Dialogues: Bridging Literary Divide

The international following Arundhati Roy enjoys particularly illustrates how she has managed to gain audiences well beyond the borders of her country in all cultures; the text will elaborate on this. As a commentator on the world, best-selling author, and an internationally renowned public figure, she has successfully bridged cultures and languages, fostering cross-cultural dialogue, and as a result earning her the status of a roving ambassador of canonical literature. This part will focus on her works and their impact on cross-cultural relations analytically and with emphasis on union through storytelling.

Perhaps one of the most notable features of Roy's writing skill is her gift for effortlessly connecting global and local concepts relatable to readers across different cultures. Evocative prose allows compelling narratives to be crafted into stories that are Indian by birth yet universal in scope. By focusing on love, loss, identity, and social justice, Roy has provided a foundation for readers from different corners of the world to come together, share ideas, and exchange perspectives.

Moreover, Roy's social activism dedicated to the underrepresented and the marginalised socio-political issues of concern has evoked useful conversations beyond the borders of any single nation. As an activist and advocate, she contributes to understanding her community while helping forge connections for readers passionate about social change. In this context, engagement with important global issues helps remind us of the shared relationships among different communities struggling towards similar goals.

Apart from her writings, Roy's activism has provided her opportunities to speak on international platforms and has an appeal that accrues to audiences on numerous critical issues. Her participation in public lectures and interviews, alongside participation in literary festivals, has been productive enough towards conversations that go beyond geography very meaningfully. Using these avenues, Roy has interacted with a readership from different regions of the world and engaged in dialogues meant to break stereotypes and promote understanding.

Ultimately, we can analyse the profound impact of her writings in international literary discourse by considering the numerous translations of her works. The meticulous translations of her novels and essays into different languages made them available to readers belonging to distinct cultures. Thus, the translations fostered enriching dialogues on literary issues from different countries. These translations offered and exchanged perspectives and contributed to the body of culture for the value Roy's stories arranged into different languages.

Reception in the West: Acclaim and Critique

Arundhati Roy's works have echoes in Western world literature and have raised both acclaim and critique. Roy's writing has been accepted in the West because of her unfiltered representation of social and political realities, which often resonate with global issues. The God of Small Things won wide acceptance by bagging the renowned Booker Prize and became famous among Western audiences. Roy's narrative style, as well as her fearless approach to tackling difficult issues, has made her a notable figure in discussions of the Western world of literature.

Like all iconic writers, Roy has faced accolades and criticism for her work in various contexts of the West. Some have raised concerns about her depictions while others have pointed out the ideological framing of her narratives. This dual reception shows that Roy's writing is provocative but helps generate deep thoughts and discussions.

Analysis and critique in the West further showcase Roy's literary abilities and creativity as well as prove the broader global perspective on Roy’s storytelling technique. Her storytelling continues to sustain norms and provoke ideas, leading to constructive critique and scholarly analysis in the Western literary and academic world.

The impact of power relations, human experiences, societal disparities, and other aspects of Roy’s works have struck deeply with Western readers. This impact alone has triggered extensive discourse and collaboration among Western intellectuals and scholars who wish to grapple with Roy's literary genius. Furthermore, her interpretation of India’s socio-political dynamics has deepened understanding of the country and, at the same time, cross-cultural understanding and empathy towards it.

The growing impact of Roy's works on Western readers and intellectuals has amplified insight into the role literature plays in shaping views and discourse on international communication between cultures. This research comes to life through symposia, literary festivals, and other public spaces, relaying the interpretation of Roy's work from a Western lens, which is essential for constructive global dialogue. The reception of her writings in the West demonstrates Roy's enduring impact on international literary discourse while also showcasing the deep empathy her narratives evoke.

Literary Conferences and International Panels

Literary conferences and international panels form incredibly important avenues for authors to reach audiences across the globe, trade ideas, and exhibit their works. Arundhati Roy has also benefited from attending such events and is now globally recognised, but these events also enable meaningful conversations across cultures. Scholars, writers, and readers join these gatherings from all over the world and the atmosphere encourages the sharing and exploration of diverse viewpoints. Roy's attendance at these forums grants her an understanding of the writer's unique perspective regarding her creativity, her thematic preoccupations, and the socio-political factors that inform her work.

The active participation of authors in literary conferences and international panels gives them the chance to meet with their peers and readers, allowing them to explain the finer details of their stories in the context of larger questions. That is why for contemporary literature, Roy's voice has been one on identity, power, and social justice matters everywhere, beyond borders and to all people.

Aside from providing authors with a platform to address the dual aspects of cultural translation, these events host a range of international guests. As Roy has had multilingual readers, it marked her participation in international panels which exposed the intricately woven translation tapestry of her words. Roy generated discussions about translation which emphasise the relationship of culture and language with storytelling and literature. Thus, she became one of the authors who contributed richly to the sphere of international literature.

Roy has actively participated in international panels and other literary conferences which have greatly aided the advocacy dimension of her work. As such, she has intertwined narrative voices with socio-political agendas. These specific gatherings have greatly enhanced the scope of her advocacy related to social justice and environmental awareness, activism which has gone global. She has singlehandedly focused international attention on numerous important global issues and advanced the argument related to the role of literature in stimulating social debate and public consciousness.

Literary conferences and global panels have placed Arundhati Roy's voice before a global audience, showcasing the immeasurable impact of her writings and activism. Her participation in such forums illustrates the powerful role literature plays in the world in aiding cross-cultural relationships, triggering change, and fostering a more equitable globalised literary citizenship.

Translations and Their Cultural Resonance

Translations of Arundhati Roy's works have played a pivotal role in disseminating her powerful narratives and impactful messages across cultural and linguistic boundaries. The process of translation involves not only the linguistic conversion of text but also the preservation of cultural nuances, idiomatic expressions, and contextual relevance. In the case of Roy's intricate storytelling, translators face the challenge of accurately conveying the beauty and depth of her prose while ensuring that the thematic undercurrents resonate authentically with diverse audiences. This interplay between fidelity to the original text and adaptation to the target culture forms the cornerstone of the cultural resonance of translations. Through adept translation, Roy's stories have found new life in the hearts and minds of readers worldwide, transcending geographic and linguistic constraints to inspire global conversations on justice, identity, and societal change. The impact of translated works is far-reaching, as they serve as conduits for intercultural dialogue and understanding. Translators labor meticulously to capture the essence of the source text, striving to retain the emotive and intellectual essence that defines Roy's writing. By delving into the intricate layers of language and context, these dedicated professionals ensure that the spirit of Roy's narratives remains unaltered, allowing readers from different cultural backgrounds to experience the emotional and intellectual journey that her works offer. Moreover, through translations, Roy's narratives become vehicles for cross-cultural empathy, fostering connections and empathy among readers who may have otherwise been distanced by linguistic barriers.

Furthermore, the cultural resonance of translated works extends beyond mere linguistic transfer. It encompasses the assimilation of literary traditions, historical contexts, and sociopolitical landscapes, enriching the tapestry of global literature. Each translation becomes a fusion of the original narrative with the unique cultural fabric of its new audience, reinforcing the universal relevance of Roy's storytelling. As a result, her narratives are seamlessly woven into the collective consciousness of diverse communities, transcending the singular identity of their origin to become a shared reservoir of human experiences and aspirations. In light of these considerations, the cultural resonance of translations of Arundhati Roy's works serves as a testament to the enduring power of literature to transcend borders and unite humanity in common understanding and empathy. Through the adept craftsmanship of translators and the receptive embrace of international readers, Roy's narratives continue to shape and enrich global conversations, nurturing an inclusive literary landscape that celebrates diversity, empathy, and universality.

International Collaborations and Partnerships

Roy's powerful narratives and messages would not cross cultural and linguistic boundaries without the translations of her works. Translation is not a mere linguistic transfer of the text; rather, it is an intricate practice that includes cultural mapping preservation and contextual relevance. With Roy's complex tales, translators must contend with conveying the beauty and depth of her prose while maintaining thematically relevant messaging to various audiences. This dynamic of staying true to the original while adjusting to the target culture embodies the essence of the cultural resonance of translations. Through proficient translation, Roy's powerful stories have galvanised civil discourse across borders and inspired conversations on justice, identity, and social change, regardless of geographical or linguistic boundaries.

The scope of the effect of translated works is broad since they act as vehicles for understanding and communication between different cultures. Translators painstakingly strive to capture the source text's undertones and motifs – to remain loyal to Roy's writing – by analysing text and subtext. These specialists work at great depth into context and subtext so that the spirit of Roy's writings is celebrated and not altered for different audiences, which means that people from different cultures can partake in the intellectual and emotional voyage her literature offers. With translations, Roy's narratives serve as instruments of cross-cultural empathy, granting understanding and compassion to other readers who, because of language, would be isolated from each other.

Furthermore, the cultural impact or importance of translated works extends beyond the scope of mere language. It includes the incorporation of a certain literary ethnology, its history and political environment, thereby deepening the heritage of world literature. Every translation is at the same time an addition of the original story and its culture to the story told to the people who provide their own culture; this phenomenon strengthens the applicability of Roy's tales. Thus, her narratives are said to be integrated into the minds of different societies, where instead of originating from they define their identity as stories of human experiences and aspirations and are accessible to all.

In considering such factors, the reverberations of various translations of Arundhati Roy's works within culture function as validation for the importance and permanence of literature in crossing borders to unite people in shared understanding and compassion. Through the proficient work of translators and the welcoming hands of readers across nations, Roy's stories continue to participate in important global dialogues, fostering a literary world that celebrates differences while promoting compassion and inclusivity.

Impact of Political Activism on Global Platforms

Arundhati Roy has plunged into political activism that has impacted global discussions, drawing focus to important social and environmental concerns. Her determination in supporting the rights of oppressed people and the struggle against hegemony has made a difference even on a global scale. Drawing on dangerously complex socio-political realities, Roy becomes one of the most powerful spokespeople in the global struggle for justice, human rights, and environmental preservation.

Roy has often emphasised the contesting socially unjust practices in her interventions at global platforms. She is both a prolific writer and a strident activist—terms that can hardly capture her multifaceted personality, but as a silenced writer, she has risen to capture public attention through systemic oppression. Active participation for the Roys in global organisations such as the United Nations and other human rights advocacy organisations draws global attention to urgent matters and raises them to the level of global concern.

Additionally, Roy has affected borderless civil-society cooperation and coalition building through her active participation in international meetings and conferences. By advocating for indigenous peoples, the environment, and social discrimination, she has brought forth tangible collaboration amongst diverse actors globally and helped facilitate collaborative approaches to resolve common problems.

Roy's political activism goes beyond spatial confines and is general in nature addressing wide-ranging audiences worldwide. Her explanation of local struggles in relation to the global context has raised awareness and support for grassroots actions across the globe. She has written numerous essays and given many passionate speeches highlighting the correlation of social, political, and environmental issues and calling upon citizens of the world to take action towards these challenges.

In summary, Roy's influence across international platforms is not simply voicing phrases, but is the change that comes as a result of their advocacy. She has changed world conversations and mobilised people to act on exposed exploitation in the form of corporate subsidisation, forcible relocation of peoples, and the militarisation of society. Roy's political activism and its attitude underline the possibility of changing the world. This is the strongest evidence of the effectiveness coming from global political activism people can do at the world stage, and her political activism is the key.

Leading Voices: Influencing International Thought Leaders

Advanced intellectuals are deeply affected by Arundhati Roy's work. For years, Roy has advocated and authored on a myriad of themes that attract global attention and push people to take steps towards positive change. Her intellectual prowess makes her able to engage in meaningful discourse towards action and advocacy where her presence fosters action among thought leaders globally. As a result, she has cemented her position as a leading voice on various topics globally. Arundhati Roy's literature and global issues are interlinked; she remains fearless and willing to take risks. Thus far she has pricked power-sensitive political and social issues where world-renowned thinkers, scholars and policymakers speak on. Due to functioning as a leading voice, she has gathered the attention of multiple marginalised communities and oppressed groups such as environmentalists and humanitarians residing in dire conditions alongside paying attention to everlasting socio-political conditions. With this commitment, a form is traceable because of belief in speaking truth to power. Other international thought leaders as followers want to create collaborative efforts based on the principles of righteousness, justice, and equality for all, and through Roy's admired honesty, garnered admiration through international collaboration.

As noted, Roy's eloquence added value to critical discussions on social justice, gender, and environmental issues. Global leaders were compelled to reconsider their positions because of her persuasive reasoning on complex matters. Her thought-provoking essays, speeches, and public appearances stirred intellectuals to act on confronting problems by offering novel solutions.

Roy is not only captured in academia, but also in the world of diverse and non-diverse influencers such as performers, activists, and socio-political movements. Her network beyond mainstream scholars and activists helped advance the perspectives of change agents that enrich social discourse and advocate for an inclusive and intersectional approach to social issues.

To sum up, the efforts of Arundhati Roy as a change advocate in sociocultural conversation around the globe are remarkable for bringing various scholars to work towards a more empathetic and just world. She has been, and still remains, an empowering figure who induces decisive action on issues of justice, human rights, and social transformation.

Shaping Global Narratives: A Case Study Ap-

proach

Taking into account the global scope of Arundhati Roy's writings, it makes sense to utilise an approach that brings together various case studies in order to appreciate her impact on global narratives. Understanding specific cases of her activism and literature helps us appreciate the effect of her work.

These case studies would illustrate how Roy's social justice and environmental writings galvanised political dissent in different parts of the world. These are the case studies of the translation of her texts into different languages, her international speeches and essays, and global public support for the causes she advocates. Such analysis shapes an understanding of the impact her writings have made on people's lives globally.

An intriguing case study might concentrate on the consequences of her activism on some indigenous people across the world. From this perspective, we can articulate the parallels between the struggles of marginalised populations around the world and how Roy's advocacy has helped build some of their voices on global platforms. Moreover, we can assess the impact of her advocacy on other human rights issues and the ensuing debates on the rights of these communities, including their silenced struggles for human dignity and nature conservation.

Another relevant case study could focus on the reactions to Roy's fiction from countries with different socio-political contexts. Analysing the reception and critique of her novels in various cultures adds to our appreciation of the overarching affection as well as the multifaceted intricacies that are central to her narrative. This inquiry highlights the role of literature in connecting disparate global societies and encourages reflection about the unity and diversity of human life.

Also, a case study strategy can portray the collaborations and partnerships that Roy made with other international organisations and advocates. Analysing these interdependencies enables us to trace the web of influence her relationships form beyond her borders. These case studies illustrate the magnitude of her influence on international narratives and strengthen the assertion of her transnational presence and impact.

Restating the above points leads to a conclusion that the case study method is the most appropriate strategy for examining Arundhati Roy's narrative on international relations. There are particular moments when her actions, words, and partnerships have been boundary-defying; these are the moments that validate the extent of international attention and engagement. Through this investigation, we reaffirm her legacy as a catalyst in global storytelling and highlight the enduring gaps in humanity into which her work is critically essential.

Conclusion: The Enduring Global Legacy

Roy's enduring global legacy is a mark signifying the reach of her literary and activist pursuits. Roy's relentless advocacy and profound work have had a lasting impact on the world and continues to transcend borders and cultural divides. It is clear that the realm of literature and activism is not where Roy's influence ends and it is apparent that she continues to touch numerous lives across communities and nations as, during our discussion on her impact beyond borders, she became universal.

Noting the global legacy of Roy demands one to appreciate how her voice transcends borders. Roy's thoughts have been discussed and debated from the streets of India, across Europe and into

America. Her ideas, which traverse the divide of different cultures, have fostered understanding and empathy. As an advocate for social inequality, environmental decay, and political turbulence, she has become, for many, a changemaker on the scale of a whole world.

Roy's influence, whether via translated literature resonating within remote communities or her commanding engagements at international conferences and forums, continues to motivate various audiences towards action. Additionally, her global message, which is one of compassion, justice, and unwavering integrity, has been highlighted through her collaborations and partnerships with prominent figures across different countries.

There is warmth accompanied by critique and praise to be found in the reception of Roy's work in the West. Some praise her vision and courage, while others critique her revealing disheartening truths. Through these dialogues and debates, Roy's legacy perpetually evolves, thrives, and strengthens in global narratives subverting power structures.

To conclude, Roy's influence as a literary figure, socio-political activist, and humanitarian allows people to transcend borders and ideologies, shedding light on the importance of her global legacy. Arundhati Roy's enduring legacy challenges humanity to unite in empathy and take meaningful action towards the issues that define us.

When future generations take the mantle of change and progress, they will undoubtedly look up to the strong legacy of Arundhati Roy which she has bestowed upon the world. A strong legacy that gives us hope and love.

Chapter Eleven

Essays as Instruments of Resistance

A Detailed Look

Introduction to Roy's Essays

The essays of Arundhati Roy capture a striking feature of her work: they showcase great concern for socio-political issues. In an India which was still coming to terms with its contemporary history, Roy's essays heed to the interplay of power, politics, and social justice prevailing in the country. As a novelist and an activist, Roy tackles a variety of subjects with incredible insight and persuasive writing, which demonstrates her uncommon ability to represent opposing views articulately with striking force. The striking balance of Roy's essays rests on the fact that they have influenced public opinion, policy discussions, and scholarly critique, thereby silencing debates and controversies and forging a new path. In this particular part, we will focus on the essays written by Roy concerning the issues of society and politics, taking into account the various aspects of her non-fiction works.

Historical Context and Background

Arundhati Roy's essays are an elaborate form of activism that is intricately woven within a profound historical context and a deep background. When attempting to analyse the impact of Roy's essays, it is important to comprehend the historical phenomena and the societal structures that guide her worldview and way of writing. Roy's intellectual life largely evolves in the postcolonial context of India, which bears the twin scars of a struggle for independence and the tortuous process of nation-building. The legacy of colonialism, the partition of the subcontinent and the unending socio-political strife deeply influence the underlying issues Roy seeks to address in her writings. Additionally, the rise in neoliberal economic policies and the yawning gulf between the rich and the poor have been crucial in developing Roy's critique of power, capital, and justice. Not to forget the context of her work which covers an entire array of authoritarian rule, globalisation, and environmental exploitation that all form the basis of Roy's essays. These come along with her life as a public figure and activist who adds to deepen the context of her essays.

Roy's personal experiences and engagements in the socio-political life of India have added layers of authenticity to her essays which, deeply rooted in personal insights, are a critique of state policies and an active participation in social movements as an outspoken champion of oppressed peoples. While looking into the historical context and the antecedents that Arundhati Roy's essays are set in, it is clear she put a remarkable effort in these essays not simply out of her creativity or intelligence but out of the many complex multi-causal factors that exist globally and within her surroundings which bear tremendous influence on her advocacy work.

Themes of Resistance and Dissent

Resistance and dissent are some of the most significant themes found in Arundhati Roy's body of work. Through her penetrating and fascinating essays, she attempts to solve complicated social problems by focusing on upended power dynamics and sidelined voices. Some of the major themes of Roy's essays include a critique of imperialism and capitalism as well as the curtailing of civil liberties. She explores historical and contemporary examples of movements that are often termed 'resistance movements' and studies the intricacies of their struggles along with the outcomes on the socio-political systems of the region. The idea of dissent is found in all of her writings, highlighting the weakness of democratic spaces and the worst sides of power without limits. While showcasing how people and societies fight back against dominant structures, Roy highlights the critical role of social movements of and for people to bring about change. Additionally, Roy's writings demonstrate the essential link between struggle and the demand for justice while exposing the paradox of state power and the power that is denied to the people. This discourse challenges readers to reflect upon the issues of civil disobedience and the ethical responsibility of dissent, provoking thought on the consequences of uncompromisingly exercising state power.

Ultimately, the undertones of resistance and dissent in Roy's essays represent a clarion call, inciting the readers to challenge the existing order and put efforts into creating a more fair and just society.

Analysis of 'The Algebra of Infinite Justice'

In 'The Algebra of Infinite Justice', Roy critically assesses global power relations with strong regards to the interplay of economics and politics and human rights using some of the most powerful prose. In 'The Algebra of Infinite Justice,' Arundhati Roy describes how powerful countries falsely consider themselves to be 'all giving' nations while simultaneously spinning webs of neoliberal socioeconomic policies that disempower people, destroy their environment, and worsen their living conditions. Roy also explains the impacts of hyper militarization and imperialism while explaining the rationale for wars particularly those fought in the name of democracy and so-called security.

Roy goes beyond global occurrences and investigates the cultural aspects of domination and resistance. In analysing dominant power systems, she reveals the hegemonic potential of individual and group action. In her detailed research, Roy explains the authority myth of boundless justice, which in reality is devoid of infinite justice, and challenges those in power, fighting for the subjugated populace.

The Algebra of Infinite Justice is also a conduit of self-scrutiny, as it urges one to reflect upon their role in perpetuating systems of oppression while using their agency to force change. Arguments presented by Roy are a clarion call for collective action and responsible protest, galvanising attention toward major violations of social justice and human rights across the globe. This does not come without consequence. Her pursuit of unmasking lies and giving a voice to the suppressed puts readers in a position where they are forced to engage with truths that are necessary yet heavily concealed.

In the end, **'The Algebra of Infinite Justice'** serves as a powerful reminder of the role of literature in resistance and social change. It is Roy's analysis and her passionate call to action that creates a story that reminds readers to think of the new possibilities of justice and fairness in the world.

Dissecting 'Listening to Grasshoppers'

In Roy's "Listening to Grasshoppers," the author analyses the themes of power, disenfranchisement, and the destruction of democracy in relation to India. Roy focuses on describing the depth of the political corruption, the collusion of corporations, and the state violence which is downgrading the living standards of the people in India. Roy's work is a powerful and sophisticated argument that exposes the nefarious forms of violence targeted at oppressed communities and builds a strong case for social responsibility. Her work highlights the blinding depths of human inequality and attempts to portray the political violence that resides in the heart of every society. This encourages a response that no one desires to give.

Roy has not limited her analysis to social inequality but has appealed to the emotions of populations that have suffered desensitisation as she empowers them with the society's upper echelons. She presents them through remarkable narratives and insightful work that profoundly illustrates blunders occurring under oppression. Moreover, Roy tackles the question of nationalism and religious extremism, explaining their catastrophic consequences on freedom and peaceful coexistence. Her analysis not only exposes social constructs, but also alerts people regarding the uncontrolled abuse of power and drives discussion about proper governance and shared moral obligations.

Together, these arguments form the hallmark of Listening to Grasshoppers, demonstrating with periodic details Roy's artistry and her heartfelt approach toward writing.

Crafted with excellence, her sentences and metaphors contain literally art, and still pack a punch. The vigorous blend of creativity and social concern in her writings stands testament to the ability of language to enable social change and deep compassion. In waging that artistic weapon of sorts, Roy widens the scope of civil disobedience as well as the literature that impacts society, restoring its place within culture ontologically.

Towards the end of 'Listening to Grasshoppers', Roy undoubtedly takes all of her readers through a journey where they have no choice but to analyse their existing reality and contemplate what it could be. Her speech was astonishing, proving that there is still power behind dissent and that without reasonable dissent, someone able to probe behind the veil of fairness and justice suffers. It is clear that Roy placed 'Listening to Grasshoppers' alongside the most unforgiving and compassionate critiques to offer humanity where she raises the question of reasoning and global politics through ideas of resistance and freedom.

Resistance through Elegance: Style and Tone

What makes Arundhati Roy stand out for me is the boldness of her essays, laced with touching undertones and elegance of style. By the careful whispering cadence of a tale and language, Roy's texts accomplish the visceral quality of writing and stir emotions to an intellectual and emotional level all at once. A piece of her work can truly be called prose as it is so rich in sonnets and lyrics which stand in stark contrast to the issues under attack and hotly debated. With the use of far-reaching metaphors and vivid images, Roy's writings sculpt words so eloquently that their power stays permanently ingrained into the reader's psyche.

What also makes her texts stand out is her sharp tone as combined with her distinct style makes Roy's essays compelling. Her prose is elegant, complex, and sensitive—everything that draws the reader's attention. They help shift readers' minds towards reflection instead of rushing to conclusions about carefully chosen issues. In these words, she invites people to develop thinking about socio-political realities devoid of violence. Roy does not shelter from provoking thoughts; she rather shields them in art and grace towards resistance and sore lines of society's issues.

Moreover, the beauty of Roy's sophisticated style goes deeper than artistry; it is an act of defiance in and of itself. Her aesthetic underpinning confronts powerful existing structures and frameworks of discourse, daring the notion of how resistance and dissent are expressed. Such grace disrupts nativism and compels people to reexamine what activism and advocacy look like.

Her sharp prose is thoughtfully constructed using simple yet powerful sentences and words. This precision in her work, alongside eloquence, aids her in captivating the audience, with some even arguing her work changes policy discussion while simultaneously persuasively arguing, assisting in bolstering her public credibility. From environmental justice and human rights to global politics, the structured reasoning of her unchanging tone exhibits her works as a benchmark for blunt and kindly reasoned discourse towards humanity's most pressing matters. Through such emotionally charged, intellectually robust, and aesthetically pleasing frameworks, Roy's essays become not simply acts of resistance but sobering expressions of defiance and determination.

Impact on Public Discourse and Policy

Through the breadth of Arundhati Roy's essays, public discourse has been greatly influenced and policies have been set/narrated/told in a particular manner, ranging from crucial social to political concerns. With compassion and powerful articulation of her views, she has managed to promote the rethinking of policies and norms across society. Roy is well known for her incisive analyses as well as compelling arguments that challenge the established power structure and fight for the people at the bottom of the hierarchy. Her writings act as sparks that evoke citizens from their political apathy in order to engage with pressing issues. The accessibility of Roy's prose enables the public to discuss and debate policies and politics, making them active participants in democracy.

As a public figure serving the public, Roy continues to democratise fierce debates through fearless critique of sometimes abstract and other times clear-cut systems and institutions. Such powerful critique has already affected society by enabling healthy debate/discourse and influencing public opinion. Her work has fostered critical consciousness about the forgotten and voiceless, raising awareness for justice and equity. Thus, her essays act as a catalyst for social movements and ethical governance by enabling the people to demand change.

Besides influencing discourses in society, Roy's essays have also transformed public policy decisions and their execution. Her critical scrutiny of government policies and human rights abuses has lifted the standard of accountability and transparency. Roy has been able to shift the focus of policymakers towards systemic injustice and has advocated for the protection of the neglectful dominated groups. The intensity of her involvement in policies propelled the reflection on the possibility of using literature to foster real change in society.

Also, Roy's foresighted policy reform advocacy emphasised as critical self-examination of the policy's impact and scope has shifted policy change towards action. She overrides legislative procedure, prompting lawmakers to take up moral responsibility and undertake the work due conscientious policy development. Roy's essays demand active consideration of the impacts of dominant policies.

As a result, the literature of Arundhati Roy affected society far beyond the life of literature. The socio-political landscape of the society is fundamentally altered, galvanised towards responsible citizenship. Her writings remain powerful tools that motivate new social movements working towards social justice and equality.

Roy's Influence on Contemporary Writers

Arundhati Roy's artistry does not only lie in her works but rather in the contemporary writers she motivates to seek the truth and justice. Roy has made her mark in contemporary literature as an unapologetic societal and political concerned figure.

Engagement with writing contemporaries was drawn to Roy for her storytelling blend with axiomatic narrative advocacy of social change. She creates the story in a way that is unyielding to fight physically, meaning challenging social injustices and giving the oppressed a voice through systemic injustices, without consideration to having a mentor guide on how pressing global issues can be tackled.

The effect she has had on contemporary writers is striking. Roy claims that all unyielding modern writers need to focus on is the way in which they craft their work for the purpose of bringing down the prevailing power structures that interfere. Writers of every kind were encouraged to use their voices to fearlessly challenge inequities and suppressed issues. Roy's fearless tackling resonates throughout the body of work written by those under oppression.

Also, the literature and activism intersection has been interrogated deeply by Roy, and this has inspired contemporary authors to think about the impact of their words. Writers are crafting novels, non-fictions, essays, and other genres aimed at bringing positive change in the world, embracing the responsibility that comes with the power of the pen, similar to what Roy has done.

From Roy's impact on contemporary literary voices, it is clear that her bold intellect and commitment to speaking the truth have inspired a new breed of writers willing to challenge contemporary oppressive systems. With remarkable compassion for the oppressed and unshakeable faith in the role of literature in society, Roy has motivated her contemporaries, amplifying their voices and urging writers to feel a sense of passion in their storytelling that mirrors her own works.

In the case of Roy and her works, it would be reasonable to note and applaud the wrath that injustice receives and how empathy is sought from her. It is this very stance that bears Roy's unsparing gaze on the demand for justice towards marginalised groups which enables contemporary writers to tread on the delicate linking paths of activism and art. Contemporary writers who in one way or another confront the issues of concern respond to Roy's challenges and preserve her legacy through her endless and fierce literary analysis of truths.

Criticisms and Controversies

Arundhati Roy has faced essay-related critique and debate like any other public figure. She has been critiqued for being aggressive in her specific writing and blurbs that seem to attack rather than serve dialogue. This kind of approach, while effective in garnering attention, raises questions on the ability to sustain constructive change in society. In the case of Roy, a number of critics will lean towards one extreme or the other. Whatever side they choose, it is more often than not the case that Roy's arguments will evoke controversy. She has also been transformed into critiquing liberalism and contesting one at a time mandating authorities which at some points can come off as too extreme or radical within one single space. Roy's harsh words to the superpowers have blanketed the difference in approach from different political and rhetorical spectrums leading to a ton of debates. Her policies do bring heavy debate mostly around geo-political happenings, more precisely the internal workings of India and geo-political jointures of Israel and Pakistan. These two major pieces of land can provoke her into fire and stoke some harsh criticism. Her being a bit too concerned with ecological environmental changes has pushed her into becoming critiqued by changing the sensitive phrases and arguments emanating from the opposite directions.

Such controversies have, in some cases, clouded her primary focus in the essays, resulting in them missing the points that she desperately wishes to communicate. Regardless of the problematics and accusations put forth, it stands correct that Roy's essays have indeed triggered fundamental discourse and advanced conversation on important socio-political matters. While inviting discourse in dissent, they still remain oxidative and pivotal in countering the existing systems of power to extend the scope of silenced voices, thus proving literature's important essence as a transformative instrument for social change.

Conclusion: Lasting Impact of Roy's Essays

In contemporary literature and social critique, Arundhati Roy's essays are still considered pioneering works given the significant influence they have disseminated. Challenging the dominant narratives is a task deemed impossible, but with the power of the written word and Roy's insightful, poignant, and at times provocative writings, it has transformed into a possibility. Her essays possess the unparalleled ability to challenge critical social and political issues. Even after her works have been posted, and years have gone by, this legacy continues to inspire countless readers, activists, and intellectuals.

Roy's enduring impact is rooted in her grappling with uncomfortable truths and her steadfast commitment towards truth-telling. With her essays set against the backdrop of a society overwhelmed by shallow din, they stand out as remarkable displays of intellectual bravery, awakening the readers towards interrogating power structures and uncomfortable realities. Roy has reshaped public discourse and fostered a culture of accountability by tackling controversial issues head-on and revealing systemic injustices around us.

Roy's essays stand out, not only for their nuanced arguments but also for the clear call to action they provide to their readers, showcasing how deeply introspective reflection can lead to transformative action. As a masterful researcher and searing critic, Roy challenges the readers to actively engage and not just passively consume her work. Her essays do not remain confined to the academic realm; rather, they go on to inspire individuals and communities to advocate for justice, equality, and human rights on the local and global stage.

The timeless impact of Roy's essays has endured for this long because of their remarkable ability to endure shifting socio-political changes. Roy's essays address contemporary issues and ever-changing themes through a multifaceted lens that guarantees resonance with diverse audiences. The society we live in today still feels the ramifications of her questions, which stands testament to the timelessness of her work. It also showcases why her work is, and will continue to be, important for generations trying to understand the reality and inequities of power.

In Roy's essays, the most clear and powerful impact is the unending dialogue they have created within new generations of writers and activists. The change Roy encourages and contributes to through her unapologetic stance gives her words a strong feeling of empowerment. Society's women pursuing justice are a part of the rich tapestry of dissenting voices and social necessities, further concluding that change in Roy's mindset encourages dissent for a more inclusive future.

Heavily condoned and ignored, the transformative impact of Arundhati Roy's essays is widely regarded as extreme. They are most commonly perceived through the scope of harsh truths that one should face, disregarding reason and further invoking the wrath of change through resistance.

Roy integrates her themes so powerfully that they incite moral dilemmas, ultimatums for action, dismantle perspectives, transform accounts, and most of all, promote indignation.

Chapter Twelve

The Personal and Political

How Biography Informs Work

Overview on Arundhati Roy's Early Influences

Arundhati Roy in particular has had her literary pursuits greatly influenced by certain aspects of her life, starting from her childhood and persisting to this day. Growing up in the state of Kerala, in India, Roy already had access to a vibrant cultural landscape that later found expression in myriad creative writings. Her drawing parallels with imagination received a powerful boost from the rich culture and traditions of Kerala which required honing of her deep empathy for the humane and sociable world. The familial structure and relationships within her family also greatly impacted Roy and these nuances had to be dealt with in her stories that focus on relationships and their dynamics. The complex yet serene landscapes she encountered early on in her life served as a source of inspiration and aided in developing the reverence for nature that Roy writes about, often providing metaphors or backdrops to her narratives. The richly multicultural and multilingual nature of the state of Kerala also aided Roy in bearing the creativity to juxtapose personal narrative with societal critique which makes her perspective unique.

Her social interactions during her formative years, compounded with her early schooling, equipped her with a practical grasp of the prevailing social injustices and inequalities, which she sought to address through her writing. It is clear that Roy's life experiences have shaped her perceptions of the deep complexities of existence, revealing a formative period of wonder and disenchantment—motifs that echo throughout her powerful narratives.

The Role of Childhood Experiences

Early life events greatly impact an individual, most usually setting the foundation of their worldview and activities for years to come. In the case of Arundhati Roy, her childhood in the state of Kerala was instrumental in shaping her understanding of sociopolitical issues and culture and later became a central focus of her writing and activism. Roy's childhood is filled with rich and vivid memories from the landscapes of her hometown to the detailed weaving of family relations which served as a fountain of motivation. The nurturing environment provided by her family was thoughtful; it not only offered comfort and safety but also sparked her imagination and natural empathy. While drifting through the turbulent sea of her teenage years, she became increasingly aware of the society and history of modern Kerala which served as an active backdrop for her literary imagination later in life. The synthesis of personal and social experiences crafted her worldview and enabled her to thoughtfully approach several issues in her later works. Furthermore, her exposure to different people from an early age gave her a new lens to examine the world and appreciate human life which fostered social consciousness and diversity in her writing.

The vivid experiences, valuable lessons, and wondrous stories from her childhood undeniably shaped her in some remarkable ways. With deeper reflection, Roy's childhood experiences highlight the beginnings of her storytelling compassion, which tells us captivating stories but also serves as deep insight into humanity.

Family Dynamics and Their Impact

Family relations have the greatest impact on an individual's perception and values, and Arundhati Roy is no exception. The different forms of family relations, customs, and even an individual's socio-economic class tend to shape how a person views the world. For Roy, her family has impacted many aspects of her life in a complex way owing to the different influences it possesses, a impact that she can carry throughout her whole life. The influences that arise from the family tend to emerge from her complex family relations and the family dynamics that shaped her growing years. Roy's family-based experiences have tremendously shaped her literary body of work, such as the multi-faceted family conflicts, deeply-rooted rivalries, and powerful emotions that are portrayed through her writings. Considering the complexity of Roy's literature, it is possible to argue that her early family life profoundly impacted interwoven themes within her stories. This concurrently explains the vivid depiction of relationships focused around conflict, authority, social class, and control in her works.

Additionally, it gives a deeper understanding of the relationships and disconnects she attempts to unravel through contrasting expectations, complexities, and pairing pairs and groups in society and relationships, family and society. Roy's exploration deepens through the understanding of human relations based on the contradictions set by society.

Roy's writing brings out emotional complexity unlike any other author. As we analyse the familial structures and their seemingly interwoven ramifications, it becomes obvious how vital these components are in understanding the emotions in Roy's writing. The combination of her childhood experiences has led to Roy understanding the intricacies of families and conflicts surrounding them beautifully. Exploring the details in family structure offers a captivating way to think about the powerful emotions woven into Roy's work.

Educational Journey: Shaping Critical Perspectives

Roy's approach stems from extensive criticism of her surroundings and such theories are rooted in her education. Each stage of Arundhati's life is critical for her intellectual growth, starting from the first day of school all the way to university. It began in Roy's native state of Kerala, a southern state of India best known for its rich culture and heritage. The microcosm of politics, society, and culture alongside nature makes Kerala beautiful. These elements, being abundant in Roy's formative years, encouraged her growth.

While completing her education, the different disciplines and philosophies she encountered deepened her understanding of societal complexities. This interdisciplinary approach propelled Roy to academic stratospheres beyond standard boundaries, shaping her understanding of the world, and ultimately influencing her ability to weave intricate socio-political commentaries through her prose. She possessed a profound appetite for knowledge and delved into numerous subjects, considering them to be a part of the same holistic web.

Academia sparked Roy's activism and advocacy work. During university, like most of her peers, she had some powerful eureka moments that brought to light the systematic exploitation that existed in society. The realisation, without doubt, impacted how powerful structures are challenged and voices of the oppressed are heard, but it also signalled the marriage of academic pursuits with social consciousness. Her writings and public activism heated with the desire to make change.

Consequently, Roy's educational history along with her appetite for intellectual inquiry provided her with a discerning lens to analyse emerging inequalities and dominant narratives from different angles in a society exposed to so much information. It is also this critical acumen that provides her literature with depth, allowing her to address contentious themes and dissect power dynamics rigorously. Roy's approach to analysing contemporary issues distinctly emerged from her training.

In a nutshell, Arundhati Roy's life readily demonstrates the intersection of activism and education, portraying the value of education as a facilitator of critical thought and constructive social change. Her intellectual journey shaped her profound understanding and strong values, while also preparing her to become a social justice activist and a towering figure in the world of literature.

Cultural Context: Kerala's Influence on Thought

Kerala, often referred to as 'God's Own Country,' possesses a distinct charm in the intellectual and cultural map of India. Arundhati Roy's childhood in this beautiful and green state continues to influence her as a person and a writer. The stunning culture and traditions of Kerala, with its rich social heritage, surely must have impacted Roy's thinking. She tries to include the feeling of Kerala in her writings by drawing from its rich past, folklore, and social landscape to strengthen her narratives with reality.

One cannot delve into the influence of Kerala without appreciating the vibrant literary tradition that permeates the state. The folk stories and other modern masterpieces offered by famous Malayalam novelists are a great source of literature for Roy. Her immersion into the local literature and the narratives about the people displays a unique awe for the creative wealth of the state. This profound connection with the literary legacy of Kerala helps Roy provide her work with emotional depth and a keen understanding of human life.

Besides, the progressive movement, along with socio-economic reforms, has characterised the socio-political environment of Kerala over a period of time and has been further entrenched by a sense of communal harmony. It is in this background that Roy's sensitive multicultural social justice activism and her advocacy for the oppressed peoples of the world have blossomed. The socialist sensibility and democratic ethos that have been dominant features of Kerala society must have profoundly impacted Roy's sociopolitical sensibility.

Keralites, apart from their profound religiousness with strong beliefs, also have colourful and artistic forms of festivals, dance, and drama, which adds to Roy's creativity. She argues that her works on different issues, which have no geographical borders, are rather the brainchild of the diverse cultural heritage of Kerala. In this way, Kerala is not only frozen in part of Roy's life but also comes alive in her works as she expresses the beauty and depth of this place through her words.

To put it simply, it can be said that Arundhati Roy, owing to her close association with Kerala, has crystallised her creative thoughts and sharpened her ethics. Her use of rich and artistic prose in her exquisitely crafted literary pieces highlights her engagement with the unparalleled culture of Kerala, which now and forever remains the mark of her works.

Navigating Social Issues Through Personal Lens

Roy's childhood in Kerala, India, was crucial for her understanding of social issues with a compassionate gaze. She encountered the problems of caste, class, and gender relations in India at a very young age. Such experiences of societal inequities helped her cultivate a sense of responsibility to fight for the oppressed.

Roy has been an astute observer of life inherent in society, taking her life's sceneries and struggles, which became part of her literary and activism pursuits. This perspective contributed to her writing and activism on important social issues with a great deal of compassion. Based on her life experiences, Roy handled issues of injustice, oppression, discrimination, and inequalities with hope and realism.

Roy's involvement in numerous sociopolitical activities assisted in broadening her perspective and strengthening her ability to empathise and connect with different communities. It would not be an exaggeration to claim that Roy's writings have been focused on providing social justice, explaining the mechanisms of oppression, and uniting people for the cause of justice. Along with revealing the stark truths of inequitable social arrangements, I believe her work serves as a means of guiding a collective movement toward sustained constructive action.

Roy effectively blends her narratives with experiences that she observed, her friends' stories, and the people belonging to the marginalised groups that she interacted with. By taking ownership of the narrative, she does much more than tell a story; she compels her audience to face gnawing truths that demand action to uproot the system. This approach empowers the reader on a personal level and serves to widen the impact of her literature beyond the pages, motivating the willing souls to step forward and work toward achieving social justice.

In essence, Roy's social navigation through personal issues highlights the scope of her advocacy, transforming literary engagement and fostering critical attention to issues of social justice, equity, and human rights. Her unparalleled contribution to global literature and activism reflects the significance of individual experience positioned within a collective context, forever defining her legacy as a source of inspiration for all times.

Political Awakening: Personal Encounters with Activism

Arundhati Roy's innovation with activism came about because of the circumstances of her life, and not just as a response to existing societal injustices waiting to be dealt with. Her journey to activism began when she travelled to Kerala and saw the face of barbarous development cutting into tribes in backward regions, as well as the ecological disaster development projects bring forth. These awakening experiences of her tribe's suffering ignited in her the desire to work for other people. It was in Roy's internal compassion and understanding blend crucible where she actively began participating. Culturally rich spaces she travelled to as a youth opened her mind towards systemic inequality, aligning social issues across her country and trying to dismantle its root oppression. Her actions demonstrate clear trust in the ability of ordinary people to bring about sociopolitical change through unmediated forms of intervention. Having seen the impact of ordinary civilians on policymaking from the ground up, Roy became actively involved in post-development movements as an anthropologist working on policy strategies aimed at defending human rights, environmental issues, and the sovereignty of indigenous people.

This form of participation opened up new and intricate understandings of activism and sharpened her skills in connecting personal experiences with sociopolitical issues within her literature. Roy's activism enhanced her interpretation of systemic injustices and increased her determined efforts to advocate for those who suffered from oppressive social structures. Through her writings and advocacy, she incessantly demonstrates how individual actions relate to wider systems of politics, understanding that narratives are vital in defining and dismantling systems of injustice. Roy's crisis of politics exemplifies the impact of direct encounters with activism on an individual's life and how these experiences can infuse the arts with tenacity, compassion, and an unwavering commitment to social equality.

Integration of Personal Narratives in Fictional Worlds

Arundhati Roy's personal intertwining of fiction shows both her creativity and deep knowledge of people. It also reveals the significance of emotions and complex stories. In her iconic book The God of Small Things, Roy integrates parts from her life into her works wherever she can, including her experiences from Kerala. Because of this, readers understand Roy at a deeper level. She manages to capture fragments of her childhood through her character Rahel, making the novel a personal account about society. This is one of the strongest defining aspects of the book and the novel shows a surreal reality where personal experiences of Roy's life blend with social issues like norms and constraints. Such mastery helps Roy take readers on a journey that feels, at once, both real and imaginary. While exploring the realities of caste, class, and gender, she recalls her own experiences of such structures, making Roy's work vulnerable yet honest to humanity.

Roy's blending of personal stories into fictive realms began well before 'The God of Small Things' and persists in her later works like 'The Ministry of Utmost Happiness'. In this work, she continues to contemplate the complexities of self and sociopolitical violence drawing from her life as a witness to these events in order to forge her characters and their stories. In doing so, she merges the personal and the political to push beyond the limits of fiction and deliver striking comments on the reality of conditions, and humanity's relentless suffering and resilience. The blend of fiction and personal stories that Roy constructs to make worlds with blurred lines of reality and autobiography showcases her depth of imagination and skillful use of literary devices, creating worlds that capture the reader's attention while provoking deep reflection on the nature of society and existence.

Intertwining Biography with Broader Societal Themes

Arundhati Roy's literary works stand out due to their distinct blend of personal experience and deeper societal issues. By integrating her biography into major socio-political matters, Roy highlights the relations among individual stories and the society's conscience. This chapter examines the astounding ways Roy weaves her biography to foster understanding of broader societal issues and appreciate her work. Roy's sharp depiction of characters and situations has some basis in her life and experiences, which makes them empathetic towards the conflict and reality she presents. Roy, along with expressing delicate and broad insights from her lifetime, offers a direct narrative about socio-political dilemmas raging in every society. Additionally, she uses her experiences to take up most pressing problems in society and makes the audience contemplate them deeply and, at the same time, appreciate her artistry.

This integration aids in the perception of social issues such as gender, class, power, and other intricate conversations that require attention while cultivating deeper empathy toward necessary social issues. Moreover, Roy's artistry uniquely appeals to her audience by portraying the deeply personal as something universal. Her life experiences make her narratives compelling due to the authenticity of her self-depictions of the societal inequities and injustices that she endures, her insight, and raised by her truths. Scrutinising the manner in which Roy intertwines her biography with profound societal issues deepens appreciation of her work and enables us to understand the personal is political. In other words, examining how Roy ties her biography to broader contextual frameworks offers fresh perspectives on the discourse surrounding narrative, reflection, and society. In conclusion, Roy's deft blending of the private and public spheres affirms that literature is more than an art — it is a critical tool that encourages engagement and exploration to expand one's understanding of the world.

Conclusions on the Symbiosis of Life Experience and Literary Expression

The relationship between personal history and literature is distinct, intricate, and interconnected, creating opportunities for both the writer and the reader. As discussed in the previous chapter, merging an autobiography with a larger societal context offers a remarkable means of writing and social critique. With this merging, there is greater compassion and understanding towards the characters and issues presented in the story.

It now becomes clear that Arundhati Roy's life experiences have profoundly influenced her work, often blending it with rich personal history. Roy's life in Kerala nurtured her multicultural outlook which she later splendidly captured in her writings. The deeply entrenched stories within her works evolved through her personal experiences with the politics of dissent and active citizenship.

Furthermore, these distinct elements have allowed Roy to reach beyond geographical and cultural borders because of her blend of personal experiences with overarching concepts. Creating bases for her works in the realm of feelings and sufferings nurtures people's engagement with the narrative as it encourages people to connect with the very essence of humanity without immunity to underlying ideologies.

Such life experiences create within a person sentiment that is far better than any imposing abstraction, while literature gives such experiences the imaginative dimension and depth they require: both provide a link between the personal and collective experiences. Addressing her journey, Roy deals with issues like social disparities, eco-sabotage, and the postcolonial intricacies of India. The readers are granted insight into difficult socio-political realities from a personal lens due to her blending of the personal and the political.

To conclude, merging biography and fiction demonstrates not only how stories are stitched together but also how literature offers a voice to social consciousness. Arundhati Roy's body of work presents an exemplary case of how life bearing witness to deep and complex realities inspires dramatic action. Strong, caring, understanding and above all, life-affirming literature emerges when personal accounts and public issues are deeply interwoven. An ever greater sympathy for the power of literature, which has the ability to change the world, is born from such symbiosis, fostering a growing movement of young authors and readers.

Chapter Thirteen

Roy's Poetic Prose

Language and Style

Introduction to Roy's Linguistic Craft

Through Arundhati Roy's auspicious command over language, a story is no longer just a tale, but rather a depiction of a beautiful masterpiece. Her works encompass striking imagery due to her unique approach. Roy uses metaphors and imagery with such brevity that it is almost second nature for her to transport the audience into the depths of her world.

Roy transforms language into a symphony of emotions that intertwine with profound themes, evoking profound feelings through every meticulously chosen word. Be it the emotionally tumultuous lives of her subjects set in picturesque Kerala or relationships riddled with complexities, Roy's unmistakable mastery over words paints vivid pictures alongside rich, dynamic emotions.

As Roy skillfully combines metaphors and descriptive sensory language, her prose takes on a quality which draws readers into the intricate and rich worlds of her stories. Her careful word choice and imagery evokes a world that goes beyond the page and commands the readers' sight, sound, and touch. Her craft does not only put on display her artistry but reveals the depth of her grasp regarding the phenomenon of language and story.

Roy's strength comes from the remarkable visual representations that can be created through her words. In Roy's hands, words do not only serve to describe settings and characters; they are means to unveil the complexities of human thoughts and feelings. With her carefully crafted prose, she invites the reader to confront and grapple with her stories' lived realities and sensations—thereby establishing a bond that goes beyond the text.

Roy's construction of her prose demonstrates that her mastery of language is not simply in the expression of beauty but rather in how language connects with readers on a personal and emotional level.

The Role of Metaphor and Imagery

The art of writing greatly depends on metaphor and imagery since they seek to evoke aesthetics and feelings and make works more pleasurable to their readers. In Arundhati Roy's writing, metaphor and imagery evoke emotions and feelings from the readers, making them personally attached to the narrations. In Roy's writing, a metaphor is essential in the analysis of difficult concepts because readers are given the opportunity to delve into rich human experiences through her narratives. The readers, through Roy's poetry, have transformed into her rich and vivid multi-faceted imagery, which places them in the heart of the dense, colourful world of Kerala, where they can hear, see, and smell the beauty of the place. By creating imagery full of colour and life, she gives her writing's settings and characters vivid movement and vitality. Apart from beautifying her writing, the use of imagery and metaphor becomes increasingly more powerful because it gives the prose meaning and produces intellectual and emotional responses. Roy uses imagery and metaphors to blend multiple themes to take the readers through an intense journey of self-exploration and contemplation. The pair of metaphors and imagery serves as a pointer to numbingly deep thoughts about social and political systems and their interconnectedness with mankind.

Roy meticulously intertwines symbols and images, merging her stories seamlessly. This careful layering of metaphor and imagery showcases her great understanding of human nature, enabling readers to connect with her work on a deeply personal and intellectual level. As such, every metaphor and image captures, at a deeper level, the paradoxes of our reality and the psyche of man, blurring the boundaries of the external world and internal reality. By sophisticated use of metaphors and imagery, Roy does not simply tell a story; rather, she gives it a profound effect that lingers after the last page has been read.

Syntax and Rhythm: Crafting Melodic Narratives

Combining elements of literary style, such as syntax and rhythm, makes writing an aesthetic feat. Roy demonstrates the sheer mastery of the language through her ability to narrate in a manner that, quite remarkably, sounds musical. While studying her prose, one cannot fail to notice the charm that her narrative bears. It is in the arrangement of her sentences together that, much like a piece of music, strikes deep emotions in readers, just like listening to a beautiful tune does.

Roy's mastery is apparent in her ability to strategically manipulate the lengths and structures of her sentences, harnessing their potential and control over the flow of her stories. Through shifting between long, flowing sentences and shorter, staccato sentences, she creates prose that pulsates with life as it captures the movement and rhythm of thought. This kind of manipulative approach to sentence structure becomes a medium through which various complex ideas can be blended without boundaries, resulting in captivating narratives that flow like a magical spell captivating readers' minds and eyes.

Roy's rhythmic control becomes more than just linguistic performance; it marks a deeper appreciation of the art of telling a tale. The rhythmically controlled prose pulse, which is a characteristic of her narrative, resembles the pulse of the characters, making them alive and real for the reader. The strokes of her pen, both upward and downward within her sentences, are full of emotion and carry within vibrant tremors that win her readers more into the narrative world.

To these features, Roy's cultivation of melodic narratives stems from her skillful application of repetition, parallelism, and pauses. These devices not only add to the rhythmic quality of her prose but also work to highlight important themes and motifs, enabling a more profound engagement with the material and aiding in the storytelling's underlying layers.

Roy's devices are clearly visible in her cadence and syntax because Arundhati Roy goes beyond traditional prose in her writing, evoking a different form of art, one where words compose an enchanting melody. Moving forward to the next section on the 'Symbolism in Language: Layers of Meaning', it is easy to notice that Roy's creativity is not skin-deep when it comes to her use of language and she goes as deeply as nature in symbolic representation and many more profundities.

Symbolism in Language: Layers of Meaning

Language is undeniably an emotional vehicle, or a cultural bridge, and thus needs mastery on the part of the user. Arundhati Roy's use of symbolism in writing offers her readers a lot of value along with prose. Each word that the author uses in her writing is consciously selected such that it conveys important meaning beyond the obvious. The language of Roy's is full of nature's symbolism as it becomes an overriding technique which goes effortlessly beyond the basic understanding and leads to a breathtaking reading experience. There are nature's endless themes like light-dark, nature-objects and nature-setting relationships that form their own meaning in Roy's language. In her works, she also depicts nature in such a way as to remind every human being of the relationship that people share with nature while narrating stories that ooze with ecological consciousness and environmental care. Likewise, the way she describes light and shadow serves as a reminder of the complexity of people and the reality they go through while also bringing forth their resemblance to hope and despair, love and loss, and changes of humanity. In contrast, objects and settings in Roy's works are more than mere surfaces; they describe the character's mind and social context and give them an allegorical meaning.

By employing the nuanced use of symbolism in her language, Roy encourages readers to delve deeply into emotions, social issues, and philosophical ideas. The impact of these symbols lingers beyond the text, accompanying readers throughout their everyday lives and allowing them to search deeper within themselves. As proof of Roy's skillfulness as a writer, this use of language adds more layers and details to the stories, thus making a great and shocking effect on the audience all over the world. When readers analyse and interpret the underlying details and immerse themselves into the world of Roy's symbols, they are made to stop everything and think about the powerful realities nudging around them. It is in this careful use of symbols that Roy's speech becomes prose that looks like a complex mosaic, capturing everyone through a single thread and leading them down the path of life changing literature.

Dialogue as a Reflection of Character and Culture

Literature without dialogues would be very different from what we know it as today. Dialogue not only propels the story but gives us a glimpse of the character's psyche as well as the culture that surrounds them. In the case of Arundhati Roy's works, dialogues largely influence the cultural context of the society she writes about and the relationships of people within it. Her mastery of placing true-to-life dialogues demonstrates her deep comprehension of human interactions and social structures. It is as if the people in the factual world speak using particular slang, jargon, and other speech attributes that colour the narratives. These conversations go beyond mere talking; they reflect the beliefs and principles of the sociocultural context where the characters exist. For her, what is most significant is how dialogue gives life to her story by making them believable and transporting the audience to the settings of the stories she writes. The dialogues not only divulge the character's persona but go further to provide a social critique. In the conflict and social interactions of the characters, Roy exposes the social class systems, dominant and subordinate powers, and many issues of discrimination which better the purpose of her writing.

Moreover, dialogue offers Roy the ability to delve deeper into the multiple layers of interpersonal relationships and the feelings of her characters. From the ethno-biographical interview, it can be seen that Roy seems to focus on the telltale features of speech that are parts of human social interaction, which adds complexity to her storytelling. Besides, the adoption of multilingual dialogues as well as code-switching in Roy's texts corroborates her intention to picture the diversity in vernacular languages as sociometric markers of the populations she depicts. This too reinforces the multicultural spirit of the narratives but also speaks of the sociopolitical conditions of the contexts she examines. In the analysis of the relationship of dialogue to character and culture, Roy shows that her stories are much more than narratives because they bring together a multitude of voices appealing to the human condition in particular and to humanity in general.

Literary Influences and Unique Voice

Arundhati Roy's literary influences highlight the intricacies of her voice as a writer. Roy's work as an activist fiction writer shows that she uses a variety of sources which have shaped her style and thematic explorations. Many scholars and critics have researched the various aspects of her literary heritage, adding the multi-layered richness that captivates readers.

Roy interlaces her works with Indian literature, postcolonial theory, and global narratives, allowing her to craft a unique voice that is structured in tradition and boldly innovative. Drawing from such a diverse body of literature, Roy displays a profound engagement with the letters, which allows her to elevate the richness of her work. Not only do the traces of fragmented narrations shape Roy's voice, but also her keen social and political critiques. Striking the perfect balance between unyielding advocacy and poetic prose fuses her work with a potent synergy that sets her apart in the literary landscape.

Critics have often remarked upon the presence of Salman Rushdie's magical realism in Roy's work, as well as the incisive social commentary of Toni Morrison and the multilayered storytelling of Gabriel Garcia Marquez. This appreciation of various influences highlights the breadth of her literary preoccupations as well as the distinctiveness of her voice. Roy's distinctive voice rests on her own reality and her lived experiences, demonstrating a keen awareness of social disparity and inequality, environmental issues, and human rights abuses. Such experiences lend her work a sense of authenticity and connection to humanity. It is this combination of experience and influence from world literature that allows Roy to express herself in ways she seeks to impact through. Ultimately, the literature of Roy's influences is instrumental in developing her unique voice, one that draws on these cultures and still echoes through time for countless readers and writers to come.

Interweaving Vernacular: Authenticity in Representation

Arundhati Roy's weaving of vernacular languages in her prose shows her cultural authenticity towards the communities she represents. In her works, Roy incorporates vernacular expressions, dialogues, and phrases which help her to construct the reciprocal identity of her characters and their local nuances. Roy includes vernacular pieces to help her readers experience her storytelling at a new level by understanding the culture and language intricacies through her writing. The volunteers brought food for us all so that we could share a meal together. The phrases highlight Roy's attempt to tackle the oppression of language expression and emulate the lower forms of communication which have long been considered inferior. Roy's incorporation of regional speech captures the essence of identity while demonstrating the shared understanding across cultures and languages. By depicting vernacular languages truthfully, Roy argues against linguistic standards that are often seen as oppressive and showcases plurality in language that exists within different communities.

By deliberately integrating the colloquial languages, Roy goes beyond telling a story and begins the work of culture protection and resisting language suppression. Roy's readers strive to understand her use of language and as a result, they begin to peel off different parts of the layers of identity and belongingness that are interconnected to language. As a writer, she not only enriches her stories but also empowers marginalised people by capturing the attention of others who have been silenced, which allows them to claim their heritage through language. With the inclusion of the vernacular in her fictional works, Roy endorses the maintenance of languages alongside culture, and the existence of diversity and equality within written works, thus making everything fair and balanced in the literary world.

Emotional Resonance through Poetic Devices

Capturing a reader's emotion calls for the use of different poetic devices that help in evoking deep feelings. Arundhati Roy's poetic language and style are breathtaking, as she applies so many devices that aid her in achieving that emotional reverberation which stays long after the engagement. In "The God of Small Things", Roy enchants her audience with metaphorical emotions behind similes and symbolism. She paints vivid imagery that places readers in a world which reverberates on emotional planes and feeling empathy becomes inevitable. As masterfully layered prose invites readers with rich allegory and allusion, complex emotions through stories crafted within deep themes tell them to not stay at surface level. Additionally, the cadence and syntax control allows for graceful shifting of musical elements into the narrative which crafts an emotionally moving story. By setting pace in rhythm, Roy builds words into waves, flowing on feelings to bond the readers profoundly with the feelings of the characters.

Analysis of the dialogue shows that it serves as a window into culture and emotions, and in turn adds depth to Roy's writing. Every conversation has a delicate touch of underlying emotion which communicates the character's pain and yearnings. Also, the other influences Roy draws upon, along with the distinctive voice she shapes for herself, add layers of feeling to her prose. Roy makes use of many cultures' and literatures' traditions which creates a bond of emotions that knows no borders, reaching the souls of people everywhere. Critics have praised her emotional weight and mastery of the poetic devices so much that she has emerged as a leading contemporary writer, one whose writing profoundly impacts her audience. Readers, as they engage with the nuances and the powerful emotions etched into each page by Roy's hand, find themselves inexorably drawn into an unparalleled emotional voyage. A sustained exploration of Arundhati's work shows that her command of poetic devices places her prose in a realm beyond reach, striking a chord with the reader's heart.

Critical Reception of Roy's Language

Readers and critics have been captivated by the prose and the poetic style of Arundhati Roy that has elevated, igniting conversations and debates over how her choice of language features in the world of literature. Critics have vigorously discussed Roy's imaginative application of poetic elements and other poetic devices, claiming that the overwhelming emotion present in her works derives from her skillful manipulation of language and style.

Roy employs complex metaphors and imagery alongside informative language, further submerging the readers into her narratives. Her writing draws appreciation for the ease with which she renders diverse scenes, characters, and places through the use of poetic devices and vivid descriptions. Critics continue to praise her skillful portrayal of complex emotions and even abstract ideas through carefully curated phrases and her exceptional word choice.

Moreover, Roy's manipulation of syntax and rhythm has been both celebrated and critiqued in the world of literary criticism. Critics have focused on how the rhythm of her prose, which is often musical in nature, is shaped by her choices on sentence construction and the pacing of the narrative. The combination of choppy, brief thoughts with soft, flowing passages creates a balance that reflects the rise and fall of human feeling, encoding her words with meaning that transcends communication and evokes strong emotions in the process.

Along with her use of poetic language, symbolism in Roy's diction has been critiqued extensively. Roy's motifs, representative of allegorical references, are employed with purpose and deepen the complexity of her narratives, encouraging readers to go beyond the surface to extract reality. Roy's approach to language, rich in symbolism, cements her status as an author who captures the attention of readers and scholars, forcing them to think critically about the realities she uncovers.

Consequently, the evaluation of Roy's language has been splendid over the years, appreciating her as a premier master of words which marks her uniqueness as a writer. With her dissimilar but captivating words, Roy has transformed the limits of what is deemed achievable in literature, thus elevating her status among the great authors of all time.

Conclusion: The Enduring Impact of Roy's Style

Apurva has single-handedly transformed the typical lenses through which modern literature is perceived and approached through her breathtakingly creative perspectives. Beyond the measures of country and culture, Arundhati Roy's impact resonates across the globe; she is considered a literary giant for a reason. As significant as her impact is, it has surpassed Roy's personal boundaries. Meaningful discussions stemming from strong discourse and peaceful movements have been outsourced to the public's imagination due to the deep and subtle impact Roy leaves. Her gentle but searing prophecy has created a blend of critique and exciting language that results in a sharp incision, allowing her readers to resonate with her words and experience a literal bounce between worlds where nothing falls flat. Roy's command over language is anything but marred; her militant form of expression and artistic acumen sways public opinion, driving motion and lending itself to activism. Rather, it is a phenomenon that allows rupturing ideas to escape the confines of oppression, as shifting metaphors, along with vivid explanation, form multiple layers that unveil various facets of humanity. Collectively, the Roy effect possesses the unmatched ability to create a sense of ease that endures through hypnotising — captivating readers well after they have turned the pages. But this talented author does not merely stop at crafting each line syntactically as a masterpiece; each sentence is enriched with perspective, metaphor, synesthesia, and a tactful ear for prose. It goes without saying that the cadence enables the building of vivid imagery that lingers with us, allowing every conscious critique to engage and foster proactive social sharing of the narrative.

Roy's dialogue showcases her profound mastery of characterisation and human culture - a mastery of accurate interaction. Drawing from various literary works, Roy has crafted a voice that is uniquely striking. By incorporating colloquialisms, she portrays the myriad groups that populate her stories, rendering them with tangible authenticity. The connections she creates with her audience using poetic devices are achievable due to their detachment from the language itself. Aside from the multitude of awards she has received, Roy's comments have also come under scrutiny, but this is what reveals the lasting impact of her style. Observing her writing with self-critique unveils the beauty of her craftsmanship and the wealth of reportable conclusions her work offers. Above all, it is clear that the impact of Roy's stylistic features lingers long after her written works. It emphasises the notion of literature being capable of instigating change, defying societal boundaries, and engaging diverse voices to narrate one common story of humanity.

Chapter Fourteen

A Critique of Power

Dissecting Capitalism and Nationalism

Introduction to the Intersection of Power, Capitalism, and Nationalism

The interconnection of power, capitalism, and nationalism has always influenced the growth of society, government, and the resources in a society. This intersection is a socio-economic phenomenon that controls the flow of wealth, power, and politics. Arundhati Roy's analysis reveals the rational and philosophical centre of this triad and how power functions under capitalism and nationalism maintains.

Roy's view on the dynamics of power and nationalism indicates that capitalism has a history and evolves over time and that Roy follows its lineage from mercantilism to present capitalism. Her evaluation encompasses a longitudinal approach of capitalism that is initiated from trade economies to industrial revolutions, then to market economies. In this timeline, Roy gives an explanation of capitalism power and nationalism by demonstrating how businessmen propel economically to ensure power is structured and defended firmly.

Moreover, Roy's focus is not limited to purely economic considerations and incorporates an aspect of nationalism together with capitalism. In her critique, Roy explains how nationalism is used as a cover for capitalism and how, in the name of patriotism, money-making endeavours are often exploited out of nationalist sentiments. This examination illuminates the ways nationalistic zeal is exploited to reinforce and perpetuate existing systems of domination.

To put it differently, it is the combination of power in conjunction with capitalism and nationalism that acts as a support for the lower and middle strata of society. In these strata, as deep Roy's analyses go, gives the knowledge of the configuration and distribution of power and resources available in a society. By studying the past and present, she hopes to find a society in which power, capitalism, and nationalism are justly balanced to promote equity and uplift every member of society.

Historical Context: Evolution of Capitalist Structures

As the primary economic and societal system in contemporary life, capitalism has a sharp and differentiating history spanning centuries. The mercantile activities in the late medieval period marked the beginnings of capitalist structures with the trade routes and circulation of goods and wealth forming the basis of commercial capitalism. This system of trade was further supported during the European exploration and colonial periods, where powerful trading companies and imperial ventures capitalised on resources harvested from colonised countries. The industrial revolution in the 18th and 19th centuries further advanced the processes of production and gave birth to industrial capitalism, which in turn nurtured the growth of urban centres.

The development of capitalism was not an exclusively European phenomenon, as it spread and exploded into international markets with imperial and colonial exploitation. Moreover, along with the soul paradigm of an economy revolving around capital accumulation, new financial institutions and stock exchanges imposed strength on capitalism. With time, the system underwent drastic changes and embraced varied new models such as laissez-faire capitalism, state capitalism, and neoliberal capitalism, marked by unique rules of governance and control.

Examining marks of early Capitalism and its present-day forms shows that it has undergone periods of attainment and distress in its development. Periods of recession, significant economic falls, and rampant poverty highlighted the inherent flaws and imbalances of Capitalist systems. Moreover, the Capitalist system's merger with nationalism has globally altered the trajectory of historical events by changing policies, wars, and international power relations.

Knowing how deeply rooted Capitalist frameworks are within history will enable a person to fully analyse these frameworks' sociocultural consequences. This examination enables an understanding of the disproportionality of wealth and income, the persistence of social stratification, and the tangled web of globalised economic relations. This foundation also helps understand the problems posed by capitalism along with its unsettling nationalism and sovereign power of nation-states at the core of economic dominance amid shifting global boundaries.

National Sovereignty vs. Global Capital: A Delicate Balance

The dilemma of national sovereignty and global capitalism remains a dominant problem in the geopolitical world as countries become increasingly integrated. This analysis is broken down profoundly by Roy where she aims to understand the tension that lies with the combination of national self-determination and the requirements of globalised capitalism.

The most prominent feature in this narrative is striking a balance between defending national policies while dealing with the overwhelming force of multinational corporations and international financial institutions. There's a fight nowadays due to sovereignty within national borders because there are currently existing transnational treaties, capital and investment flows, and integration of markets. Roy unpacks these elements and illustrates the struggle of how countries are able to defend their self-identity, self-determination, and self-governance in the face of globalisation.

The interplay of national sovereignty with global capital shows complex power relations and ethical issues. In order to achieve economic growth and development, governments frequently reach a compromise between protecting their domestic industries and granting foreign investment access. This opposition mandates consideration of the impact on labour rights, environmental protection, and social justice within the country's territorial limits.

Roy's nuanced scrutiny explores the impact of such choices, providing analysis beyond traditional frameworks.

Also, the balance of national sovereignty and global capital does not end at the borders of the economy, but also expands into ideological and cultural territory. The spread of entertainment media and technology from one country to the entire world raises concerns regarding the preservation of unique national identities and cultures. Roy deftly underscores the need for intellectual autonomy and self-determination in crafting a nation's narrative as it succumbs to the torrents of globalisation.

Through his or her suggestions to support the balance of national sovereignty and global capital, the author calls attention to the fundamental issues of justice, human rights, and participatory democracy. By exposing the problems that lie within this merging, she stimulates the discussion on the changing relations of power and the need for ethical leadership in modern times.

Critical Examination of Economic Policies in India

Each of the economic policies in India has brought about fundamental changes over the years, and has, in turn, become crucial in defining the socioeconomic character of the country. Renowned for her insight and equally sharp criticism, Arundhati Roy explores the intricate web of economic policy formulation in India. The assessment of policies is invariably complex and demands a thorough and holistic study of its colonial imprint, post-independence period, and the neoliberal turn towards the end of the twentieth century.

Roy's insightful analysis does not remain confined to classifying micro and macro, as is frequently practised. Roy reflects on the consequences of 'globalisation rationalised' neoliberal policies on the social fabric of India. She analyses the policies which have systematically dispossessed vulnerable sections, deepened divides, and led to rampant exploitation of resources by corporations.

Additionally, Roy studies the problematic coexistence of industrial development and ecology as the environmental and sociological impacts of certain economic policies suggest the presence of development of industries, which has led to extensive ecological damage and displacement. Additionally, Roy examines how the power dynamics influence the formulation of these economic frameworks, resulting more oftentimes than not, in hyper-concentration of wealth and power.

It is in this analysis that Roy delineates the paradox of social welfare enhancement alongside capitalistic development, and critiques the poverty bred by the most extreme capitalism and aggressive privatisation policies. His analysis sheds light on the deep and systematic denial of modern democracy to citizens through the principles of crony capitalism, revealing the cruel reality inflicted upon the societal outcasts.

To sum up, Roy's examination of the economic strategies of India draws attention to the relationship between power, capitalism, and nationalism while at the same time makes the public aware of the need for an integrated and fair approach which takes into account all citizens, not only a few economically powerful individuals.

Arundhati Roy's Analysis of State Power

Arundhati Roy deeply analyses how state power operates, paying attention to how subtle forms of control enable a government to assert power. She makes critical observations about the structure of the state and its myriad forms of governance, including control, regulation, and coercion, based on existing empirical data. The intricate relationships among the state and its corporate and peripheral constituents are analysed deeply by Roy within the context of their forces that perpetuate inequalities within society. Roy looks not just at the state as an institution but also at the informal structures and social networks that are involved in policy making and provide a holistic view of power. She connects this scrutiny with sociopolitical currents to locate state authority in historical contexts of power struggles, contrasting ideologies, and social justice agendas. By conducting painstaking documentation of social resources alongside meticulous research, she highlights the impact of state authority on the distribution of social resources, environmental care, and human rights advocacy.

Roy's work reveals how the actions and policies of the state inflict systemic violence which captures the commitment of the power in authority on the sociopathic scale of existence. Her analysis of state power brings out its scrutiny within the context of appropriate critique, which fosters the much-needed democratic accountability and equal governance. Their vigilance against the flagrant and unapologetic use of state power is not enough; it is equally important to transform society from one level of injustice to a significantly more just and socially equal system.

Corporatisation and Its Impact on Local Economies

The process of gaining greater control over economic resources and policymaking is referred to as Corporatisation, and it has great effects on local economies. Arundhati Roy's incisive analysis offers insight into the sociocultural divide spawned by this trend. The fundamental problem is that of the inequitable allocation of the resources and disappearance of traditional avenues of employment.

The advancement of multinational companies into local economies comes with many consequences. One of the most pertinent issues is the removal of Indigenous peoples and farmers out of the lands they traditionally inhabit and work. The commercialisation of natural resources, often alongside government agencies, leads to the exploitation and neglect of these vulnerable people. Roy highlights the commodification of land, water, and forests as a major problem claiming that the most brutally impacted communities in the face of rampant corporatisation have lost their existence or identity.

The arrival of large-scale businesses may also disturb the local economies and further plunge them into dependency and hopelessness. With this, small businesses and traditional craftsmen have been pushed aside, and whole branches of uniquely artisanal work and local economies have been driven to the wall. Roy's keen insights unravel the intricate effects of corporatisation, particularly the complete disempowerment of the local entrepreneurial ecosystem.

However, the social problems raised by corporated modernisation also lead to further elevation of ecological problems and environmental pollution. Practices such as clear cutting, over-industrial waste dumping, and resource overuse have a dramatically negative impact on the environment that sustains regionally based economies. The environmental devotion in today's society,

Arundhati Roy's harsh critique of the corporate world also covers their collision with nature as she reminds us how, in order to widen their profit margins, eco-friendly but economically useful actions are completely ignored.

Moreover, when large corporations dominate the economy, their power leads to the poor treatment of employees and the creation of difficult working conditions. In doing so, Roy teaches us about the exploitation of workers, the denial of their basic human rights, and the desperate conditions many of them work under due to corporatisation's ever-tightening grip on reality.

Roy's analysis of the processes of corporatisation alongside its impacts on local economies marks a strong appeal to action as a compelling threat to social order to fight for imbalance of power, oppression, and inequality. In highlighting the concerns of those who have been affected, Roy builds the discourse on the need for reconstruction of dominant economic paradigms based on social justice, ecological balance, and self-determination instead.

Media as a Tool for Power Dissemination

Today's political and social climate is increasingly shaped by the media. Arundhati Roy unpacks this complex web as she studies how media is used as a weapon by those in charge. Information flow, be it through news sections or popular digital platforms, comes with specific motives, often undermining the public with constructed realities that serve their interests. Roy painstakingly captures the complexity of media abuse and highlights the importance of defeating public censure that is perpetuated by media control. Roy eloquently explains how media works to further state and corporate sponsored narratives on the public while constantly drowning out other perspectives. By examining control of media, she uncovers the underlying ideas that govern, strategically guiding the flow of information, and bare the biases that shape public discourse. Roy also analyses media's relationship with political power to expose the dangerous coupling of capitalism and nationalism. Roy showcases the impacts through case studies. In doing so, she highlights the dangers of monopolising the media on democracy, highlighting the need for independent media free from control.

As advocating for critical media literacy, she analyses the impact of media through their historical precedents and draws from global contexts. Roy makes readers understand how media disseminates power to enable them to grapple with reproduction of information and become informed citizens who can resist negative representations and dominant narratives.

The Role of Literature in Political Discourse

Literature has so far been defined as an important tool in the expression of political views and even in social activism. Shining a light on Arundhati Roy, who is an acclaimed author, we can see that she has used literature to reflect critically on the interrelatedness of power, capitalism, and nationalism. Roy's writings provide stories that defy established notions of power and challenge the prevailing hegemonic thought in authoritative modern politics.

In Roy's own words, small things do define individual identities, but in her landmark books, 'The God of Small Things' and 'The Ministry of Utmost Happiness,' she reveals powerful aspects in society and she captures power relations between people and systems through literature. The storytelling prose is evocative, colourful, and powerful. Its appeal lies in narrating the tales of people who suffer because of cruel systems. By providing vignettes alongside the bigger picture, Roy's writing turns into an instrument of struggle by the politically subdued people.

Literature often helps readers reflect and process the ongoing consequences stemming from capitalist exploitation and nationalist fervour. It does this by acting like a reservoir of collective memory and historical consciousness. Roy's narratives had an impact on readers by encouraging them to come face to face with painful realities through stories, profoundly examined by her, challenging the consequences of state violence and socio-economic stratification. By bringing forward silenced voices and revealing the darker realities of governance and power, literature challenges society to undergo ethical self-examination and change.

Also, the blend of art and activism through Roy's work exemplifies the role writers play in inspiring action against social injustice and the power it holds in inciting grassroots resistance. She uses her passionate writing and elegant style to convey urgency in addressing the issues created by neoliberal capitalism and hyper-nationalism. She blends her literary work with moral obligation in order to create blueprints for new realities of social order in which readers are invited to refashion relations of power.

The examples by Arundhati Roy showcase how literature does not only play a role in political discourse for entertainment or aesthetic reflection, but also deeply impacts 'engaged' literature, as we call it. It highlights the stirrings of critical engagement amongst the readers that defines the very political reality of their life. Literature in its many forms scaffolds civic awareness by informing them of the consequences of action or inaction, inviting empathy for the very complex set of forces at work, and striking at the very structures that inform their being. Civically engaged literature urges readers to not resign to accept the course predetermined for them by society, but become actors of change.

In the case of her literary works, Roy invites readers to reflect on their roles within society, and which by virtue of their imagination and intellect become active defenders of social change, thus a testimony to the power of politically engaged literature.

Case Studies: Movements Against State-Endorsed Capitalism

At this stage, we consider captivating case studies of the resistance movements against state endorsed capitalism which are equally terrains of struggle with various approaches and results. First, let's focus on the Narmada Bachao Andolan (NBA), a peaceful social movement aimed at opposing the construction of large dams on the Narmada River.

From the lopsided conflict over capitalist systems, it is possible to unravel a multitude of political, environmental and even social intricacies or the issues raised with developmental projects are multi-faceted and so is their human toll which is captured so poignantly by Arundhati Roy's advocacy for the development's displaced people. Next is an examination of the Narmada River social movement, which draws attention to the expansive civic activism in Kerala for the dismantling of commercial tribal expropriations.

It is possible to piece together both the exploitation of land by state policies and the oppression of people through painstaking narrative documentation. These cases sharply delineate the portrait of ethical governance against the harsh reality of economic growth, revealing the underlying tension emergent in power relations.

As previously stated, we examine the efforts put forth by agrarian movements in combating the corporate takeover of agriculture, particularly focusing on the farmers' plight regarding biotechnology and seed monopolies. The sociological aspects of these movements provide insight into the relationships between socio-economic policies and social justice, featuring well-balanced perspectives to explain the difficulties encountered when dealing with state-sponsored capitalism. With these case studies, we seek to illustrate the courage and ingenuity of those communities defying the prevailing conditions while recognising the underlying social and economic inequities of the situation.

Reflections and Conclusions: Pathways to Equitable Power Dynamics

The focus of this investigation into movements resisting state-backed capitalism leads us to an important point of reflection from which conclusions can be drawn to better navigate the route towards establishing balanced power relations. The case studies selected have provided evidence reinforcing the concentration of power which has remained the primary enduring feature of state-sponsored capitalism. These powers have social, economic, and environmental consequences and have created an ecosystem of inequality that serves the marginalised.

It is clear that any attempt to dismantle these sociopolitical structures involves complex tactics and multiple actors. The works of Arundhati Roy have repeatedly pointed out the need for bottom-up organising as well as cross-societal alliance and solidarity in dealing with established systems of power. From the theoretical perspectives of the movements studied, we learn about the success of community-based movements in transforming power relations and working towards policies that are holistic in nature, benefiting all individuals.

Additionally, this study fosters constructive scrutiny concerning governance and policy formulation aimed at resolving systemic imbalances. In such efforts, there is a need to pay attention to systems and ideas used that are hostile to egalitarian relationships based on respectful power. Acknowledging these limits, focus should be placed on creating frameworks that defend sustainable development, social justice, and human rights. From Roy's sharp critique, there is always an overriding control politically and economically that shapes the lives of people on the margins, leaving them with negligible options resulting in the gains of an uneven society that requires urgent attention for the restructuring of power.

Equally important is the contribution of education and awareness in the development of a constructive social consciousness to contest hegemonic paradigmatic systems of power. The unprecedented social changes happening all over the world can be traced back to the education system in which people are taught to think and analyse complex issues rather than accept the information presented to them without questioning it. Roy's involvement in public discourse brings to light the very essence of activism that seeks to hold the powerful to account, and to ensure that systems of governance are accountable and transparent.

With all those considerations in mind, one's reflection on the movements that are forming in response to state capitalism reveals the experiences that underpin emerging and existing narratives of power. This reflection helps in formulating new approaches to instilling change while simultaneously reminding society of the entrenched structures that need to undergo fundamental change. In the course of this contemplation, it is our responsibility to use reflections from these considerations in an attempt to promote dignified and equitable power relations for both current and future generations.

Chapter Fifteen

Reception and Criticism

Navigating the Literary Landscape

The immediate impact of Arundhati Roy's first blockbuster

Arundhati Roy's notoriety as an author emerged with the brand new novel 'The God of Small Things,' with its captivating plot as well as its postcolonial era rich setting. The novel has set frighteningly high expectations for Roy, owing to effortless storytelling within elaborate frameworks of humanity. This 'new talent' was critically acclaimed for her exquisite English literature, making it an instant classic and earning her the Man Booker Prize in Britain.

Roy's work on 'The God of Small Things' was not only about intricate family relationships set against deep-rooted societal hierarchies, but also about unclaimed love that transcends societal norms. Critics were divided on whether Roy delicately portrayed the beauty of Karela or masterfully captured Indian societal expectations surrounding race, religion, and gender dynamics, flooding literary circles and societies with fervent discussions.

Equally praised were Roy's obscenely poetic descriptive passages and deeply evocative prose. As warm Karela breezes met the readers, they too became advocates for social activism, empowering them to see the grotesque injustices and emotional conflicts human beings are bound to face and endure throughout the deep-rooted expectations set upon them. Roy received both admiration and stark critique for uncovering such stark social injustice realities.

Consequently, the unparalleled success of 'The God of Small Things' propelled Roy's rise as a fierce literary force that would, through her later works, defy expectations and deeply incite reflections. The reception of the novel signified not only an encouraging start to Roy's literary journey, but also set the foundation for an enduring legacy that transcends borders and resonates through the ages.

Literary Acclaim and Prestigious Awards

The literary scope of Arundhati Roy's work has brought her accolades of high regard which have catapulted her to the top levels of contemporary literature. After 'The God of Small Things' was released, Roy has been in contention for winning global prizes and has won many prestigious ones, making her and her literary works strikingly known. The attention from the public and critics for her debut work was immediate due to its astonishing elegance in depicting family relationships within the socio-political framework of India, and the novel did allow the readers to take the much-needed deep breath of fresh air. It was the 1997 Man Booker Prize for Fiction winning book that defined Roy and her skills as a writer, after which there was no stopping her and people understood the fact that she was anything but ordinary. Along with the Man Booker Prize, 'The God of Small Things' was also awarded the DSC Prize for South Asian Literature, showcasing the longevity, sustainability, and relevance of the India-based novel. This indicated that the novel was much more than what people perceived it to be. As Roy advanced in her career, she earned respect from across the globe because of her unconventional style of writing without boundaries, which definitely put some cautiously difficult angles around the relatively simple sides of the human experience that we live.

Her work was recognised with awards such as the Sydney Peace Prize and the Lannan Foundation's Cultural Freedom Award, highlighting the importance of her writing outside the realm of fiction. All of these awards acknowledge Roy's literary genius, but more importantly, they also recognise her unwavering commitment to fighting for justice and equality. The scope of her impact is also illustrated by the Anisfield-Wolf Book Award which Roy received for her outstanding scholarship on racism. The ability of Roy to blend the personal with the political makes her a global leading literary figure and the force of reflection and debate that she incites is unmatched.

Critical Voices: Divergent Opinions on Narrative Techniques

Her narrative style has been analysed by a range of scholars, resulting in differing opinions within literary discourse. Some applauded the unconventional and lyrical aspect of her prose as it paints an intricate emotional landscape while others criticised the added complexity as an unwanted barrier to genuine engagement with the work.

One group as part of a school of thought acknowledges and appreciates the purposeful obscuring of conventional narrative structures as one in which Roy subverts the status quo, appealing to readers to engage with the text more actively. On the other hand, some critics claim that such an approach, while innovative, may alienate parts of the audience and that it comes off as self-indulgent. The adoption of non-linear narratives and the shifting of points of view alongside rich symbolism has drawn admiration and skepticism in equal measure. Some hail the heightened emotional impact and profound thematic exploration made possible through these techniques while others argue that such devices may distract from the focus of the story and weaken its telling. Discourse around the representation of characters and cultures through language and dialect has sparked passionate discussions. Critics have focused on the blend of authenticity and modernity, asking if the inclusion of linguistic quirks is a strengthening detail that enhances the text or a frustrating detail that offends readers who are unfamiliar with the specific dialect. Roy's layering of voices and stories has drawn different responses about the narrative's coherence and readability, showcasing the importance of narrative design and readers' impressions in reconsidering the boundaries of reception and acceptance.

Such distinct views on narrative strategies show the ever-evolving nature of Roy's work, which offers deep appreciation of her writing.

Interpreting Themes: Political Undertones in Literary Works

There is a wealth of scrutiny concerning Arundhati Roy's oeuvre. One critical bone of contention especially focuses on politics and the intertwining storylines within her literature. The artistry with which Roy weaves together multiple dimensions of socio-political issues evokes a plethora of interpretations and fuels intellectual arguments. The way she captures volatile matters like class conflict, environmental devastation, and post-colonial identity is highly representative of her concern toward contemporary issues.

While assessing the sociopolitical aspects in Roy's literature, it is hard to miss the reasoned depiction of power relations and societal hierarchies. She gives voice to many of the oppressed people, subverts the grand narratives, and denounces authoritarian regimes. Often, such unpacking of themes serves to provoke and challenge the reader to reflect on critically important societal concerns.

Roy's stories carry an allegorical importance that inspires readers to consider the consequences of political choices and ideological battles. Her sharp criticism of globalisation, capitalism, and counter resistance movements makes people act by changing pre-defined norms and supporting essential changes in the social structure. The mixing of self-storytelling with broader socio-political issues is exceptional while at the same time inviting people to analyse how deeply politics affect their lives.

The politics in Roy's works go beyond just the critiquing shadow of politics; it becomes a space of hopeful change. Roy marks the beginning of hope and resistance against defeat by empowering the silenced and bringing down the system that has oppressed people for so long through her writings. She uses her vivid writing to prove to the people the reality of social justice, equality, and equity by changing their perception of political engagement and responsibility to active engagement, agency, and civic duty.

It is clear from Roy's literature that it cannot be easily classified as her political themes are complex and multi-layered. Her works reflect richly layered comments that challenge the reader to think deeply and offer fresh insight on the realities of the times. Arundhati Roy illustrates the importance of literary discourse in social change and critique by navigating carefully through the details of human life intricately woven with larger political systems.

Public Discourse: Engagements with Key Social Issues

Roy's controversies concerning her works showcase as much literary attention as Arundhati Roy herself has generated over, or rather because of, several social matters that escalate in importance quite rapidly. This part focuses on how Roy's crafting stories has affected public attention as well as concern towards important issues. Candidly, Roy's literature aims to provoke concern and debate on caste, gender, environmental issues, political issues and corruption, and at the very least, the inequality and injustice structures of power relations accompanying them all. Roy goes beyond the reality of traditional storytelling with a range of critical analysis of her societal frameworks. In her writings, Roy creates characters and settings that compel the reader's imagination beyond the wish to passively accept social realities, to actively engage with deeper and often uncomfortable truths. The way Roy writes is crafted vividly under complex narrative frameworks and pressing worldly issues which, like it or not, places Roy squarely at the association between literature and social advocacy. Of course, as many people as there are who care little for what she has on offer, there is an equal number who is never left indifferent or untouched and willing to engage with contentious perspectives. The public debate ignited by all of the above is great, not only appealing to men's self-suggestive attitude of a crisis in society, but also empowering the discussion audience as an inspiration to the suppressed.

Their narratives extend far beyond the country's borders, aiding in shaping the global zeitgeist and encouraging priceless intercultural dialogues. Using a sweeping lens, this part analyses the multifarious effects of Roy's works on social discourse, paying attention to their fundamental importance in instigating and participating in crucial social conversations.

The Global Perspective: International Acclaim and Criticism

Arundhati Roy's works of literature are no longer bound by the borders of India. They have received worldwide attention from both readers and critics. The merging of personal and political narratives makes Roy's prose truly captivating—this work has brought both praise and criticism from all over the world. Roy became a household name with her debut novel 'The God of Small Things', which won the prestigious Man Booker Prize in 1997. The book gained immense acclaim worldwide, leading to multiple translations and adaptations selling in different languages.

She became a part of global literary conversations. But for every commendation Roy earns through her writings, there has been a fair share of intense critique and debate stemming from different perspectives. Some have supported her on the basis that she portrays an unapologetic standpoint on sociopolitical matters, deeming the work brave in the face of much-needed criticism of existing systems. Others, however, are disappointed by what they see as a focus on politics at the expense of art within Roy's prose. Roy's writings have a reception that is heavily intertwined in the web of literature and criticism. What's more, Roy has been widely discussed on the international literary stage due to her arguments on intense debates about environmentalism, human rights, and even globalisation.

Her works have been engaged with in numerous interpretations by scholars, thinkers, and literary critics all over the world. Her global perspective is more than just a literary critique as it deals with issues of decolonisation, social justice, and resistance. Regardless of whether she is viewed as a voice for the silenced or reprimanded for writing too much, there is no doubt that Roy's powerful narratives and critical examination of societal issues elicits both admiration and critique from every corner of the world. As her works continue to spread around the world, culture, literature, activism, and global awareness intertwine through the duality of acceptance and discontent, enriching the debate on the subject.

Academic Analyses: Scholarly Interpretations and Debates

In the field of academic research, Arundhati Roy's literature has incited immense academic attention which keeps growing in the interpretation and discussion aspects within the scholarly world. Scholars and critics have examined deeply the multi-layered narratives of Roy, looking for rich thematic elements and critically analysing the relations between literature and politics. The reception of Roy's works has grown within various disciplines like postcolonial studies, feminist theory, and critical race studies. Many scholars have paid attention to the complex issues of power, social injustices, and contradictions in her fictional world and attempted to relate her fiction to actual political realities.

Moreover, the discussions stemming from Roy's writings have fostered new opportunities to examine different narratives and perspectives which are not easily accepted. Applying postcolonial theory, some scholars have examined Roy's fiction from a different perspective, focusing on the dismantling of Eurocentric value systems and highlighting the voiceless within her words. The combination of environmental advocacy and literature in Roy's work brings forth new ideas regarding the representation of ecological issues, including the ethics of human relationships with nature.

The scholarly disputes concerning Roy's literature have also focused on culture and national identity, questioning how her stories engage with and subvert dominant discourses of nationalism and cultural nationalism. This focus has led to the study of hybridity and the multiplicity of identities, especially with regard to Roy's consideration of the Indian subcontinent as a palimpsest of narratives and contested histories.

As readers engage with Roy's commanding prose and keen insights into sociopolitical issues, interpretations remain fluid and dynamic, facilitating exchanges across disciplines. Such discussions deepen appreciation of Roy's literature while expanding understanding of how literature engages with urgent issues facing the world and the development of critical awareness.

The Role of Media: Amplifying Controversies

With respect to literary reception and literary criticism, media's impact is of great significance. The arousing of controversy regarding Arundhati Roy's works of literature has always received massive coverage in both print and electronic media. As a consequence, the newspapers, magazines and even blogs and social media platforms have started discourse regarding her writings and have, to a great extent, shaped the narrative regarding her literary works. Owing to the need to capture the attention of the audience, most media platforms tend to focus on the narratives that Roy has presented and explore her literary works in greater detail only to reach conclusions that are quite different from popular opinions, surmising that media has sensationalised certain narratives regarding Roy's work, thus leading to contrarian debates and conflict-fuelled discussion.

Balance of power: the politically charged narrative focus and the media's need to sell content. In his prologue to the collection Race and the Politics of Memory, John R. Kenneth Chains argues that the Roy-centric narrative stems from motives other than those suggested in her writings, raising a very important aspect of debate. Parts of Roy's prose which are most engaging are filled with contrariety. Diversity is present not only in the themes but also the views and arguments, which are often unknown to the general public. Also, the lack of coordination among those covering the media tends to work with full ignorance to the adjective-laden language, thus contributing to the pulpy, text-marked prose, failing to pay attention to the satirical strategy symbol guarding Royce's style of prose, lavishly contributing to her wonderful work disguised as her work.

The advancements in technology have played a role in the media's scrutiny of controversies in regard to Roy's literary career. Critics appreciate and attack authors almost immediately, and this culture of instant recognition often leads to awards and condemnations poised in opposition to each other. Any developing controversies revolving around Roy's writings are bound to receive attention due to the speed and scope provided by the internet, which often results in passionate discussions and opposing views within societies all across the globe.

The media does not only amplify an issue that needs further debate; it also tackles the issue head-on and critically examines Roy's literary works. Engaging interviews, detailed journalistic pieces, and academic critiques of her works in prominent literary journals serve to enrich the dialogue on her works by bringing new perspectives and broadening the conversation around her creativity. The media fulfils a double duty, not only drawing attention to controversies but also providing an intelligent examination of Arundhati Roy's literary work with the purpose of looking deeper into the ideas and themes of Roy's writings.

In the case of the media's framing of reception and criticism of Roy's works, it reflects the complex relationships of perception, journalism, and literature as a body of work in constant flux. While traversing the complex pathways of media portrayals, it is crucial to assess the impact of such narratives on Roy's legacy in literature, considering the dynamics of literary reception, especially the risks and opportunities presented in today's media environment.

Reader Feedback: A Spectrum of Reader Experi-

ences

The feedback given by readers is a critical element of the literature associated with Arundhati Roy. The range of reader responses is quite broad, which speaks to the extent and reach of Roy's writings. On one side, readers admire Roy's narratives and how they have unmasked the politics and social dynamics of the region in question. Many have spoken fervently about the emotional resonance they experienced while immersing themselves in Roy's fictional worlds, empathising with the struggles faced by the characters. This profound connection to humanity is a common response in feedback, which speaks to the impact of Roy's work. On the other side, critical voices go to the other extreme to offer constructive critique of the contentious issues and stylistic features of Roy's writing. Some readers who consider the issues and character motives tend to challenge the portrayals and offer alternative representational frameworks within the literary framework. It is in this wide range of responses that the appreciation of Roy's literature lies.

The dialogue that reader feedback offers contributes to the reinterpretation of Roy's literary work. Each new addition to the readership brings with it a different viewpoint that looks at untold aspects of her narratives. The interaction between the author and reader demonstrates the importance of her literature. The different encounters readers have is proof of the impact that storytelling has for people coming from diverse cultural and social backgrounds. The full range of responses to Arundhati Roy's work reveals the true extent of her influence.

Reflections Over Time: Evolving Recognition and Impact

Roy is regarded as a multifaceted figure whose recognition and impact throughout her literary career has changed over time. Her catalytic entrance onto the global literary stage as an astute social commentator came after writing the groundbreaking novel 'The God of Small Things' which helped her to win numerous international accolades and awards. She adeptly fused compelling narratives with strikingly perceptive and sharp social commentary. Her account of India's socio-political issues, Roy's writing achieves a level of resonance that begs for contemplation long after its consumption, impact getting more defined over time. Within scholarly circles, there remains an enduring engagement with her remarkable works, wherein the intricacies of her fluid narratives are dissected, revealing deeper layers of rich meaning. A widening spectrum also views Roy through the lens of discourse on power relations, social justice, activism, and environment considering her literary contributions. Such a widening spectrum of perspectives denotes the shift expanding the amplitude of her influence but also depicts increasingly relevant contemporary conversations. Roy's work, whether through literature and art, becomes multi-dimensional in purpose, showcasing the shifting socio-political milieu illustrating diverse ideological currents and their attitudes making her ideas far more important. Grave seminars and colloquiums are only the tip of the iceberg when considering the superficial impact of her contributions.

Without a doubt, Roy's impact has crossed borders as well as national frameworks to inspire and provoke reflection globally. While her writings continue to be a source of controversy and conflict, their impact on literature and socio-political debates is still indisputable. In the world of reader reception, Roy's narratives have established enduring bonds and captivated many generations with their relevance. As her work gradually enters the literary canon, its profound impact will serve to influence other writers and activists in the years to come. All in all, the increasing acknowledgment and appreciation of Arundhati Roy's work proves that she still carries strong influence in an ever-changing world.

Chapter Sixteen

Legacy and Influence

Inspiring Future Generations

Introduction to Legacy: Defining Roy's Unique Contributions

As an author, Arundhati Roy weaves intricate narratives alongside socio-political commentaries that are out of the ordinary, shattering literary boundaries, and therefore encouraging both novice and seasoned writers. Her astonishing literary works reflect the tumult of human experiences on a societal scale and aid writers grappling with the intention of embedding social relevance into their works.

Her unflinching embrace of complex character portrayals from varying levels of socio-economic standing is one of the most captivating elements in Roy's work. Intertwining a myriad of human emotions and social relationships set into motion by vastly contrasting sociopolitical systems, Roy has carved a niche for herself which compels emerging authors to explore the very depths of the ocean that is human experience with astonishing nuance and insight. Moreover, the exploration of power structures alongside social injustice and self-identity is bound to attract authors who aspire to create counter-narratives to overpowering authoritarian worlds.

Roy's artful blending of poetic language with sharp critique serves as a guide for writers aiming to produce socially conscious art within the bounds of literature. Her ability to wield language as both a vessel of beauty and as a weapon of protest fuels a new generation of writers, urging them to flow with intent crafted with grace and incisiveness, to capture the fluidity of life in jerky motions of urgency.

Also, Roy's steadfast commitment to telling the truth, no matter the opposition she faces, serves as a motivational guide for writers confronting hard-hitting themes and subjects. Her unapologetic stance on controversial topics while holding powerful figures accountable inspires other writers to be bold in their own explorations, nudging them to face the painful truths of human existence without flinching.

Roy's intricate characterization paired with her unrelenting social criticism, together with poetic yet inflammatory prose, and devotion to truth serve as a source of motivation to contemporary writers, which explains why Arundhati Roy's literature stands unmatched. A legacy that sets standards of literary brilliance beyond measure to transcend norms is the hallmark of Roy, inviting within and beyond fathomable limits established meanings.

Literary Influence: Inspiring New Voices in Contemporary Fiction

Roy's work is known for its intricacy alongside her sharp socio-political analysis, and this clearly has implications for aspiring writers looking to hone their craft. Her impact can be witnessed through the mastery of prose achieved by writers shaped by Roy through her political engagement, unapologetic themes, and evocative style. She intricately weaves stories with compelling narrations and vivid characters. Even the most passive readers have been stimulated by her words, forcing them to reimagine reality. Because of this, many writers have sought to explore new avenues, giving them motivation to amplify their creative selves. Such innovations in contemporary fiction that capture the tension of culture, power, and the deeply personal political are a product of her influence.

It is evident that Roy's influence can be seen from authors inspired by the absence of literary boundaries. These writers are willing to embrace norms unlike anything seen before, radically transforming the surrounding world through literature. Emerging voices are now more engaged with societal issues not just as topical referencing, but with the urgency that demands thoughtful engagement and reflection alongside creative storytelling. Roy invites writers to be bold, allowing them to make their mark.

Consequently, an ever-increasing number of writers has emerged, contributing to an evolving literary world that bears the unmistakable impact of Roy's narrative boldness and thematic depth. Rather than only attempting to replicate her writing style, these authors have adopted the spirit of fearlessness and sociopolitical awareness that characterises Roy's stories. In so doing, they have redefined contemporary fiction to include more diverse, provocative, and challenging narratives, similar to those in Roy's best-known works. Roy's enduring legacy as a literary figure continues to provoke new authors to explore underdeveloped frameworks, constructing silenced perspectives while employing the art of telling stories to bring about change. The consequences of Roy's literary ripple effects assure that her legacy will serve as a beacon for countless upcoming storytellers.

Activism as a Catalyst: Shaping Social Movements and Dialogue

Arundhati Roy's activism has inspired social movements in India and across the world. Roy has always sparked crucial discussions during her undeterred fight for social justice, ranging from environmental destruction to human rights violations to economic discrimination. The way she presents complicated societal issues is both persuasive and easy to understand, and this has certainly empowered the oppressed and mobilised people. Roy's impact is, and will always be, felt in contemporary activism. She has passionately voiced the issues of the oppressed and marginalised people, raising crucial challenges against state power and corporate capitalism. By unapologetically calling out systemic injustices, Roy has dealt with social movements stressing intersectionality, and through this, activism becomes more holistic. This unique fusion of understanding different movements and working in unity marks the legacy of Roy's advocacy work.

Roy's involvement with grassroots movements and marginalised groups has helped to change the social inequities that directly affect them. Additionally, her understanding of power relations and the impact of absolutism have deepened the understanding of the experience of oppression, forcing people to face hard realities and do something about it. As a public intellectual and activist,

Roy's work is not limited to writing; she also participates in large public rallies, makes numerous public appearances, and works to unite various groups under one cause, which helps her reach a wider audience and encourage more people to fight for social change. Moreover, her publications, speeches, and critiques have been powerful tools and resources for both activists and scholars. Roy has relentlessly and tirelessly fought for numerous progressive issues, capturing the attention of many, and blending the efforts of diverse groups to work towards a single goal of a fairer society. With her constant advocacy, Roy has become one of the most important leaders in the fight for social change, thus revolutionising the approach taken in movements aimed at achieving social justice.

The Intersection of Art and Advocacy: Bridging Two Worlds

For Arundhati Roy, art and advocacy are intertwined to form a gateway that opens two disparate worlds. Roy's storytelling features social justice prominently and she advocates for social justice through literature; her powerful words create and compel a captivating image that garners the attention of readers worldwide.

The intersection of advocacy and art is perfectly exemplified in Roy's fearlessness towards suppressive societal norms showcased in her novels. With her eloquent and moving narration as well as strong characters, she moves readers, activists, and the audience while simultaneously advocating for socio-political issues. The enhancement of social issues and activism is the reason behind her artistry; she uses literature to comment and spark dialogue on different social norms and socio-political changes.

Roy engages in advocacy outside the boundaries of literature, using art to further her point and strengthen her argument. Whether it be awe-inspiring essays, captivating speeches, or evocative paintings, Roy uses art to advocate and advance her arguments. This form of activism by Roy emphasises the need to use the bounds of creativity to embrace change in society.

Art's ability to evoke empathy and self-reflection holds significance in this intersection. Sympathy towards socio-political complexities through understanding is created by Roy when she harnesses the emotive power of art to inspire empathy in her audience. By merging artistry and advocacy, she captures the attention of readers and advocates to guide them toward self-examination, fostering social awareness while nurturing a collective responsibility towards becoming effective catalysts for change.

Finally, the integration of advocacy with artistry proves to embody the change that can be evoked through creative expression. The way Roy approached this issue demonstrates how art can stimulate social movements and transform public opinion. She has proven that art can be blended with unwavering advocacy, which not only gives those who follow the courage to act but allows them to create social impact through art, making them resonate profoundly as influential changemakers for years to come.

Educational Impact: Inclusion in Academic Discourse and Curriculum

Her works like 'The God of Small Things' and 'The Ministry of Utmost Happiness' are part of many university syllabi as rich resources for diverse storytelling integral to complex social, cultural, and political discourses in modern India. Like any progressive writer of her calibre, Roy has elevated the standards of education at school and university levels. Her writings enrich the literature, humanities, and even social studies portions of the syllabus. Academia appreciates her rare ability to bond compelling narratives and socio-political commentary encompassing nearly all contemporary power relations, human rights abuses, and environmental degradation disputes. Students are introduced to postcolonialism, feminism, globalisation, neoliberalism, and much more, all through the lens of Roy's work.

Roy's work further adds a practical dimension to academic discourse through her advocacy activism. Her humanitarian works advocating for people which cover environmental justice and anti-globalisation movements add a real-world aspect to the curriculum. This inspires critical thought among learners while developing empathy to explore the course material beyond literature and advocacy to consider societal issues around the world.

Furthermore, educators have acknowledged the relevance of Roy's essays and speeches in contemporary social and political contexts as pivotal captures even in basic educational analysis. The undermining of existing oppressive frameworks through claims of justice is eloquently pronounced in class. It enables students to understand inequalities within systems and provides them with the potency to alter them constructively.

Aside from her official teaching responsibilities, Roy goes to other universities where she participates in global lectures, workshops, and symposiums. To advancing crucial conversations in an academic setting, she also motivates many emerging writers and activists. We can appreciate the impact of Roy's insights related to interdisciplinary studies and literature by understanding her firsthand accounts and her interdisciplinary approach to advocacy and social issues.

To summarise why Arundhati Roy's work is essential, it is not only for appreciating contributions to academic assignments and disciplines. There is impact in critical thinking, self, call to action, and soft empathy thanks to the frameworks Roy provides. The blend of literature, activism, and intellectual rigor underscores her enduring influence on educational policy while fostering an emerging generation of scholars and changemakers to engage compassionately in addressing today's challenges.

Mentorship and Encouragement: Direct Support to Emerging Writers

Arundhati Roy has many legacies and two of them include proactive mentorship and encouragement. As a gifted author, Roy has made it her mission to serve underemployed and unemployed writers and has advocated for them through literature. She understands from her own experiences how important it is to build pathways for nurture and tell stories that matter through the experiences that influence today's world. I want to highlight the ways Roy has relentlessly mentored and supported writers from all corners of the globe. For Roy, mentorship is much more than technical guidance. Rather, she takes a full spectrum approach to mentoring that fosters creativity, resilience, and ethical narrative crafting. She has actively participated with emerging writers through workshops and seminars and also on a one-on-one basis. By sharing her personal struggles and creative processes, Roy's aspiring writers begin to develop confidence in their abilities. Her mentoring goes beyond the walls of writing to include advocacy, critical thought, and even ethical responsibilities of public intellectuals. The fruits of Roy's mentorship are evident with the launch of diverse socially oriented literature and discourse from public platforms.

Numerous beneficiaries of Roy's mentorship are now creating masterful works of literature. In one way or another, all of these narratives pay homage to Roy's activism, which involves fighting against dominant paradigms and oppressive power structures. Roy's mentorship knows no borders, as it extends to writers of different cultures, languages, and socio-economic backgrounds. This diversity has given rise to an exhilarating pool of emerging writers influenced by a variety of ideas and perspectives. Consequently, Roy's impact on the world continues to grow as she deepens the international discourse on social justice, human rights, and the myriad complexities of life. The future, however, seems certain: the impact of Roy's guidance will ripple across generations, enduring within the literary canon while encouraging new storytellers to bravely untangle our world's complexities.

Global Reach: Influencing International Perspectives and Policies

The impact of Arundhati Roy stretches far beyond her native land as it captures people worldwide through her impassioned advocacy and writings. Social justice issues have always been a concern for her which led her to international prominence and now influence global views and policies.

A key feature of Roy that fosters her global reach is her ability to speak across cultures and regions. Human rights, protecting the environment, social inequality, and many other pertinent topics splashed across the media have garnered the attention of peoples across the globe due to the manner in which Roy presented them. Particularly the areas of concern that she and her supporters focus on continue to spark debate around the world. Roy's works as an activist and a writer have been translated into a variety of languages which ensures her audiences span across the globe. This has greatly increased the good conversations that allow her to inspire many people across the world. Alongside her influence on public discourse, Arundhati Roy has transformed international policies and governance as they currently exist. Her sharp analysis on the political economy of power, corporate capture, and state terrorism has echoed in politics everywhere and has influenced many politicians to try and deal with issues that they would not have attended to otherwise. This is because there is no doubt that Roy's scathing criticism of enduring inequalities has brought about some policies and laws in many countries, thus furthering her influence as a change agent.

Roy's work with international organisations and other world forums has exposed her to the needs of the locals and the global forces shaping their realities. In bringing awareness to the relationships between political, environmental, and social issues, she helped develop solutions that seek to bridge these national problems. Her direct involvement in these multi-spheres has shifted international discourse and common practices, leading to new goals that focus on social justice, ecological balance, and comprehensive policy frameworks.

In the end, it is more accurate to state that with how far-reaching Arundhati Roy's impact is, it has completely changed how we respond to the world's pressing issues. Her struggle towards greater social justice has impacted the very foundation and landscape of advocacy and activism concerning social justice at a global level. There is no denial that the world is poised to change along with future generations and it is precisely due to the global policies that will remain due to Roy's strong storytelling and bold claims.

Cinema and Media Adaptations: Broadening Artistic Legacy

With respect to Roy's artistic legacy, her novels have directly been integrated into adaptations in the medium of cinema, which in turn, greatly contributes to the legacy's expansion. Adaptations of her novels, ranging from the God of Small Things to the Ministry of Utmost Happiness, have already been developed into movies and these movies have graced audiences globally. An adaptation helps in marketing Roy's storytelling but at the same time, drives conversations on real social issues prevalent around the world, something Roy intricately captures in her works. The visual aspects of these adaptations allow for an interaction with the melodrama and multi-dimensional exploration of the themes and characters Roy captures so beautifully in her works. The straight exposure into the cinematic domain itself showcases how these legends have endless relevance all over the world irrespective of culture and age.

In working closely with filmmakers and creatives, Roy is able to keep the prose intact while adapting the narrative to the screen through the visual medium. In addition to literature, Roy's work has an impact in other forms of media like podcasting and social media. These adaptations foster public discourse concerning the dominant themes in Roy's writing, enabling her ideas to reach wider audiences and encouraging critical examination of socio-political issues. The scope of the connection between literature and visual art highlights the significance of aside from literature leaves a mark on society in literature and other field literature, underlining the impact of socio-political issues through Roy's visual artistry. Adaptations in cinema and other media serve as a powerful instrument in promoting Arundhati Roy's body of work fostering an everlasting stamp that nurtures one's curiosity about literature and invigorates discourse on the human condition.

Philosophical Legacy: Encouraging Intellectual and Critical Thought

The legacy of Roy's philosophy encompasses literature and activism, as it runs deeper into the society's collective consciousness, provoking critical and intellectual thought. Roy's captivating stories have inspired a great deal of debate regarding societal systems, power, and the interplay of self and society. By articulating her ideas with precision, and performing adept analytical work, Roy makes sure that the world is not inquisitive but introspective. One of the most primary portions of Roy's philosophy is her dedication towards truth and her efforts towards the commonly suppressed voices. Her writings act as an appeal for people to examine, critique, and transcend imposed opinions, exercising intellectual autonomy and fostering thoughtful discourse. Outside the world of literature, Roy has engineered a philosophy that aids in formulating a comprehensive view of the world/society. Her works on environmental injustice, territorial rights of the indigenous people, and political and social equity have changed the attention of the society's critical thinkers and intellectuals in regards to their positive societal impact.

Roy's accompanied work serves as a point of reflection and causes the readers to deeply evaluate their ethical responsibilities in relation to an intricate world. He made it possible for debates and discourse to take place in an inter-disciplinary framework in which various subjects that seem to be irreversibly fragmented could interact at multiple levels. Roy's approach to empathy, compassion, and holistic understanding not only advances traditional paradigms but also popularises philosophy for scholars and educators of other disciplines. The multifaceted civic engagement and diverse scholarship within Roy's work make it clear that they are meant to be deeply studied for the sole purpose of sparking an interest that promotes investigation and research intensively. Roy's legacy inspires ethical reflection alongside critical inquiry. Literature and civic participation can be utilised to further provoke thought and discourse on pressing contemporary issues. Even more today, Arundhati Roy offers us a glimpse of hope and an enduring inspiration through civic engagement with literature.

Closing Reflections: Imagining Future Generations Inspired by Roy

With the rich understanding of Arundhati Roy's impact, contribution, and influence, it is revisited how much more influence she will have on future generations. Her thoughts and ideas span across various fields of literature, activism, and their sheer breadth make a baton of motivation for people differing in a multitude of fields. Looking forward, it is obvious to imagine that there are many ideas originating from her work that will continue to exist and evolve long into the future.

Her approach to critical thinking and intellectual involvement cultivates fertile ground around aspiring writers, thinkers, and activists to exploit. From her challenges towards power and dissent, she builds upcoming future generation templates that show strongly why they must question the pervasive presence of authoritarianism and fight for justice. In a world suffering many problems like inequality, neglecting the environment, or violations of human rights, there are so many different approaches fearless people often take to tackle these problems, and Roy is one of them.

Exploring the impact of Roy's literary works on future generations, one expects the exploration of her themes and techniques to remain evergreen. The characterisation of social and political relationships, along with the relationships between the characters, is likely to capture the imaginations of many more writers to come. The accompanying storytelling in advocacy as seen in Roy's work is sure to ignite compassion-driven literature of mounting global concern alongside constructive criticism.

Outside the literary world, Roy's activism is likely to rouse a sense of advocacy for the already marginalised communities within aspiring changemakers. Her commitment towards the marginalised remains a great example for anyone attempting to advocate for social welfare, focusing on justice and human rights advocacy. The wake of her activism is still felt in every movement that combats the abuse of systemic power structures in the name of humanity.

Equally, as we look toward the future, it does not take much to appreciate the lasting change Roy has had, and will continue to have, on academia, art, and the media world. Her sharp critique of power paradigms and her determination to reveal the untold stories serves as guiding principles for critical scholarship and journalism. Moreover, the film and art adaptations of her works will most likely extend her reach to broader audiences, igniting discourse on the issues she passionately addresses.

This forward-looking perspective comes hand in hand with the notion that Arundhati Roy is a herald of hope for compassion, relentless truths, and equity. The Roy effect is bound to be felt through new generations of writers, scholars, and even artists who will change the world for the better.

Chapter Seventeen

Conclusion

Arundhati Roy's Enduring Impact on Literature and Activism

Recapitulation of Arundhati Roy's Literary Journey

Roy has authored a number of critical essays and nonfiction works compiling the harsh realities within the government and its societal outlook. Some of these works include: Capitalism: A Ghost Story, The Ministry of Assault and Obsession and War Talk. Most of her works speak of the social issues and the erasure of people who live in poverty. Almost all her works have met praise, making her one of the most talked-about authors of contemporary literature.

Claimed to be a woman without a world, Roy has received acclaim in the form of benediction published by many of her critics. The harsh realities of capitalism and neoliberalism heavily impacted Roy during her childhood, which is reflected in her works.

Fueled by anger and rage, A Ghost Story furthers her fight against capitalism by claiming that those in power brutally abuse it. Upon receiving her first acclaim for her book, Roy became a public target in Britain but defended herself through War Talk. Most of her writings stem from the pure fact of needing an outlet to explode, which makes her one of the most engaging authors to read.

Roy continued to push boundaries while incorporating her art into activism, and as always, she was outspoken against oppressive systems. Her writing has kept her in the limelight—however, this has also motivated young writers to use their work towards change. Roy's works throughout her entire career go beyond categorisation as fiction or non-fiction; there is an emerging territory of literature and activism, and her work carved this space. Readers, scholars, and even activists draw inspiration from her as she continues to make a mark on the world, demonstrating how art can change social consciousness and society as a whole.

Reaffirming the Intersection of Literature and Activism

The intersection of literature and activism, highlighted by the life and works of Arundhati Roy, showcases the power which creative work holds in social and political change. In every era, writers and artists have had command over words and imagery, and have utilised them to fight against oppression, raise societal awareness, and push for change. In Roy's case, her transformation from an award-winning novelist to an ardent activist represents the balance of storytelling and action. She has reimagined the frontier of authorship by combining prose with passionate engagement, claiming active participation in the global discourse on human rights, environmental conservation, and social justice.

Literature, as a guiding statement, is one of the mediums of the truth, complexities, and empathy. Writers are able to illuminate societal issues through critical introspection and healing with their diverse scope of compassion. Roy's socio-political description in her fictional narratives like 'The God of Small Things' and 'The Ministry of Utmost Happiness' showcases the beauty of concern and understanding which can be built from storytelling. Her incredible accounts of marginalised peoples and their turbulent histories serve to highlight the disparities and encourage readers to confront the stark realities required to make transformative societal changes.

At the same time, Roy's literature is marked by a distinct sense of civic activism, which validates the impact of change-oriented storytelling. As a public figure, she does not shy away from participating in the public debate concerning the rights of indigenous peoples, environmental issues, or civil rights. Roy's reasoning and ethics are deeply critical while her advocacy is multifaceted. Through public address, speeches, and other forms of literate activism, she illustrates the need for greater involvement with people who do not read. Roy's actions show that social justice cannot be entirely devoid of the arts and demonstrate how these fields intersect to motivate low-level changes and important reorganisations through artistic expression.

This combination of creativity and civic activism shifts focus from single endeavours to a phenomenon that has no specific region or cultural markers. The contemporary world is characterised by greater economic, political, and cultural integration. It is during these times that artistic activism gains power, effectively mobilising different people for common campaigns across national borders.

Exercising dual roles as an acclaimed novelist and passionate activist, Roy demonstrates the power of literature and calls other creators to join her in realising the vision of social change that can leave a mark on society.

Revisiting the life and work of Arundhati Roy affirms her prowess as literature holds the power to transform not only the world, but civilisation at large. Where there is hope, there is change, and that intersection can be abundantly found across the narratives Roy has wielded. She certainly casts a beacon into the borderless gulf between creativity and morality – where literature meets activism. As long as morals and social equity are in balance, artistic influences will continue to guide society towards a more evolved and fair world.

Evaluating Global Influence: A Diverse Resonance

There is no trace of doubt regarding the global impact Roy has had, and that is reflective of how she influences individuals from varying cultures and societies across continents. This exposure stems from her literary genius alongside an implacable drive in the pursuit of human rights. These two are bound to spark conversation, forge alliances, and move nations beyond borders. Through her words, and rather passionate dedication to activism, Roy challenges norms which leads to her being regarded as a pioneer of the voiceless in the contemporary world.

Roy has gained recognition for her literature as it has been translated into many languages which increases the diversity in readership able to appreciate her work. The ideas she explores – such as inequality, autonomy, and oppression – are compelling enough to be relevant to many people from different socio-cultural contexts.

Through exploration of different societies, Roy's literature sparks cross-cultural critical dialogues and self-reflection, which enable change in perception beyond local societal norms within different cultures.

Apart from literature, Roy's influence is evident in community organisation and policy advocacy which shows the extensive reach of grassroots activism. Her strong remarks on the existing order of power and neglect of the environment have mobilised many activists and organisations around the world, striving to achieve social and ecological balance. Roy's thoughts have built bridges between diverse groups of people from the Amazon jungle to metropolitan cities, bringing them together in the struggle for environmental justice and balance.

Assessing the worldwide impact of Arundhati Roy shows that her moral and intellectual contributions have profoundly influenced the world's mindscape. Roy's articulate storytelling, which exposes deep-rooted inequalities and the ravages of corporate predation, has sparked global outrage and made people rethink their responsibilities as aware citizens and stewards of the earth. Roy's work is a reminder of the synergy unbounded by geography; the hope for a world that is just, humane, and full of compassion remains ubiquitous and ever-present because of her activism and writings.

Bridging the Personal and the Political in Contemporary Contexts

The blending of personal and political spheres in Arundhati Roy's works for both literature and activism is striking. In today's world, this integration matters because it captures the essence of how personal lives and societal issues are structured. The weaving of the complexity of human relations, culture, and power dynamics is one of the most important things Roy has done since it allows readers and activists to grapple with many issues in the contemporary world. The combination of politics and personal stories creates vivid accounts that help fuel her social justice advocacy. Roy brings personal identity to life amid systemic violence and political storms by weaving a narrative of systemic suffering and struggle through personal identity stories. This particular strategy advances the understanding of intricate problems by making them relatable, igniting compassionate interaction and constructive discussion. Additionally, in devoting her energy and efforts to addressing unheard issues and focusing on women, children, and the subaltern, she effectively blends the personal with the political.

Her works exemplify the notion that personal stories are fundamental to appreciating change at the societal level. Further, in the context of Roy's work, which reminds us of the value of understanding the personal-political dichotomy boundaries in contemporary times of relentless change and unyielding social inequities, is quite striking. Navigating through modern terrains, Roy continues to grapple with these dualities, and it is her ability to reconcile these opposites that provokes critical thought and action. Her stories and activism constitute a clarion call for the need to engage with contemporary issues — personally and politically — affirming the notion that personal narratives are as urgent as social narratives. She urges those with the power to engage with the complexities of the contemporary world to embrace challenges with empathy, fortitude, and resolute faith.

Impact on Emerging Writers and Activists: Inspiring Change

With regard to budding writers and activists, Arundhati Roy has had an unparalleled impact irrespective of their geographical or cultural contexts. Roy's steadfast struggle for justice and outspoken opposition to tyranny has inspired countless young people across the world who seek to make a positive impact. She has shown that literature can indeed be a powerful tool for transformation, driven by one's personal experiences and convictions that activism and literature can be seamlessly woven into one formidable tapestry.

Roy's fierce advocacy has encouraged emerging writers and activists to change troubling sociopolitical and environmental issues within their own communities. Through Roy's example, writers have begun to approach storytelling as more than just an art—it is a powerful catalyst for change.

Roy's impact can be felt in the works of younger writers who aim to expose injustices as well as amplify silenced voices. Her activism has also influenced many of her peers; her outspoken approach to addressing atrocities was a game changer for people confronted with deep systems of social inequality and oppression. This shift in mindset has sparked numerous literary and advocacy initiatives, all seeking to shift the paradigm to improve conditions for marginalised groups.

At the same time, Roy's relentless dedication to the causes of social and environmental justice became encouragement for young advocates looking to propel real change. By merging the personal and political, she empowers a generation of activists to tackle multilayered issues with compassion and, in turn, inspire a new approach to advocacy. Fostering a range of perspectives and empowering marginalised voices has enabled Roy to cultivate a global community of emerging writers and activists dedicated to dismantling the hindrances to progress. Such individuals, through her work, have realised the impact that storytelling and non-violent resistance can have on fostering social change and shifting collective consciousness. Arundhati Roy will be remembered for her literature, but equally for motivating a new generation of writers and activists to pursue their creativity and relentless spirit towards meaningful contributions for a more just and equitable world.

The Evolution of Public Perception: From Criticism to Admiration

Today, we celebrate Roy, but many do not realise that her public image used to be that of controversy. This admiration is due to the perpetual impact of her advocacy work, giving Roy a deeper public image than she received throughout her life. Readers saw her as a radical, antagonistic, and an idealistic woman devoid of any literary talent. Towards the beginning of Roy's career, her unapologetic activism was bound to garner attention, both negative and positive. It is safe to say that critics were highly divided in their opinions. Eventually, the quality literature Roy produced over the years created a shift in society's perception.

Critics recognised and re-evaluated her impact on society's literature and began to underscore her indefinably essential contributions. In the modern day, her works are greatly admired. Not only because of her stunning mastery of literature, but also for her work of bringing critical issues of Roy's society to the forefront. Readers appreciate her work and these efforts transform Roy back into a woman of courage, earning her admiration across the board and further accentuating her reputation as a symbol for those who stand against systemic oppression.

Furthermore, propelling her into the realm of admired public figures are her efforts to face challenges head on, believing strongly in her vision, and articulating it insightfully and eloquently. With every spiral of her narrative, the public perception also transformed and ultimately was in complete awe of her unyielding commitment and dedication towards social issues, the environment, and marginalised people. This change in the public's feelings indicates the power of Roy's words and rhetoric but also the undeniable reality that society, as a whole, is beginning to appreciate these words. This shift in public perception describes the impact of her work and illustrates its astounding ability to forge societal shifts, transforming her from a controversial character to a beloved voice.

Contributions to Global Discourse on Human Rights and Environmental Issues

Arundhati Roy is and will remain a significant contributor to the global discussions of issues concerning the environment and human rights. Through her impactful works of fiction and non-fiction, she has highlighted some concerning issues at the societal and global level and ignited movements that bring about real change. Her abilities as an author and as an activist have impacted society in regard to some critical issues, which is visible in her efforts to propel social change through literature.

In her non-fiction works like 'The Greater Common Good' and 'Field Notes on Democracy,' Roy does not shy away from discussing the human rights violations and environmental destruction due to the extensive development works in India. Her powerful advocacy for marginalised communities did not only dismantle existing systems of oppression but also built awareness and mobilisation.

From the onset, Roy has aligned herself with grassroots movements, propelling sustainable environmental change, which illustrates a different side of critique altogether – advocacy. Her consideration of social injustices arising from environmental exploitation provides a stark reminder of how — all the things we see as different spheres are, in fact, profoundly intertwined.

Roy's fictional works, 'The God of Small Things' and 'The Ministry of Utmost Happiness,' highlight the stories of people suffering from systemic oppression, violence, and environmental violence. Exquisite character development and rich storytelling help turn the pain of the invisible into something tangible, urging people to step into the shoes of the marginalised and the silenced.

Roy's impact cuts across regions and often propels people into action. It is her boldness on issues like displacement from homes after the construction of dams and the danger of uncontrolled capitalism that makes her stand out as one of the prominent advocates for socio-environmental justice.

In an age when the world is grappling with severe challenges such as the widespread violation of basic human rights, environmental destruction, and other abuses, it is Roy's relentless work to shine a light upon the oppressed, as well as deconstruct the nature of power, that is profoundly needed. The way she tells stories and advocates for neglected causes makes her an important figure in the struggle for human rights and environmental protection while also shaping the way these topics are discussed worldwide. She continues to impact the collective consciousness and emphasises the need for change while offering hope for a future that is equitable and environmentally friendly.

The Role of Prose in Shaping Public Consciousness

Roy's prose is an exemplary case where literature has helped shape public consciousness and awareness in a global context. She engages with social and political issues that are intricately layered and painstakingly crafted within narratives, projecting the plight of the marginalised with intense attention. Her storytelling deeply resonates with the readers because it is vividly powerful and awakens empathy towards issues that are usually considered distant. By portraying the grim picture of life at the societal and individual level, Roy makes the readers uncomfortable and forces them to rethink their notions and assumptions. Her prose aids in achieving progressive change in society by helping the readers challenge their own realities.

Roy transcends borders through her usage of language and imagery, which speaks to audiences globally. Her keen observations and bold proclamations accompany her text and render the complex issues humanised and relatable for readers across the globe. Such prose evokes empathy and becomes essential for fostering a sense of responsibility and urging them to attend to the severe social and environmental issues that we face today.

As noted, Roy's narrative style is a mix between poetics and stark realism, which makes readers grapple with the harsher effects of injustice. She tells her stories in a way that makes her audience perceive unsolved social problems as hardships that are relational and complex in character. Through personal accounts and political context, Roy intricately poses the question for her readers to reflect deeply, confront, and strive to make a change by dismantling these structures.

Furthermore, Roy's prose does not simply record the social ills of society; it also looks into a future that deserves planning as it sparks the spirit of togetherness and change. In hopeless situations, her stories provide hope, which motivates readers to work towards building a more empathetic society. By providing readers with compelling views of these problems, Roy enables people to bring about change by igniting a sense of responsibility regarding the socio-political struggles.

In simpler words, Arundhati Roy's prose goes far beyond mere storytelling – it can and has been used to shape and raise the public's consciousness. Her powerful command of language and narrative urges readers to not only empathise but also take action against injustices. With these qualities, she demonstrates the still unmatched ability of literature to invite deep thinking, spark conversations, and facilitate meaningful changes in society.

The Enduring Legacy: A Template for Future Endeavours

The literature we have today and changemaking activism attached to it gives us an idea of Roy's legacy. As we reflect on Roy's impact, we see that her work provides a striking model for future actions and ventures directed towards social justice, human rights, and even literature itself.

Her legacy stems from compelling stories that evoke deep emotions alongside unyielding advocacy directed toward marginalised communities. Future activists and writers have now been provided with a new vision: profound narratives and determined activism combined create deep, meaningful impact. This can change the way we work through the words we have.

As a socio-political and environmental issues champion, Roy has demonstrated how one can tackle complex problems in the world while providing a fearless perspective on inequity. She single-handedly takes on difficult topics while ensuring the silenced are given a platform. Because of this effort, every aspiring activist and writer draws inspiration from her work.

Established power structures have differing perspectives, which is precisely the reason why Roy's work enables future generations to attempt to dismantle institutionalised discrimination without fear. The work she has done is a prime example of literature spurring social change, encouraging young writers to construct their stories from the herculean efforts to oppose tyranny.

Going further, Roy is not just an author; her work as a social activist engraves her as a changemaker. Because of her unrestricted access to upfront political debates as well as enduring commitment to defend justice, Roy is seen as an authoritative figure in modern-day activism.

Roy's work has certainly shaped empathy and dialogue toward social movements. It also defines the importance of artistic literature as a means to take relentless action toward framed policies. Roy's exceptional work is fuelled by the belief that literature is a means through which society can be transformed.

In summary, Arundhati Roy's ever-lasting influence serves as a source of optimism and potential for future literary and activist pursuits. It is her fierce nature and steadfastness towards telling the truth which breathes life into a myriad of movements. It will compel the forthcoming youth to carry out social transformations by harnessing the power of words and actions.

To Conclude: Where to Place Arundhati Roy In Contemporary History?

Roy's powerful contributions in literature and activism earn her a spot as one of the modern contemporaries. She defies the conventional perception of an author and a social advocate, becoming a central figure in social discourse about injustice, human rights, and eco-sustainability. While pondering over her life's work, it becomes increasingly apparent that, unlike other recorded figures in contemporary history, Roy will not be bound to a particular timeline and location. Instead, the echoing impact of Roy is global and persistent throughout various discourse communities and movements.

Roy's intertwining of personal experiences with political issues has helped redefine the responsibilities of writers and intellectuals in contemporary society. Confronting power dynamics, inequality, and oppression head-on serves as a beacon for future generations to follow in exercising their agency. These transformations, along with her compelling critiques of state policies and her advocacy for underserved populations, exemplify the power of literature as an enduring testament to social change.

Additionally, Roy's advocacy of the silenced and powerless influences her place in the context of modern history. Her multifaceted literature, alongside her passionate activism, gives voice to the unheard members of society. These powerful intersections of empathy with socio-political phenomena portray her as someone wielding her power far beyond the conventional borders of a writer.

Evaluating Arundhati Roy's modern historical significance requires working appreciation of the impact her prose still holds today, which skillfully dismantles dominant myths while clarifying the interdependence of human life and relationships. The compassion and social awareness integral to literature, even in this day and age, shines through in her deep and attentive treatment of diverse characters and captivating plots. Roy's deep understanding of identity, trauma, and resistance alongside her deft skill in weaving those concepts into stories has shaped narratives that impact audiences globally, allowing them to cultivate awareness of the profound complexities of humanity.

In the case of Roy, modern history is not confined to how we have so far understood it, because it is both eluding and adding to any timeline we wish to create. While she broadens literature's horizons, Roy also integrates and shapes political discourses. Roy possesses boundaries of fierce intellect alongside equally fierce spirit and loyalty towards what is right, making her one of the many known faces of history we will encounter.

Selected Bibliograpy

Arundhati Roy'sWorks

Fiction

Roy, A. (1997). *The God of Small Things*. Random House

Roy, A. (2017). *The Ministry of Utmost Happiness*. Hamish Hamilton.

Non-fiction

Roy, A. (1999). *The Cost of Living*. Modern Library.

Roy, A. (2001). *Power Politics*. South End Press.

Roy, A. (2003). *War Talk*. South End Press.

Roy, A. (2004). *An Ordinary Person's Guide to Empire*. South End Press.

Roy, A. (2004). *Public Power in the Age of Empire*. Seven Stories Press.

Roy, A., & Barsamian, D. (2004). *The Checkbook and the

Cruise Missile: Conversations with Arundhati Roy*. South End Press.

Roy, A. (2005). *The Algebra of Infinite Justice* (Revised ed.). Penguin Books.

Roy, A. (2009). *Listening to Grasshoppers: Field Notes on Democracy*. Hamish Hamilton.

Roy, A. (2011). *Broken Republic: Three Essays*. Hamish Hamilton.

Roy, A. (2011). *Walking with the Comrades*. Penguin Books.

Roy, A., Mishra, P., Chatterji, A. P., Alam, T., & Ali, H. (2011). *Kashmir: The Case for Freedom*. Verso.

Roy, A. (2013). *The Hanging of Afzal Guru and the Strange Case of the Attack on the Indian Parliament*. Penguin Books.

Roy, A. (2014). *Capitalism: A Ghost Story*. Haymarket Books.

Roy, A., & Cusack, J. (2016). *Things That Can and Cannot Be Said*. Penguin Books.

Roy, A. (2017). *The Doctor and the Saint*. Haymarket Books.

Roy, A. (2019). *My Seditious Heart: Collected Nonfiction*. Haymarket Books.

Roy, A. (2020). *Azadi: Freedom. Fascism. Fiction*. Haymarket Books.

Roy, A. (2023). *Geographies of Privilege*. Penguin Books.

More on Roy's Work

Anglo-Indian literature (2007). In Stringer J., Hahn D.(Eds.), (3rd ed. ed.). Oxford University Press.

Brajesh Kumar, et al. (2024) Resistance and Empowerment: The Representation of Women in Arundhati Roy's 'The God of

Small Things' and 'The Ministry of Utmost Happiness. International Journal for Research in Applied Science and Engineering Technology. https://doi.org/10.22214/ijraset.2024.6390

Doraiswamy, R. (2005). In Benson E., Conolly L. W.(Eds.), Film and Literature (India) (2nd. ed. ed.). Routledge, Taylor & Francis Group.

Doyle, L. (2010). Geomodernism, postcoloniality, and women's writing. In M. T. Linett (Ed.), The Cambridge Companion to Modernist Women Writers, Cambridge (pp. 129-145). Cambridge University Press.

Frost, A. (2001). Roy, Arundhati. ProQuest.

Globalizing Dissent: Essays on Arundhati Roy (2008). In Ghosh R., Navarro-Tejero A.(Eds.), Taylor & Francis Group, Taylor & Francis Group.

Goh, R. B. H. (2021). The (In)Significance of Small Things: Data, Identity, and the Dilemma of Recovery in Arundhati Roy's The Ministry of Utmost Happiness. Studies in the Novel, 53(1), 1-19.

Gowralli, M. (2022). Azadi: Freedom. Fascism. Fiction by Arundhati Roy (review). Ariel, 53(4), 180-183. https://doi.org/10.1353/ari.2022.0038

Jagadisan, Nagarajan, M. S., & Narayan, S. A. (2005). In Benson E., Conolly L. W.(Eds.), Short Fiction (India) (2nd. ed. ed.). Routledge, Taylor & Francis Group.

Joshi, P. (1998). In Schellinger P., Hudson C. and Rijsberman M.(Eds.), INDIAN NOVEL. Fitzroy Dearborn Publishers.

Kanjirakkat, J. M. (2017). The Ministry of Utmost Happiness. Transnational Literature, 10(1), 1-2.

Kapoor, M. (2021). The God of Small Things Versus the Devil of Big Things: Narrative Technique and Arundhati Roy. IUP Journal of English Studies, 16(2), 46-55.

Kendall, J., & Silva, P. (2000). The God of Small Things. Literature and Psychology, 46(4), 61-62.

Kirpal, V. (2005). In Benson E., Conolly L. W.(Eds.), Orality in Indian Literature in English (2nd. ed. ed.). Routledge, Taylor & Francis Group.

Lutz, J. (2009). Commodity Fetishism, Patriarchal Repression, and Psychic Deprivation in Arundhati Roy's The God of Small Things. Mosaic : A Journal for the Interdisciplinary Study of Literature, 42(3), 57-74.

Mahajan, R., & Mudgal, A. (2023). Multicultural elements in Arundhati Roy's the god of small things. International Journal of Applied Research, 9(2), 155–157. https://doi.org/10.22271/allresearch.2023.v9.i2c.10580

Marx, J. (2004). Postcolonial literature and the Western literary canon. In N. Lazarus (Ed.), The Cambridge Companion to Postcolonial Literary Studies, Cambridge (pp. 83-96). Cambridge University Press.

Mittapalli, R. (2018). Novel as Counter-Narrative of the Nation: Arundhati Roy's The God of Small Things †. IUP Journal of English Studies, 13(2), 42-49.

Morton, T. (2006). Receptions. In T. Morton (Ed.), The Cambridge Companion to Shelley, Cambridge (pp. 35-42). Cambridge University Press.

Mukherjee, M. (2005). In Benson E., Conolly L. W.(Eds.), Novel (India) (2nd. ed. ed.). Routledge, Taylor & Francis Group.

Narayan, S. A. (2005). In Benson E., Conolly L. W.(Eds.), Devadoss, Manohar (1936-) (2nd. ed. ed.). Routledge, Taylor & Francis Group.

Pei, T. (2017). The Minor-narrative of Transgression in The God of Small Things. Contemporary Literary Review India, 4(4), 1-13.

post-colonial literature (2007). In Stringer J., Hahn D.(Eds.), (3rd ed. ed.). Oxford University Press.

Poyner, J. (2018). Subalternity and Scale in Arundhati Roy's The God of Small Things. Mosaic : A Journal for the Interdisciplinary Study of Literature, 51(3), 53-69.

Rafiee, B., & Deedari, R. (2015). A Spivakian Reading of Louise Erdrich's Track and Arundhati Roy's The God of Small Things. International Journal of Applied Linguistics & English Literature, 4(2), 134-142. https://doi.org/10.7575/aiac.ijalel.v.4n.2p.134

Roy, A. (2009). The Title of The God of Small Things: A Subversive Salvo. ANQ, 22(3), 56-63.

Roy, Arundhati (2007). In Stringer J., Hahn D.(Eds.), (3rd ed. ed.). Oxford University Press.

Swan, J. G. (2001). Perspectives on Addressing the White Gaze: Arundhati Roy's The God of Small Things and Othello. The Upstart Crow, 21, 138-153.

Uma, A. (2005). In Benson E., Conolly L. W.(Eds.), Feminism (India) (2nd. ed. ed.). Routledge, Taylor & Francis Group.

Annotated

Anwer, M. (2014). Resisting the Event: Aesthetics of the Non-Event in the Contemporary South Asian Novel. *Ariel, 45*(4), 1-30.

This essay interrogates the ways in which contemporary fiction from the subcontinent responds to the preoccupation with the spectacular event in Western philosophy, historiography, and popular media discourse. Today, this seemingly unanimous and all-pervasive fixation with colossal moments--revolutionary, politically progressive, or apocalyptic, terroristic ones--grips our collective global imaginary like never before. The collapse of the twin towers and the post-9/11 context of the war on terror have produced dominant discourses that accept, willy-nilly, the cloying power of event-centric narratives. In this context I study Vikram Chandra's Sacred Games , Arundhati Roy's The God of Small Things , and Mohsin Hamid's The Reluctant Fundamentalist to suggest that contemporary literary experimentation emerging from South Asia proactively resists the catastrophic event's magnetic power to create an inescapable force field that keeps everything constantly aligned in relation to it.

Baneth-Nouailhetas, É. (2002). Cet obscur objet du désir : la transgression dans The God of Small Things. *Études Anglaises, 55*(4), 435-443.

Transgression is the central, structuring axis of The God of Small Things. The term seems to be deliberately left undefined, however, giving the narration the opportunity to suggest, through its typical use of connection and repetition, an equivalence between all levels and types of transgression. This provokes a significant conflation between simple rules and fundamental taboos, between social laws and moral laws. The danger of such a juxtaposition lies in the blurring of the narrative's ideological discourse, which--among other consequences--diminishes the impact of its statements against the caste system.

Basu, B. (2014). Postcolonial World Literature: Forster-Roy-Morrison. *The Comparatist, 38*, 158-187.

In the last fifty years or so, we have seen the emergence of new discursive for- mations, among them, certain "new" literatures, some even finding homes in new programs like African American Studies, Womens Studies, and others. During the same time, we have also seen the emergence of theory, literary theory, as continuous but also discontinuous to literary criticism. Among these new discursive formations is postcolonial literature and postcolonial theory, which are, however, fortunately or unfortunately, unhoused in any particular department or program. I will offer an algorithm of sorts, marking the spatio-temporal co- ordinates for a reading of world literature but without removing it from the historical realities of race, gender, and other markers of differential power relations. My reading is also a close reading, a close textual analysis that reinstates the literariness of literature as one of its important qualities.I focus on Arundhati Roy's The God of Small Things and some of Toni Morrison's novels, particularly The Bluest Eye and Beloved. The postcolonial text executes a double articulation or a dual spatio-temporality, a vertical and temporal articulation on one hand and a horizontal and spatial articulation on the other. The former maps the text's relation with the past, the Indian, the British, and African American past, although here the primary coordinates are the history of British colonialism in India and specially the literary representations of it, as in Forster and Orwell.

Baysal, S. M. (2020). *Trauma, Survival, and Resistance: Possibilities of Recovery in Monica Ali's Brick Lane and Arundhati Roy's the God of Small Things* (Order No. 31679174). Available from ProQuest Dissertations & Theses Global: The Humanities and Social Sciences Collection; ProQuest One Literature.

This thesis analyses Monica Ali's Brick Lane (2003) and Arundhati Roy's The God of Small Things (1997) through the perspective of cultural trauma theory in order to lay bare the ways in which survivors respond to trauma and strategies of survival and resistance and possibilities of recovery these responses point to. Building on but also criticising earlier and Caruthian approaches to trauma, this thesis argues that the novels under study stretch and extend the definition of survivor from a helpless victim imprisoned into an incomprehensible event and its uncontrollable traumatic symptoms to a complex characterisation which involves both elements of insightful resistance through means of silence, indifference, and bodily encounter against various traumatogenic systems, and destructive after-effects of trauma. By focusing on novels written in different styles and forms which not only illustrate insidious and event-based trauma models individually but also emphasise the need for divergent textual and narrative strategies to represent the experience of trauma, this thesis also problematises the gaps of earlier trauma theory and calls for a more contextualised and pluralistic approach to trauma to acknowledge and be attentive to the multifacetedness and variability of traumatic experience and its literary representation.

Bertrand, C. (2008). *Identity and female agency in three postcolonial texts* (Order No. 1452495). Available from ProQuest Dissertations & Theses Global: The Humanities and Social Sciences Collection; ProQuest One Literature. (304825831).
Utilizing postcolonial theory, this thesis explores the positions of women in Bharati Mukherjee's Jasmine, Jhumpa Lahiri's Interpreter of Maladies, and Arundhati Roy's The God of Small Things. Although immense unbalances of power exist that work against the women in these 3 texts, they are neither completely powerless nor voiceless. It is not possible to simplify the struggles of the characters by looking at only 1 factor such as race, gender, class, or caste; the matrix of factors influence each character differently, and consequently each woman finds herself alternately marginalized and empowered. The women actively resist (with varying degrees of success) the dominant culture's hegemonic structures. This thesis aims to expose how women exercise agency in their own lives, while still recognizing the multiple factors hindering their voices. Ultimately, these restraints do not completely muffle these women; instead, the unique conditions of their existence enable

new forms of creative self-expression.

Vitasse, J. (2008). The Blurring of Frontiers in Arundhati Roy's The God of Small Things. *Études Anglaises, 61*(1), 68-82.
Arundhati Roy's The God of Small Things transcends many a boundary between cultures, fine arts, visual arts, performing arts, genres, genders and religion at large. Thus, the author endows her novel with an operatic dimension, abolishing time and space, intermingling myths, legends and tales, fiction and reality, the sacred and the profane, as if she were weaving a printed mythological-patterned canvas.

Cassity, G. K. (2005). *Narrating transcendence: The temporal potentials of Arundhati Roy's "The God of Small Things" and Tom Tykwer's "Run Lola Run"* (Order No. 1430451). Available from ProQuest Dissertations & Theses Global: The Humanities and Social Sciences Collection; ProQuest One Literature. (305358590).
This study investigates the temporal arrangements of narrative and how the interplay of these forms influences---and perhaps determines---narrative outcomes. The inquiry considers conceptions of narrative intimated in J. Hillis Miller's description of coherence and closure in narrative fictions, Frank Kermode's notions of narrative concord and readerly skepticism, Edward Branigan's idea of narrative efficacy, and David Bordwell's explication of knowledge and ambiguity in film narration. The examination proceeds to assay the narrative cast of language; the iterative disposition of language and narrative; the connate natures of personification, determinism, and temporality; and the lyric temper of narrative. Two texts, Indian author Arundhati Roy's novel, The God of Small Things (1997), and German filmmaker Tom Tykwer's movie, Run Lola Run (1998), are appraised from these theoretical frames of reference. Finally, this analysis proposes an account of the figu-

rative effects of temporal dialectic and metanarrative rupture and their redemptive potentials.

Ch'ien, E. N. (2000). *Worlds of exile: Nabokov, Rushdie, Kingston, Roy, and Díaz* (Order No. 9954425). Available from ProQuest Dissertations & Theses Global: The Humanities and Social Sciences Collection; ProQuest One Literature. (304637325).

In "Worlds of Exile," I define exile as a phenomenon of migrants who cannot surrender their past lifestyle, language, or culture without great anxiety. In the cases of Vladimir Nabokov, Salman Rushdie, Maxine Hong Kingston, Arundhati Roy, and Junot Diaz, their new language is English; their original homelands are Russia, China, India, and the Dominican Republic. Although exile entails highly personal experiences, these writers from a variety of different cultures describe them in astonishing similar ways. They create hybrid languages as if language itself could become a kind of abode from which they reorganize their new worlds. Exile apparently frees these writers to play with language. Each writer invents his or her own version of English: Nabokov's English is fastidious and acrobatic; Rushdie delights in linguistic eclecticism; Roy emphasizes the capacity for language to be design by manipulating letters, saying that she enjoys their "look on a page"; Kingston marvels at the way English can create Chinese sounds; and Diaz shows how English and Spanish together form a musical hybrid. They all speak of having a passion for English: Nabokov delights in his "love affair" with English in Lolita; Roy says "I love English" and Kingston confesses an early attraction to English in her meditations on language. For these writers, language is less a pragmatic tool than a creature for which they have great feeling. Their shared habit of indulging in linguistic fetishes appears to compensate for their psychic uneasiness in a new physical environment.

Cilano, C. N. (2000). *Place -ing postcolonial identity in contemporary literature by women* (Order No. 9993761). Available from ProQuest Dissertations & Theses Global: The Humanities and Social Sciences Collection; ProQuest One Literature. (304586214).

This project focuses on the identity of the Anglophone postcolonial location in M. Nourbese Philip's Looking for Livingstone: An Odyssey of Silence (1991), Grace Nichols' I is a Long-Memoried Woman (1983), Jean Rhys' Wide Sargasso Sea (1966), and Arundhati Roy's The God of Small Things (1997). With the dissolution of the British Empire as its historical context, the central premises of this project hold, first, that the operative power dynamics characteristic of decolonization are place-specific manifestations of social, cultural, political, historical, and economic discourses and, also, that these power dynamics, particularly in the ways the individuals and groups living in a place interact with them, shape the numerous identities that a given place can signify. Moreover, these power dynamics, while always circumscribed, are forceful in their positioning of people in certain roles and yet also vulnerable to alteration as people collude with and/or resist the asymmetrical relations that characterize/-d the (post)colonial encounter. Each of the project's four chapters engages with these primary premises in unique ways. The first chapter concentrates on how Philip's volume re-conceptualizes language's meaning-making functions so as to highlight the potential for the co-existence of multiple senses of place, identities, and histories. The second chapter foregrounds how the slave women in Nichols' poems construct, among other things, a new sense of "place" in the New World that denaturalizes the colonizers' power. The third chapter explores how Rhys's novel forwards a conception of identity's relationship to place as a shifting and provisional process that varies according to context and to an individual's or a group's social position. Finally, the fourth chapter on Roy's novel examines the impact of global and local discourses on the potential for a resistant though limited agency.

Doğangün, S. (2023). THE SEMIPERIPHERAL SUBALTERN AND LITERARY EXPRESSION: NARRATIVES FROM TURKEY AND INDIA. *Metacritic Journal for Comparative Studies and Theory, 9*(1), 5-29. https://doi.org/10.24193/mjcst.2023.15.01

The onset of neoliberal capitalism has endowed the concept of "peripherality with significant relevance for literary scholars investigating the dynamic interaction between aesthetic structures and the consequences of evolving socioeconomic and political terrains. Building on the theoretical foundations of subalternity, world-systems theory, and theories of combined and uneven development, I intend to present a comparative, constructive exploration of three distinguished novels from India and Turkey. These include Latife Tekin's Berji Kristin: Tales from the Garbage Hills (Berji Kristin hereinafter), Arundhati Roy's The God of Small Things (Small Things hereinafter), and Aravind Adiga's The White Tiger (hereinafter White Tiger). My analysis delves into the intricate intertwining of familial dynamics, communal relations, gender violence, and patriarchal norms with the mechanisms of neoliberal market operations. In doing so, I strive to delineate the manner in which semiperipheral subalternity surfaces as a consistent theme of discourse within the distinct cultural landscapes of Turkey and India.

Gardner, B. J. (2012). *Speaking voices in postcolonial Indian novels from Orientalism to outsourcing* (Order No. 3515337). Available from ProQuest Dissertations & Theses Global: The Humanities and Social Sciences Collection; ProQuest One Literature.

(1020380256).

In Orientalism, Edward Said identified how the Westerner "spoke for" and represented the silent Orient. Today with the burgeoning call-center business with India, it seems that the West now wants the Orient to speak for it. But is the voice that Western business requires in India a truly Indian voice? Or is it a manipulation which is a new form of the silencing of the Indian voice? This dissertation identifies how several Postcolonial Indian writers challenge the silence of Orientalism and the power issues of the West through various "speaking voices" of narratives representative of Indian life. Using Julie Kristeva's abjection theory as a lens, this dissertation reveals Arundhati Roy as "speaking abjection" in The God of Small Things. Even Roy's novelistic setting suffers abjection through neocolonialism. Salman Rushdie's narrative method of magic realism allows "speaking trauma" as his character Saleem in Midnight's Children suffers the traumas of Partition and Emergency as an allegorical representation of India. Using magic realism Saleem is able to speak the unspeakable. Other Indian voices, Bapsi Sidhwa, Khushwant Singh, and Rohinton Mistry "speak history" as their novels carry the weight of conveying an often-absent official history of Partition and the Emergency, history verified by Partition survivor interviews. In Such a Long Journey, Mistry uses an anthrozoological theme in portraying issues of power over innocence. Recognizing the choices and negotiations of immigrant life through the coining of the word (dis)assimilation , Jhumpa Lahiri's writings are analyzed in terms of a "speaking voice" of (dis)assimilation for Indian immigrants in the United States, while Zadie Smith's White Teeth "speaks (dis)assimilation" as a voice of multiple ethnicities negotiating immigrant life in the United Kingdom. Together these various "speaking voices" show the power of Indian writers in challenging the silence of

Orientalism through narrative. INDEX WORDS: Postcolonial, Orientalism, Narrative, Abjection, Ecocriticism, Trauma, Magic Realism, Carnivalesque, History, Anthrozoology, (Dis)assimilation, Assimilation, Edward Said, Arundhati Roy, Julia Kristeva, Salman Rushdie, Rohinton Mistry, Kushwant Singh, Jhumpa Lahiri, Zadie Smith

Gillis, S. (2013). *Hybridized identity and "going native" in Arundhati Roy's The God of Small Things and Paul Theroux's The Elephanta Suite* (Order No. 1543115). Available from ProQuest Dissertations & Theses Global: The Humanities and Social Sciences Collection; ProQuest One Literature. (1426853355).
Within the past decade, critics such as Aarti Vaade, Peter Mortenson, Janet Thormann, and Pumla Dineo Gqola have examined various facets of Arundhati Roy's landmark novel, The God of Small Things (1997), investigating topics from ecological collectivity and the environment to ethical subjectivity and the caste system, respectively. However, scholars have yet to assess the hybridized identities that function as an attempt made by the characters in Roy's text to challenge the Indian caste system. Furthermore, while scholars largely regard "going native" as a literary trope that is localized to various nineteenth-century travel narratives and fictional works, novelist Paul Theroux's The Elephanta Suite (2007) presents itself as fodder for a contemporary examination of "going native." In assessing Theroux's body of work, including his highly regarded travel narratives, critics such as Terry Caesar, Tim Youngs, and Elton Glaser have gleaned notions of what Theroux considers to be the meaning of travel and travel writing, yet no scholar has studied identity construction and performance within The Elephanta Suite. To this end, my thesis examines hybridization and "going native" in these texts. Through the use of small-scale character studies, I argue that both texts present char-

acters whose identities have become hybridized as a result of an obsession with, attraction to, or sexual contact with a character of an opposite cultural group or a lower caste. Based upon this interaction, I contend that these texts portray the unsustainability, shame, or danger associated with hybridization and "going native." I develop this thesis in the course of two chapters and a coda. The first chapter examines hybridity in order to determine how the characters in Roy's novel are changed as a result of their interaction with British colonizers. The second chapter analyzes how hybridized identity constructions are achieved through sexual experimentation and forays into "going native" by the characters in Theroux's text. Finally, the coda investigates how the boundary-crossing relationships in these two texts depict what a postcolonial India looks like by assessing one family's fall in family status within the caste system as well as the advent of transnational capitalism in India.

Goh, R. B. H. (2021). The (In)Significance of Small Things: Data, Identity, and the Dilemma of Recovery in Arundhati Roy's The Ministry of Utmost Happiness. *Studies in the Novel, 53*(1), 1-19.

Arundhati Roy's second novel, The Ministry of Utmost Happiness, was published in 2017, twenty years after the appearance of her first novel, The God of Small Things. Despite some thematic continuities between the two novels, there are also significant narrative differences that can be attributed to Roy's evolving socio-political consciousness (elaborated in her large body of essays and commentaries), but also to what might be seen as a changing view of humanity and human society post-9/11. What comes to prominence in the later novel is a concern with the individual subject as a site of surveillance, rumors, reports, and (dis)information—what, following the novel itself, we can collectively call "data"—and a corresponding novel form which relies on textual bricolage and narrative fragmentation. "Data," in this sense, is the expression of a social sensibility that stems from the trauma of loss and the absurdity of geopolitics post-9/11—and, in Roy's vision, how this absurdity plays out in the context of India under Narendra Modi. In its formal evocation of this traumatic milieu, the novel—embodying the dilemma facing the 9/11 novel—may ultimately reinscribe and reinforce the fragmentary identity and disjointed knowledge that it critiques.

Gupta, R. (2022). Reconceptualising Family in Arundhati Roy's The God of Small Things and Kamila Shamsie's Broken Verses. *Contemporary Literary Review India, 9*(4), 71-86. http://ezproxy.univ-paris3.fr/login?url=https://www.proquest.com/scholarly-journals/reconceptualising-family-arundhati-roy-s-god/docview/2800680677/se-2

Both Arundhati Roy and Kamila Shamsie, as profound South-Asian women writers, have often been associated with postcolonial politics or feminist agendas. However, this paper attempts to recontextualise their works, The God of Small Things and Broken Verses, respectively, to uncover the particularities of their politics. While enmeshed in the ideas about the nation, patriarchy, and colonialism, these texts deal with the specificities of individual families. Yet, the representation of the family, in these works, is not conventional as these authors attempt to either reveal the interstitial spaces within the family, or try to restructure a normative bond, or finally, even reject the family to accommodate individual desires. Ultimately, their postcolonial or feminist politics do not overshadow the multiplicity of a family: as an ever-evolving and diversified entity.

Jani, P. (2001). *Before Rushdie: Cosmopolitanism and the national question in the post -colonial Indian English novel* (Order

No. 3006742). Available from ProQuest Dissertations & Theses Global: The Humanities and Social Sciences Collection; ProQuest One Literature. (304681895).

This dissertation historicizes the contemporary emergence of a post-modern perspective in the post-colonial Indian novel in English. By reading novels from across the post-colonial period against the twists and turns of post-colonial modernity, "Before Rushdie" marks key ideological and formal shifts in the genre and challenges the prevalent notion that the post-modern, post-nationalist tilt of contemporary Indian English literature is a necessary product of "post-coloniality" or "cosmopolitanism" itself. In the early post-colonial period, cosmopolitan writers like Kamala Markandaya and Nayantara Sahgal wrote realist novels centered around an engagement with the national question—despite sharp differences in their assessments of Indian modernity. But the representations of the nation, the cosmopolitan figure, and "the people" in the Indian English novel shifted drastically after the late 1960s and 1970s, as a developing-yet-crisis-ridden Indian modernity produced a new cosmopolitan subject with expanded opportunities in India and abroad and a cynical view about national liberation. The writings of Vikram Chandra, Arundhati Roy, Rushdie, the later Sahgal, and Shashi Tharoor—marked by a general dismissal of national liberation and a dazzling and eclectic style that eschews linear narratives—have met the ideological and formal requirements of the new cosmopolitanism by turning their artistic focus from society to subjectivity. In short, the attempt is to redefine the post-colonial as a historical category, not an ontological one. The six novels discussed in detail are: Nayantara Sahgal's A Time to Be Happy (1958), The Day in Shadow (1971), and Rich Like Us (1985), Anita Desai's Clear Light of Day (1980), Midnight's Children , and Arundhati Roy's The God of Small Things (1997).

These close readings are ensconced in theoretical questions about national liberation and nationalism, cosmopolitanism, subalternity, and the link between form and ideology. By tying its analysis of literary representations to the history of the Indian nation-state, further, this study suggests that a critical understanding of national liberation—of its deep, emancipatory impact and its limiting structures—is crucial to grasping both the textual content and social context of post-colonial literature.

Kanjirakkat, J. M. (2017). The Ministry of Utmost Happiness. *Transnational Literature, 10*(1), 1-2.

Apart from such attention to detail, which is common to both her novels, it is hard not to notice her evolution as a writer - from someone who handled a story set in small Kerala to someone who has dealt with a large canvas depicting issues as wide-ranging as Kashmir, transgender rights, Dalit (lower caste) issues, leftwing movements in east central India and colour politics in the nation. Roy's sociological eye remains sharply delightful as she captures the larger Indian reality of the subtleties of caste system (a Baidya is a Brahmin, but not quite), describes the Hijra (transgender) community in Delhi and passingly mentions the global impact of Malayalee nurses. The rest of the story revolves around three of his friends from his college days - Tilo, the unconventional, half-Dalit, wandering woman; Naga, a radical university student who transforms to an extremely successful journalist writing about the Kashmir situation; and Musa, a quiet and sensitive man forced by circumstances to respond intensely to the insane situation in Kashmir.

Kapoor, M. (2021). The God of Small Things Versus the Devil of Big Things: Narrative Technique and Arundhati Roy. *IUP Journal of English Studies, 16*(2), 46-55.

As an astute muckraker, Arundhati Roy uses the narrative technique of "inversion" to express her concern for all categories of the marginalized, be they women, children, factory workers, etc. In true muckraking tradition, her novel touches upon a plethora of social evils-political and social hypocrisies, patriarchal property rights, ill-treatment of divorced women, caste issues, wife-battering, and so on. A strong sense of grievance lends an angry color to her work. Roy's The God of Small Things as a specimen of women's writing displays an obsessive urge to articulate anger through the technique of "inversion," in turn made possible through the novel's constantly changing perspective and its non-linear progression. "Inversion" accounts for the undertone of irony that runs through the novel. It colors the title, the ordering of each individual chapter, as well as the controversial end. "Inversion" ensures the effectiveness of the title in foregrounding the "small things" as the central preoccupation of the novel. It also works cleverly to expose the contrast between the apparent and the real and thus upset reader expectations. It also determines the ordering of the events that constitute the novel's diegesis. The technique of inversion allows the event of the punishment to precede the so-called crime. The crime is relegated to the end, and ironically makes possible the inversion of a happy ending to a sad story.

Koparanoğlu, H. G. (2011). *Colonialism, Globalization and Resistance in Jean Rhys' Wide Sargasso Sea, Arundhati Roy's The God of Small Things and John Updike's Terrorist* (Order No. 30851874). Available from ProQuest Dissertations & Theses Global: The Humanities and Social Sciences Collection; ProQuest One Literature. (2956859468).

Although colonialism seems to be an idea of the past, its subtle forms have survived to the present disguised especially as globalization. The global world, however, involves strategies of resistance to colonialism from the colonized corners of the world which have come to be called post-colonialism. Literature is one of the important areas in which the ideology of colonialism, globalization and the resistance that the people show against this ideology can be best seen. In this dissertation, I put forward that there are socioeconomic, cultural and political resistances to ever-expanding imperialism of western civilizations. Therefore, by calling attention to "the silenced" under the hegemony, this dissertation aims to show how three writers from different nationalities, cultural backgrounds and ethnic groups reveal resistance through their protagonists. In Jean Rhys' Wide Sargasso Sea, the protagonist Antoinette resists the dominant colonial ideology by trying to find solutions from her culture. She also shows her resistance by her discourse against patriarchy and colonialism. In Arundhati Roy's The God of Small Things, the protagonist Ammu protests against colonialism and assimilation in which women and "untouchables" in the caste system are silenced by the dominant system and ideology. In John Updike's Terrorist, the reader faces multicultural America, after September 11, and Updike presents the difficulties that the Muslim society in the U.S faces by portraying Ahmad, the protagonist who wants to be close to his culture by resisting the dominant ideology with a different kind of resistance: terrorism in the global world.

Kremins, K. A. (2005). *An ethics of reading: The broken beauties of Toni Morrison, Nawal El Saadawi, and Arundhati Roy* (Order No. 3166249). Available from ProQuest Dissertations & Theses Global: The Humanities and Social Sciences Collection; ProQuest One Literature. (304993895).

In the novels of Toni Morrison, Nawal El Saadawi and Arundhati Roy, torture expresses the violence of slavery, religious fundamentalism and poverty. Rather than simply revealing loss and diminishment, the areas of criticism most literary critics have focused on in the last thirty years, such works expose the possibility for transformation through transgressive narratives that discover a sense of wholeness through moral and spiritual defiance and a redefinition of beauty. Especially in fiction that explores a postcolonial response to repression, torture often functions as reality and metaphor. Thus, contemporary, postcolonial fiction demands an ethics of reading. An ethical reading involves more than the narrow reading permitted by the critics who espouse a politics of identity. To read ethically means to consider a variety of divergent perspectives as the reader engages with, and often wrestles with, the text. Reading ethically challenges the reader to make reading an act of resistance. Therefore, because of such demands, traditional literary criticism can be too confining. In studying Beloved, Woman at Point Zero and The God of Small Things, and reading them ethically, I have relied on art and film critics, cultural, political and social critics as well as literary critics who have rejected the critical traditions of the last thirty years. I have structured the study to provide for a global contrapuntal reading. Each chapter focuses on a single element and investigates how each text and between the texts the element contributes to an ethical reading. The conclusion, then, establishes why an ethics of reading is a requirement to fully unpack the violence and torture within postcolonial texts. My study of these three novels proves that an ethical reading requires an unflinching commitment to textual engagement. To acknowledge that narrative is itself memory evoked in a specific landscape is critical to an enlightened reading. A constant awareness of how the narrative shapes itself and is in conversation with other texts is also significant. An ethical reading cannot exist in isolation; for a reading to be ethical, the text must be informed by and engaged with other texts, as well as history and other art forms. An ethical reading must use the analytical techniques behind close reading, but should not be dictated by such tools.

Lutz, J. (2009). Commodity Fetishism, Patriarchal Repression, and Psychic Deprivation in Arundhati Roy's The God of Small Things. *Mosaic : A Journal for the Interdisciplinary Study of Literature, 42*(3), 57-74.

Appearing early in the first chapter of The God of Small Things, Ammu's encounter with Police Inspector Thomas Mathew establishes a repeated pattern in the narrative whereby the brutal violence underpinning the social and economic structure of patriarchy and capitalism is displaced onto seemingly innocuous trademark images, icons of popular culture, or objects for mass consumption.

Martins, M. P. (2016). *The Search for Identity and the Construction of an Idea of India in the novels "The God of Small Things" by Arundhati Roy and "The Inheritance of Loss" by Kiran Desai* (Order No. 10598163). Available from ProQuest Dissertations & Theses Global: The Humanities and Social Sciences Collection; ProQuest One Literature. (2010531473).

The main objective of this research project is to analyse how the novels The God of Small Things (1997) by Arundhati Roy and The Inheritance of Loss (2006) by Kiran Desai can help readers and scholars construct an idea of India and of the Indian cultural identity. In order to develop this theory it is necessary to look into three aspects which are crucial to the building of knowledge on a nation, its culture and people and these are, national history, identity and cultural representation through different artistic production, including fictional narratives. Historical processes are the key to the unfolding of present circumstances and fundamental to the construction of a national identity that makes sense collectively. However, the perceptions of the past change according to philosophical and ideological trends, placing historical objectivity in the hands of its subjective counterpart. It is cultural theory and how it evolves in simultaneity with the world and its social, political, economic and technological development that in effect dictates the forms and expressions that give shape to societies, nations and identities. The function of narrative whether as text, visual arts, film, architecture, dance and other creative expressions of the self, is to tell a story. And every moment of every living being can be told in a story. History too is a story and though in the past it focused mostly on the grand deeds of the European nations, with postcolonialism new stories began to emerge, revealing a world of diversity and deconstructing traditional views of the shaping of the past and the power relations involved. However, this new approach to the historical, cultural and political dialectic was achieved through the effect of the postcolonial narrative which used Western forms and structures, such as the novel and the English language, to achieve its aim. This appropriation of language and form resulted in an inversion of power relations as a cultural metaphor. For the purpose of such a debate, the present dissertation focuses on the two novels by Roy and Desai and is divided into three main sections each of which deals with one approach to the thesis. The first chapter contains the historical approach, in the second I discuss postcolonial theory and the third analyses the relation between anthropology and fiction.

Martorano, E. (2018). *Spectrality as an Aesthetic of Fragmentation: Resisting Totalizing Narratives in Arundhati Roy's The God of Small Things* (Order No. 10840917). Available from ProQuest Dissertations & Theses Global: The Humanities and Social Sciences Collection; ProQuest One Literature. (2089438485).

This thesis examines the 1997 novel The God of Small Things and analyzes Arundhati Roy's invocation of spectrality in order to establish the spectral as an aesthetic of the fragmentation inherent to the traumas of colonialism. This thesis specifically argues that by adopting a perspective that understands postcolonial trauma as spectral, we may begin to cultivate an ethic of decolonialism that claims as its foundation the understanding and acceptance of hauntings. Drawing primarily on Fredric Jameson's "Third-World Literature in the Era of Multinational Capitalism," Pheng Cheah's "Spectral Nationality: The Living on sur-vie] of the Postcolonial Nation in Neocolonial Globalization," Avery Gordon's work on spectrality in sociology and literature, Jacques Derrida's theories of deconstruction, and Dominick LaCapra's "Trauma, Absence, Loss," I establish a context and develop the resonances between the postcolonial and the spectral, and demonstrate the relationships between communal haunting and individual trauma.

McCarty, R. E. (2014). *Imprisonment and the captive body: Postcolonial reactions to Victorian gender identity in "The God of Small Things" and "Nervous Conditions"* (Order No. 1569409). Available from ProQuest Dissertations & Theses Global: The Humanities and Social Sciences Collection; ProQuest One Literature. (1638267477).

This project examines idealized Victorian gender definitions of womanhood and their appearance in postcolonial literature from the 20th century. Victorian England, a patriarchal culture, allowed the expression of femininity in limited terms: a woman was expected to behave like the unrealistic concept of the angel in the house. Often, women who expressed their femininity in ways that did not reflect this concept were criticized and labeled as madwomen, and they were treated with rest therapy, which allowed dominant male figures to confine these women to their homes. After Sigmund Freud introduced psychotherapy and after Charlotte Perkins Gilman published "The Yellow Wallpaper," rest therapy was phased out, and women could no longer be easily manipulated into behaving in an idealized manner. These unrealistic standards of femininity are found later on in the 20th century postcolonial texts Nervous Conditions and The God of Small Things. Both Tsitsi Dangarembga and Arundhati Roy trace the progression of female empowerment across multiple generations in these texts, and female characters are made to navigate the difficult intersection of Victorian culture and their native culture. When the characters understand these complexities, they are able to reconstruct femininity on their own terms.

Md Abdul, M. S., & Rahman, M. M. (2018). Intermingling of History and Politics in The God of Small Things. *Advances in Language and Literary Studies, 9*(4), 138-142. https://doi.org/10.7575/aiac.alls.v.9n.4p.138

Suzanna Arundhati Roy is a post-modern sub-continental writer famous for her first novel The God of Small Things. This novel tells us the story of Ammu who is the mother of Rahel and Estha. Through the story of Ammu, the novel depicts the socio-political condition of Kerala from the late 1960s and early 1990s. The novel is about Indian culture and Hinduism is the main religion of India. One of the protagonists of this novel, Velutha, is from a low-caste community representing the dalit caste. Apart from those, between the late 1960s and early 1990s, a lot of movements took place in the history of Kerala. The Naxalites Movement is imperative amid them. Kerala is the place where communism was established for the first time in the history of the world through democratic election. Some vital issues of feminism have been brought into focus through the portrayal of the character, Ammu. In a word, this paper tends to show how Arundhati Roy has successfully manifested the multifarious as well as simultaneous influences of politics in the context of history and how those affected the lives of the marginalized. Overall, it would minutely show how historical incidents and political ups and downs go hand in hand during the political upheavals of a state.

Menon, P. (2010). *Liminal resistances: Local subjections in "My Story", "Vidheyan", and "The God of Small Things"* (Order No. 3463444). Available from ProQuest Dissertations & Theses Global: The Humanities and Social Sciences Collection; ProQuest One Literature. (881292926).

This project investigates various ways in which resistance is explored by Kamala Das, Adoor Gopalakrishnan and Arundhati Roy in My Story, Vidheyan, and The God of Small Things respectively. "Liminal Resistances: Local Subjections in My Story, Vidheyan, and The God of Small Things" aims to examine the workings and creative subversions of hegemonic discourses of caste, class, gender and color within the local milieu of Kerala, India. By exploring the theoretical apparatuses employed in three diverse texts set in Kerala, this project identifies: firstly, Das's subversion of Nair Kerala's sense of gendered and casted normativity in My Story; secondly, Adoor's depiction of the notion of home that enables self-recognition between the exploited and tyrant ensuring both suppression and libratory self-formation for classed subjects in Vidheyan; and finally, Roy's portrayal of the conceptual category of whiteness within Kerala as being neither uniformly subservient nor stable as depicted in The God of Small Things. It is hoped that by identifying and exploring the theoretical nuances of resistances in these generically diverse texts—autobiography, film, and fiction– all set within the local realms of Kerala, this project will contribute a new scholarship in postcolonial studies that will recognize and problematize local instances of subversions and their representations within the Indian subcontinent. INDEX WORDS: Kamala Das, Nair, Caste, My Story, Adoor Gopalakrishnan, Vidheyan, Home, Arundhati Roy, The God of

Small Things, Whiteness, Kerala, Resistance

Meyer, K. L. (2014). *Transgressing Postcolonial Indifference, Recovering History: Women and Desire in Arundhati Roy's The God of Small Things, Ahdaf Soueif's The Map of Love, and Edwidge Danticat's The Farming of Bones* (Order No. 30677171). Available from ProQuest Dissertations & Theses Global: The Humanities and Social Sciences Collection; ProQuest One Literature. (2853463926).

This dissertation examines the concept of postcolonial indifference at play in three contemporary novels by female writers: Arundhati Roy's The God of Small Things (1997), Ahdaf Soueif's The Map of Love (1999), and Edwidge Danticat's The Farming of Bones (1998). All three novels are rooted in the homelands of their authors—India, Egypt, and Haiti, respectively—and a consideration of the texts in their specific historical and cultural contexts further illuminates the postcolonial worlds portrayed in the novels as well as revealing how colonialism took different forms at each site. However, by linking the three works, I establish common aspects among these postcolonial experiences that shape a framework for postcolonial indifference. Extrapolating the idea of postcolonial indifference as introduced by Rukmini Nair, my study draws from existing scholarship in postcolonial studies and postcolonial feminist critique. I also employ crucial sources from other fields of study, including philosophy, trauma studies, and history.In this dissertation, I argue that the female characters in these three novels transgress environments of postcolonial indifference by engaging in romantic relationships and expressing their sexuality. Pursuing their desires allows these women to counteract the effects of monstrous indifference in their individual lives. They experience deeply-felt personal emotions and connect intimately with fellow humans; these acts challenge the legacy of colonial indifference in the postcolonial world. From a consideration of Ammu's clear, decisive challenge to indifference in The God of Small Things and Anna's transgression of colonial apathy among the British in The Map of Love to Amabelle's subtle, perhaps incomplete breaking with numbness in The Farming of Bones, I shape a trajectory that reveals how postcolonial subjects are held captive by and, more importantly, how they can break with indifference to varying degrees. A conclusion chapter acknowledges such diverse experiences but draws on commonalities, allowing the novels themselves to establish a working theory of indifference in postcolonial literary studies. This dissertation culminates in a pedagogical essay that applies my work to the postcolonial literature classroom, where I address potential challenges and explore avenues for students to connect with difficult texts and ideas in the field.

Mittapalli, R. (2018). Novel as Counter-Narrative of the Nation: Arundhati Roy's The God of Small Things †. *IUP Journal of English Studies, 13*(2), 42-49.

In her novel The God of Small Things, Arundhati Roy offers a deeply critical perspective on modern India while riveting the reader's attention on the microcosm that constitutes the story. She unobtrusively works her commentary on issues confronting the nation into the narrative, which readily invites the discerning reader's honest reflection on them. This paper discusses The God of Small Things in terms of its engagement with three major issues-degradation of environment, commodification of culture, and degeneration of Indian democracy-and demonstrates how in the process the novel challenges the prevailing paradigms and dominant narratives of the nation that are based on a romantic concept of the nation, inadequate understanding of ground realities, and lopsided priorities. The paper then focuses on how the novel suggests alternative scenarios foregrounding the experiences of the voiceless, the underprivileged, and the disenfranchised. It further establishes how Roy's commentary underlying The God of Small Things deeply impacts imagination and how in the final analysis the novel emerges as an authentic counter-narrative of the nation.

Panwar, G. S. (2019). *Novelizing the Dissent: Cosmopolitan Literature from Latin America and South Asia* (Order No. 22619813). Available from ProQuest Dissertations & Theses Global: The Humanities and Social Sciences Collection; ProQuest One Literature. (2317596922).

This thesis endeavors to showcase this fragmented cosmopolitanism in Global South through a comparative analysis of national identity and urban cosmopolitan space in the novels The Ministry of Utmost Happiness (2017) by the Indian author Arundhati Roy, How to get filthy rich in Rising Asia (2013) by Pakistani Mohsin Hamid, Fábula Asiática (2017) by Guatemalan Rodrigo Rey Rosa and El sueño del retorno (2013) by the Salvadoran Horacio Castellanos Moya's. It explores the questions such as rooted and unrooted cosmopolitanism, and homelessness, and how these dynamics are dependent on social, political and geographical boundaries and how does it, in turn, shapes national identities? If there is a trend that can be traced across boundaries and if neoliberal politics and political unrest are part of a larger design? And lastly, how the artists and literary figures in the global south have been expressing their dissent against the nation?

Pei, T. (2017). The Minor-narrative of Transgression in The God of Small Things. *Contemporary Literary Review India, 4*(4), 1-13.

The debut novel of the Indian architect Arundhati Roy (1997) successfully won the Booker Prize (1997), offering bountiful insight into the real India through connecting dots of memory. Opposed to the master-narrative in the British canonical literary works, a minor-narrative is adopted in this novel, casting realistic light on the postcolonial India. This paper probes into the minor narrative of transgressions in various aspects: language, philosophy and ethnicity. The penetrating use of indigenous language such as Malayalam, the striking contrast between Christian God and "the God of small things", and the love affair between different castes transgress and defy the social norms, reflecting Arundhati Roy's wish for a just society in India.

Poyner, J. (2018). Subalternity and Scale in Arundhati Roy's The God of Small Things. *Mosaic : A Journal for the Interdisciplinary Study of Literature, 51*(3), 53-69.
Reading subaltern agency in The God of Small Things according to environmentalist notions of "scale" produces more complex and potentially more empowering refractions of subalternity than straightforwardly Marxist or postcolonial studies have afforded. I argue Velutha is both oppressed subaltern and prototypical eco-warrior of a new planetary order.

Premnath, G. (2003). *Arguments with nationalism in the fiction of the Indian diaspora* (Order No. 3087330). Available from ProQuest Dissertations & Theses Global: The Humanities and Social Sciences Collection; ProQuest One Literature. (305344991).
This dissertation engages with the ideas of diaspora that have become increasingly prominent in current discussions of cultural politics. While I take issue with some of the inflated claims made for diaspora discourse, I also discern in it the potential to generate a powerful reconstructive critique of postcolonial nationalism. In a context in which the postcolonial nation-state is beleaguered by obstacles at every turn, I suggest that diaspora thought might

offer a pathway for renewing national agendas—and in the process might also achieve a more fully grounded sense of its own location. With these goals in mind, I analyze the terms—and assess the consequences—of varied arguments with postcolonial nationalism conducted from diasporic sites. Occasions for these analyses are provided by a significant and newly prominent body of literature: fiction in English by writers of the Indian diaspora. This rapidly growing but still relatively compact body of work constitutes a richly interreferential discourse of diaspora, and a varied series of detours from and returns to the fateful terrain of nationalism. My first chapter sets out the theoretical stakes for the project by assessing how the thought of Frantz Fanon, one of the classic theorists of national liberation, has been reformulated within diaspora discourse. In contrast to critics like Homi Bhabha, who programmatically discredit Fanon's nationalist writings as outmoded in an era of diaspora, I argue for the relevance of these works for diasporic concerns. Four subsequent chapters set this theoretical vision in relation to significant literary representations of diaspora politics. My second and third chapters discern two poles of diasporic discourse—the communal and the exilic—in the works of two writers of the Indo-Trinidadian diaspora, Sam Selvon and V. S. Naipaul. The final two chapters treat the work of Amitav Ghosh and Arundhati Roy, both born in India, whose writings are nevertheless powerfully informed by the diasporic critique of postcolonial nationalism. While Ghosh presents nationalism as a tragic failure and emphasizes alternative forms of belonging, Roy mounts her devastating critiques of the Indian state and its ideologies of development upon, rather than beyond, the terrain of the nation-state.

Rafiee, B., & Deedari, R. (2015). A Spivakian Reading of Louise Erdrich's Track and Arundhati Roy's The God of Small Things.

International Journal of Applied Linguistics & English Literature, 4(2), 134-142. https://doi.org/10.7575/aiac.ijalel.v.4n.2p.134 The present article is the study of Louise Erdrich's Tracks (1997) and Arundhati Roy's The God of Small Things (1988) in the light of postcolonial feminism theories of Spivak. Feminist discourse shares many similarities with post-colonial theory and for this reason the two fields have long been thought of as associative, even complimentary. "Subalternity" is a very important term in both post-colonial and feminist aspects. The word Subaltern describes the lower classes and the social groups who are at the margins of a society. Tracks and The God of Small Things depict the cultural background of their authors. Erdrich Native American culture and Roy's Indian heritage has helped them in creating certain types of female characters in their novels that still carry within themselves some features of their culture. In these novels Louise Erdrich and Roy's main focus is on the female protagonists and the specific roles they have within their communities. Although these novels depict two different cultures, there are many similarities that these two cultures share. Roy and Erdrich present several different female characters in their novels The God of Small Things and Tracks, all in different ways trapped in a system of oppression but also with a substantial degree of agency. From a postcolonial feminist perspective, Roy and Erdrich have contributed to make the representation of the subaltern women more diverse, through giving us various portraits of women that, despite their oppressed and marginalized status.

Rogers, A. P. (2005). *Shattering identities: Agency and desire in Winterson, Roy, and Woolf* (Order No. 3180046). Available from ProQuest Dissertations & Theses Global: The Humanities and Social Sciences Collection; ProQuest One Literature. (304999483).

This study explores constructions and ruptures of sociopolitical and personal identity categories and examines counterhegemonic configurations of desire and agency in selected British modernist and postmodernist/postcolonial texts. Jeanette Winterson, Arundhati Roy, and Virginia Woolf produce experimental fiction in which the struggle of characters depicted as social "outsiders" drives narrative and aesthetic technique, particularly salient in Written on the Body, The God of Small Things, and Mrs. Dalloway . In each of these works, such characters challenge the social structures, normative conventions, and prevailing dominant ideologies of their respective societies through their own resistance to personal and social identity constructions. In order to maneuver through identity categories which attempt to essentialize and oppress, these characters employ strategies which subvert and destabilize the boundaries of classification, thus shattering conceptions which posit identity as solidified. Throughout, anxieties of identity and expressions of agency are traced through analyses of character, narration, and plot in the novels, developing into conclusions that celebrate ambiguity and uncertainty as a means of unsettling categorization. Butler's work on performativity is utilized to undermine identity constructs; moreover, queer theory's anti-identitarian stance broadens to incorporate the deconstruction of identity categories beyond those which denote sexual orientation. Divisions based on class, religion, and ethnicity feature prominently within these novels, as does a critique of imperialist politics. Foucault's theory of power and Nietzsche's will to power are reconfigured and subsequently applied to an analysis of poststructuralist concepts of constraining ideologies which interpellate individuals as social subjects, subjected to cultural determinism but capable of contesting such determinations. A chief concern in current theoretical debates is the question of human agency after jettisoning the individual as a timeless, ahistorical essence. Overturning charges of irresponsible nihilism, transgression and desire are asserted as strategies of resistance and refusal. Turning away from Freud and Lacan's articulation of desire as lack, Deleuze's theory of desire and Lacan's formulation of jouissance are reassessed to depict the movement of desire as excess, as a liberation of choice, and such excess is located in the narrative strategies of the three writers treated in this study.

Roy, B. (2009). The Title of The God of Small Things: A Subversive Salvo. *ANQ, 22*(3), 56-63.

According to Amar Nath Prasad, "the book shows a maladjustment between 'The God of Big Things' (Pappachi, Baby Kochamma, Mammachi, Chacko, Comrade Pillai, and Inspector Thomas Mathew) and 'The God of Small Things' (Ammu, Velutha, Rahel, Estha, Sophie Mol)" (161). ...] Big Man is held aloof from people and things around him by the grandeur of his dreams; his soaring ambition makes him single-minded and strong-willed. ...] he leaves no footprints in sand, no ripples in water, no image in mirrors.

Swan, J. G. (2001). Perspectives on Addressing the White Gaze: Arundhati Roy's The God of Small Things and Othello. *The Upstart Crow, 21*, 138-153.

Swan addresses the issue of studying white supremacy rather than race resists modernity's obfuscation of the powerful agent of knowledge. He considers the manipulation of perspective of two works that depend upon the perspective transposition for much of their remarkable achievement, Arundhati Roy's The God of Small Things and William Shakespeare's Othello. Both Roy and Shakespeare understand the power of time and space, materialist values, and objectifying subjectivities to the modern hermeneutist, and so both address themselves to these factors.

Uma, A. (2005). In Benson E., Conolly L. W.(Eds.), *Feminism*

(India) (2nd. ed. ed.). Routledge, Taylor & Francis Group.

Valero Redondo, M. (2020). Secrecy, Community and Counter-History in Arundhati Roy's 'The God of Small Things' (1997). [Secreto, Comunidad y Contra-Historia en 'The God of Small Things' (1997) de Arundhati Roy] *Complutense Journal of English Studies, 28*, 75-82. https://doi.org/10.5209/cjes.63856
This article explores the different types of communities and the role of secrecy and counter-history in Arundhati Roy's The God of Small Things (1997), a novel in which secrecy plays a crucial role and in which the most genuine human relations are characterized by a desire to participate in otherness. This article examines Roy's subversion of the operative community by considering (a) the different communitarian organizations in The God of Small Things, from the most organic (the caste system, patriarchy, religious institutions, communism and the commodification of culture) to the least organic (the community of Others and the community of lovers); (b) the connection between alterity, finitude and secrecy as preventing the unworked community from organicist fusion; (c) the link between alterity, finitude, secrecy and counter-history. Although ingrained within a deeply organicist community, the main characters in Roy's novel prove to have a vigorous capacity to trespass communitarian boundaries and to expose themselves to otherness.

Vallasek, J. (2018). FROM SMALL THINGS TO BIG SYMBOLS. TRANSGRESSABILITY OF BORDERS IN ARUNDHATI ROY'S WORKS. *Metacritic Journal for Comparative Studies and Theory, 4*(2), 161. https://doi.org/10.24193/mjcst.2018.6.09
While Arundhati Roy's first novel, The God of Small Things (1997) mostly focused on the tragic outcomes of the rigid Indian caste system and found its place in the tradition of Marquezian

magic realism and Salman Rushdie's mythical and exotic portrayal of India, her second novel offers a complex description of a divided society. The Ministry of Utmost Happiness (2017) bears the mark of Roy's vast experience in the field of political and environmental activism, her militant approach towards social injustice. The new novel is a patchwork of narratives focused around two main characters, the transsexual Anjum and Tilo, the ever revolting architect involved in the civil war in Kashmir. In the description of both hallucinatory violence and small, gentle moments of harmony and cooperation, Roy portrays the divided, postcolonial/neocolonial India where conflicts are constantly emerging on religious, political, social and sexual levels. Borders seem impossible to cross when the conflict is thoroughly interiorised like in the case of the Delhi hijras, or has grown uncontrollable like in the civil war for Kashmir's independence, yet they prove transgressable in the characters' everyday practice.

Whitt, J. B. (2011). *An appetite for metaphor: Food imagery and cultural identity in Indian fiction* (Order No. 1493573). Available from ProQuest Dissertations & Theses Global: The Humanities and Social Sciences Collection; ProQuest One Literature. (871713592).

Postmodern culture has been greatly influenced by food images and the usage of food as metaphor. Recent interest in food studies has opened doors in literary studies to examine how the use of food imagery and metaphor represents complex ideas and deeper meaning in literature. Literary food studies analyzes food symbolism to reflect on cultural identity which includes various issues from social position to sexual desire to gender relations. In three postcolonial Indian novels, Salman Rushdie's Midnight's Children, Arundhati Roy's The God of Small Things, and Anita Desai's Fasting, Feasting, food carries multiple meanings that serve to drive the action of the plots, characterize the characters, and reflect on aspects of the Indian culture. The writers use food and eating to symbolize cultural issues of acceptance, resistance, and preservation of culture, as well as symbols of memory, emotions, narrative history, relationships, power, and consumption. After examining each novel for its relevance of food images, this thesis will conclude by revealing the ways the food metaphors therein reflect directly on the Indian cultural identity as one of political and social fragmentation, postcolonial hybridity, patriarchal oppression, and repressed sexual desire.

Williams, T. A. (1999). *Matrilineaology: Mother-daughter relationships in contemporary fiction* (Order No. 1394820). Available from ProQuest Dissertations & Theses Global: The Humanities and Social Sciences Collection; ProQuest One Literature. (304564406).

This thesis examines Dorothy Allison's Bastard out of Carolina, Louise Erdrich's The Beet Queen, Arundhati Roy's The God of Small Things, and Amy Tan's The Joy Luck Club to attempt to answer questions such as, "How do a mother's experiences prior to the birth of her daughter affect the way that she raises that daughter?" and "How does a mother's history affect her attitude(s) toward her daughter?" These questions are important because they lay the groundwork for the ultimate question that this thesis attempts to answer: "Will history repeat itself?" In addition to tracing history, this thesis will identify Nan Bauer Maglin's five themes of matrilineaology (258) within each of the four texts examined.

www.ingramcontent.com/pod-product-compliance
Lightning Source LLC
Chambersburg PA
CBHW072055190726
48294CB00005B/1524

* 9 7 8 1 7 8 7 9 5 2 7 3 7 *